CLIFF

CLIFF

An Intimate Portrait of
a Living Legend

Tim Ewbank
and
Stafford Hildred

Tim: To my mother Joy, Emma and Oliver

Stafford: To Janet, Claire and Rebecca

First published in Great Britain in 2007 by
Virgin Books Ltd
Thames Wharf Studios
Rainville Road
London
W6 9HA

A catalogue record for this book is available from the
British Library.

ISBN 978 1 905264 07 0

The paper used in this book is a natural, recyclable product
made from wood grown in sustainable forests. The
manufacturing process conforms to the regulations of the
country of origin.

Typeset by TW Typesetting, Plymouth, Devon

Printed and bound in Great Britain by
Mackays of Chatham PLC

1 2 3 4 5 6 7 8 9 10

CONTENTS

PROLOGUE

The loud crowing of a lusty young cockerel is far and away Cliff Richard's favourite first sound of the day. As soon as he hears that distinctive call, he knows the sun will soon be rising over the Atlantic Ocean and bringing new life to the acres of beautifully kept vineyards surrounding the elegant farmhouse that is the singer's home in Portugal.

He silently registers relief that he is not incarcerated in yet another luxury hotel in any of the world's great cities facing a busy day in boardroom or studio – or even at home in grey old England.

'Portugal has a peaceful feel about it,' Cliff said. 'I sit on the kitchen terrace overlooking the vineyard and I feel cut off from the world. I need that sort of thing, and when I come back I'm really ready to work again. I find a great peace in the Algarve. In Portugal I can live like a recluse for a couple of weeks. I don't go out much and there's no need to shave. There are times when I need to withdraw and be ordinary.'

Cliff did not know that Portugal was Britain's oldest ally when he settled on the very edge of Europe, but it's an association he thoroughly approves of.

Ever since he took a holiday in Portugal in 1961, Cliff has enjoyed a love affair with the Algarve. He was delighted to discover the natural beauty of its unspoiled and then undeveloped coastline and soon bought a villa in Albufeira as a holiday home. The simplicity of the coastal life appealed to his yearning for peace and harmony as a counterbalance to the hectic life of the world's most durable rock 'n' roll star. Here, for once, he could anonymously join locals on fishing expeditions or dine in little restaurants unpestered and unrecognised, even when he brought out a guitar and sang.

In all, Cliff has owned three separate homes in the Algarve down the years, the latest of which is a beautiful and enchanting farm-cum-winery that he bought in 1991. The farmhouse is over 250 years old, and the vineyards surrounding it afford the maximum privacy the singer craves.

Usually the cockerel will wake Cliff at five in the morning, and in the early morning light he will venture out on to the terrace simply to gaze over the vineyards and revel in the tranquillity of the oasis of calm he has created for himself.

As a committed Christian, many's the time Cliff has sat on this terrace and pondered how fortunate he is and how far he has come. He's been knighted by the Queen, he's a friend of the Prime Minister, his success as a singer and entertainer are unmatched, and it's all a far cry from the days when he and his mother, father and three sisters existed – lived is too rich a word – in poverty in just one room in Surrey when they first came to England from India.

'It's aeons apart when I think of my humble background,' he recently conceded to his good friend, the broadcaster Gloria Hunniford, when she visited Cliff in Portugal to make a TV programme about him. 'But it's good to have the memory.

'To remember what it was like in the past stops you taking everything for granted. It's important to have a memory of what it was like, and still is for an awful lot of people. They can all come out of it, as I came out of mine, but I like being able to remember so clearly what it was like in those early days.'

Cliff will be 67 on 14 October 2007, and it's 50 years since Harry Webb, as he was then known, joined Dick Teague's Skiffle Group on 20 September 1957, and took his first steps on a career that is unparalleled in British showbusiness.

Today, as he approaches this career milestone, Cliff ranks as far and away the most successful British recording artist, with fourteen UK number-one singles, and record sales that total in excess of 260 million. Incredibly, he has spent a total of more than 20 years in the charts. He is British pop's most celebrated survivor, the only British rock 'n' roll star to ride successfully the changing musical trends over the years – rock 'n' roll, Merseybeat, glam rock, heavy metal, punk rock and rap.

Cliff has outlasted every trend with a sincerity and a commitment that is unequalled in his field. Throughout his decades in the charts, Cliff has displayed a valiant longevity. He has even been able to parody one of his earliest hits, 'Living Doll', with the comedy quartet the Young Ones and still register yet another number-one hit.

He's appeared in musicals like *Time* and *Heathcliff*, sung on gospel tours, and celebrated his 50th birthday with a move into social commentary with the anti-war hit *From a Distance*. Memorably, he even took it upon himself to stage an impromptu performance at the 1996 Wimbledon tennis championships to cheer up the crowd during a miserably prolonged rain-break. This spontaneous act endeared him to millions.

'There's never been anybody like him, and there never will be,' said Bruce Welch, his old friend and guitarist from his backing group The Shadows. 'He's had a hundred and thirty-six hits over fifty years, he's a massive star and all he's known is success.

'He's still out there performing, he's still hungry for it, and he still wants to be top of the tree. He has an enormous ego. An ego that drives him forward in anything he's doing. He's convinced when he makes a single that he's competing with Westlife or Robbie Williams, people forty years younger than him.

'But he's very contented inside. He does exactly what he wants, and works when he wants.'

It is Cliff's great sadness that his father, who died when Cliff was twenty, did not live long enough to see his extraordinary success. 'My father would have loved the knighthood and the OBE,' he said, 'the open-air concerts at castles and stately homes and seasons at the Albert Hall. I know he would have done.'

But, to Cliff, it is perhaps an even greater tragedy that in recent years his mother Dorothy, the one woman the age-defying bachelor boy has loved beyond any other throughout his life, has missed his continuing success after cruelly falling victim to dementia.

Many stars try to hide their personal tragedies, or at least shy away from speaking about them, but with his typical frankness Cliff bravely speaks out about how he 'lost' the mother he loved so much in the mid-1990s.

'She has always been the yardstick by which I've made all my decisions,' he has said. 'At the back of my mind there's always been the thought: "What would Mum think?" '

'I remember once when I appeared on stage wearing a dinner jacket, Lycra shorts and matching waistcoat, and I thought I looked terrific. But Mum called me and told me I looked like a punk. It really upset me.

'That's what I miss about her now,' said Cliff when his mother's dementia took hold. 'The only people who can clip you down are your parents. They're the only ones who can get away with it. Even now, when Mum's not well, I still feel that I'm accountable to her and I measure what I do by how she would react.'

Dorothy would be proud to know that her son would be celebrating 50 years at the top. She was the one who always had faith in Cliff right from the word go. She was the one who also advised Cliff not to get married.

Cliff Richard remains a single man, but far from lonely. He has many great, long-lasting friends. But as he sits alone with his thoughts in the early Portuguese sunlight, it's perhaps easier to understand why Bruce Welch once summed him up thus: 'He's only got Cliff Richard to think about. He's looked in the mirror since he was seventeen – he was a big star at seventeen – and all he's had to think about every day is: how good am I looking today?

'He's the biggest box-office draw in this country bar anybody. He got knighted for his work for charity and for leading a blameless life. No one's ever caught him out. And I don't think anyone ever will.'

1. CHILDHOOD

My mother had servants working for her so that somebody bathed me, someone else fed us all, and so it was all pretty good.

Cliff on his early years living in India

Cliff Richard was born Harry Rodger Webb in the King's English Hospital in Lucknow, India, on 14 October 1940. Weighing in at a healthy nine pounds, baby Harry was a much treasured first-born child for Rodger and Dorothy Webb, who had married in West Bengal some eighteen months earlier.

Rodger, who was born in Burma to English parents, and Dorothy Dazely, the young woman who was to become his wife, had arrived in India from very different backgrounds. Rodger's relatives had come to India as part of a taskforce to build a railway system, while Dorothy's English parents had left the mother country on military grounds, her father being a regular soldier.

The couple first met in 1936 when Rodger paid a visit to his sister in the town of Asansol. Pretty teenager Dorothy just happened to live in the apartment below. Dorothy was then only sixteen and Rodger was almost twice her age at thirty-one, but he was immediately captivated by Dorothy's dark, blossoming good looks and pleasant personality, while she quickly warmed to his confident, man-of-the-world approach to life.

For Dorothy, the fifteen-year age difference was not the only hindrance to any idea of romance: Rodger lived a long way from her. But the couple remained in touch, mainly by letter, and the relationship grew steadily more serious. Eventually they married on 26 April 1939, when Dorothy was nineteen.

By now, Rodger had worked his way up to become the area manager for Kellner's, a well-known catering company. Kellner's had the lucrative contract for the Indian railways and Rodger ran the restaurant cars for the Bengal–Nagpur railway. A welcome perk of the job for the Webbs was the provision by the company of an apartment above a chocolate factory in Howrah, a busy, congested town just outside Calcutta.

Rodger's job involved plenty of travel around the country from Howrah's huge railway station, which had rail connections to most of the major cities and towns in India.

He was delighted to be able to come back from his frequent business trips away to a young wife cheerfully ensconced in a well-appointed apartment with black-and-white marble floors and a team of servants at her beck and call. The Second World War might have been raging across the globe, but the horrors of the fighting seemed a long, long way away.

When he was old enough, young Harry attended the local Church of England school, St Thomas's in Church Road, an educational establishment that enjoyed the benefit of generously sized grounds ringed by banana trees.

As was customary for children of English families enjoying a colonial lifestyle, Cliff's school lunch was personally hand-delivered every day to the school by one of the Webbs' four servants. Habib, one of two kitchen staff responsible for cooking and serving meals for the family, would arrive each day with an armful of food for Cliff's delectation, the plates carefully wrapped in crisp white napkins, neatly knotted at the top.

'My mother and father had a very fine, high-profile lifestyle,' Cliff said. 'Because the British in India had good jobs there, my father made good money. We had an apartment that we didn't have to pay for provided by his company, my mother had servants working for her so that somebody bathed me, someone else fed us all, and so it was all pretty good.'

Other than the prandial pampering, Cliff's memories of his early schooldays are sketchy. He learned to speak a smattering of Hindi and Bengali, but his chief memory is of being utterly intrigued by a nature lesson, when he found he could encourage mango seeds to grow by placing them on soggy blotting paper. This simple classroom experiment demonstrating the wonders of botany elicited wide-eyed enthralment as the seeds began to sprout. It instilled in the little boy a fascination with the growing of plants generally, which has stayed with Cliff all his life, manifested most notably in his enthusiasm for the grapes that grow so fruitfully on his sixteen-acre vineyard in Portugal.

Away from the classroom, one of Cliff's favourite – typically boyish – outdoor pursuits was fishing in a nearby lake with his dad. Father and son would sit by the water with monkeys playing in the trees overhead and Cliff would try to make a catch with a homemade rod comprising a bamboo stick with a bent pin jammed in the end.

Another much enjoyed game was taking part in kite-flying battles with his pals. For youngsters in India, flying a kite was more than just a popular pastime – it was almost an art form. The skill was not in getting the kite airborne – most boys could manage that – but in deftly manipulating the strings to make it swoop on to your rival's kite and slice through his cotton controls with the aid of slivers of glass cunningly concealed in the tail of your own kite. Cliff developed a winning technique, which would leave an opponent's severed kite soaring into the sky on the wind, never to be seen again, thanks to a swift swoop and snip of the cotton strand.

Every Sunday morning the Webb family attended St Thomas's church, where Cliff had been christened. The church was sited next to the school and the young male pupils were expected to provide the treble section for the church choir. Cliff was no exception and, in his red cassock and white ruff, he was the apple of his mother's eye.

The choir provided an early introduction to music for Cliff, and at home there was also a wind-up gramophone, complete with ornate horn, to enjoy records bought mainly by Dorothy. A special favourite of Cliff's was an obscure ditty called

'Chewing a Piece of Straw' to which he liked singing along. 'Ragtime Cowboy Joe' and Glenn Miller's 'Jersey Bounce' were other numbers that caught his ear. There were also visits to look forward to from an uncle who sang to his own guitar but, young as he was, Cliff realised Uncle Tom sang and played more with unbridled enthusiasm than any marked musical dexterity or vocal ability. But the early lesson that music was to be enjoyed was certainly well received.

For a happy little child like Cliff, adored by his parents and waited on hand and foot by servants, life seemed rosy enough. But the winds of change had for some time been blowing through India and, on the stroke of midnight on 24 August 1947, the sun finally set on the British Raj after 163 momentous years. British rule of India came to an end and two new dominions, West Pakistan and East Pakistan (now Bangladesh) were created, separate from India. It was the end of an extraordinary era, and life on the subcontinent was never to be the same again.

The Webbs had, of course, long known that 'Home Rule' was approaching and, like the many other British families in India, they viewed it with apprehension and no little alarm when its advent was increasingly punctuated by Hindu versus Muslim riots.

The partition of India far from guaranteed inter-religious peace between followers of the two faiths and, nine days after India gained her independence, ten thousand died in border clashes in the Punjab. A train full of Muslim refugees from Delhi bound for the safety of Pakistani territory was ambushed and twelve hundred were massacred in the worst single incident of slaughter.

On one occasion, after gunshots were heard at the end of the street, the unrest was serious enough for Cliff and his sister Donna to spend the night at an aunt's for their own safety. Cliff always looked forward to visiting his aunt because she allowed him to eat curry and rice with his hands, as was the Indian custom. Rodger Webb was a rigid stickler for good manners and he would never have permitted this at home.

Cliff and the rest of his family later witnessed first hand a shocking sectarian clash when a terrified young Muslim boy fleeing for his life took refuge in a next-door garden to escape some Hindus hellbent on violence.

From their apartment window the Webbs could see the boy cowering next to a wall and felt compelled to help. Over several days they regularly lowered food down to him once darkness had fallen, thus allowing their act of human compassion to remain undetected. To have been seen helping the boy might have invited trouble.

When Rodger Webb was finally convinced that the lad's hiding place had not been pinpointed by his enemies, he helped him over the wall and into a truck, where he was escorted to safety by some of the Webbs' Muslim servants. Eventually, the Webbs' servants themselves deemed it prudent to head for safer surroundings as well. Much as he was sad to see them go, Rodger took it upon himself to drive them to safety.

Religious feuds were a constant worry, but there were also other serious issues to consider for British ex-patriots. After India gained its independence, British families became obvious targets for retaliation from those who deeply resented India's years of subservience and kowtowing to its white masters. Incidents of Britons being pelted with stones and worse became all too frequent for comfort for families like the Webbs.

One day, while Dorothy was out shopping with Cliff by her side, they suddenly found themselves surrounded by a group of Indians who jostled and jeered at them. The situation threatened to turn ugly when the leader of the group aggressively shouted: 'Why don't you go home to your own country, white woman?' Cliff bravely piped up: 'That's my mummy, leave my mummy alone.' He was too young to understand fully the gravity of that confrontation, although he could not fail to discern the effect it had upon his mother. Dorothy was distinctly unnerved – even more so when soon afterwards, during an Indian festival, several white women were drenched with jets of coloured water normally reserved for special effects for the local fountains on festival days.

Back in the safety of their apartment, Dorothy resolved that the family must make urgent plans to pack up and leave. It was a far from easy decision, because India was the only life she had ever known and the family she and her husband would be uprooting by now numbered five. Cliff had two younger sisters, Donella and Jacqueline, who were safely delivered after Dorothy's second child, a baby boy, had died at birth.

Another good reason to seek a new life in another country was Rodger's dwindling income. In India, his catering job had relied to a great extent on the wine trade, but when prohibition came in, he had found himself hitting hard times.

But where could they go? That was the burning question. Whatever their destination, it would be a huge step into the unknown. Eventually the choice boiled down to two alternatives on opposite sides of the world: England or Australia. Neither Dorothy, who had lived all her life in India, nor Rodger had ever been to England. Rodger was very tempted by Australia because he had a friend who was heading Down Under and was ready to form a business with him there. So keen was the friend for Rodger to join him in Australia that he was even prepared to pay Rodger's fare.

But Dorothy put her foot down. She insisted that they must try for a new life in England, where at least they had relatives they could stay with initially while they found somewhere to settle. Rodger eventually agreed, a boat passage was duly booked for the five of them, and the Webbs set about selling the possessions they could not fit into their limited baggage allowance or would have no use for in their new life.

In August 1948, almost a year to the day after India had gained her independence, the Webb family tearfully bid farewell to their friends and set off with their possessions packed into five suitcases.

The first leg of their exodus comprised a three-day train journey to Bombay before boarding the P & O ship SS *Ranghi* for a three-week voyage to England, during which Cliff quickly discovered he was horribly prone to seasickness. He spent the first few days in the cabin, throwing up and feeling desperately ill, until his father took him up on deck for some air and walked him around to get used to the pitch and roll of the ship.

Finally, early one crisp Monday morning in mid-September, the SS *Ranghi* tied up at Tilbury, the docks that regularly operated as London's passenger-liner terminal until the 1960s.

Stepping down the gangway on to British soil for the first time, Rodger Webb was a worried man. He had arrived in England with a wife and young family and he had precisely £5 in his pocket.

He was too proud a man to show his concern, but inwardly he feared for his family's all too uncertain future. He was now 48 years old, starting life anew in a country totally alien to him, and needing to find a job fast to feed his wife and three young children.

Surely never in his wildest imagination could he have imagined that, some ten years later, the cheerful little boy standing nervously beside him, gazing inquisitively up at the steel cranes towering above him on Tilbury's dockside, would take this new country's youth by storm.

2. CHESHUNT

I thought he was too nice for the showbusiness rat race.
Jay Norris, Cliff's teacher at Cheshunt Secondary Modern School

I t's not hard to imagine just how traumatic the Webbs found their transition to post-war England after enjoying the colonial luxury of ayahs and servants in India. The family experienced a staggering culture shock that impacted deeply on each member.

Prior to their arrival, Cliff's grandmother had the unenviable job of sorting out accommodation for the family and on the very tightest of budgets. It was no easy task, because men returning to Britain from the forces after the war were still searching for somewhere to live and housing was allocated on a system of points. All Dorothy's mother managed to find them was a single box room next door to her own home at 47 Windborough Road, Carshalton, Surrey.

All five members of the Webb family somehow crammed into this one room, which had to serve as a communal dormitory complete with chamber pots, as well as being both living room and kitchen. Cliff slept on a mattress on the floor head to toe with his eldest sister Donna. After the spacious and comfortable trappings of life in India, Dorothy, in particular, found the constant humiliation and grim practicalities of living cheek by jowl in a single room desperately hard to take.

There was never a single second of privacy for any of them, not even for the tears Dorothy frequently shed over her family's predicament. Lying on one of the mattresses laid out on the floor at night, Cliff could not fail to hear his mother's pitiful sobs in the darkness as she mourned the life her family had lost.

'When we arrived we didn't have any money for anything,' Cliff said, 'not even food. I can remember that three times a week our main meal would be two slices of bread with sugar sprinkled on it, no butter, and all the tea we could drink. We weren't starving, but I was always hungry and used to dream about food. Of course things did gradually become a little easier, but even then we never had any money. If ever there was a refund on the electric meter, then Dad would share out a little between me and my three sisters. If the refund was £1, then all of us would be given sixpence.'

On a practical level, life for Dorothy was challenging. In India, the cooking, the washing of the family's clothes, ironing, cleaning and countless other household chores, were all left to the servants. Now, in addition to looking after her three children herself without the domestic help to which she had become accustomed, Dorothy had to learn to cook on a hastily acquired little green primus stove. She quickly learned to prepare porridge for breakfast so she could send the family off to work and school with something filling in their stomachs. She also set about doing the family washing by hand in the bathroom sink. In those days there were no launderettes – the opening of London's first at 184 Bayswater on a six-month trial was still a couple of years away – and a washing machine was still something of a rarity in British homes and well beyond the Webbs' financial reach in any case.

Cliff and his family quickly discovered that the end of World War Two had brought peace but not plenty to England and its people. Faced with a mounting financial crisis, the British government had recently announced new austerity cuts to add to the rationing of food, clothes, petrol and tobacco, which had been in force for many years as part of the war effort. The new cuts included a stop on motoring for pleasure and a ban on foreign holidays.

To add to the family's gloomy start in England, within weeks of their arrival the country was enveloped by the worst fog in many years, leading to three train crashes, and buses and police cars being taken off the road. And for the very first time, Christmas brought no cheer for the family. They were in such dire financial straits that there were no presents to be handed out. The onset of winter made the family yearn for the warmth of India.

For Rodger Webb, the chief priority was to get a job. But with food scarce and ration books in force, the chances of using the extensive railway catering experience he had gained in India to land a similar worthwhile job were almost non-existent. While he searched for some sort of employment, the family initially lived largely on the charity and kindness of relatives. Rodger was grateful, but frustrated that they were forced to rely on the generosity of others for their survival.

Resigned to their temporary one-room existence, Cliff's parents were naturally keen to see their son settled into a local school as soon as possible. The family had arrived just after the start of the autumn term for English schools and Cliff was quickly enrolled at Stanley Park Primary School in Carshalton. He had enjoyed going to school in India, but now his parents were horrified to find their precious son frequently coming home from school battered, bruised, bloodied and in floods of tears.

A classroom can be a cruel place for children who don't fit in, and Cliff stood out from the others because of the colour of his skin. Seven years in India had given him a deep tropical tan, which contrasted sharply with the pallor of the suburban Carshalton schoolkids raised on a less-than-nourishing diet during the war.

To the ignorant eyes of some of the primary school young-sters, Cliff's dark skin marked him out as a 'wog', as they chose to call him. And the singsong lilt in his voice, which he'd acquired while in India, only seemed to confirm to the playground bullies that he was a 'nigger'.

When Cliff volunteered the information that he had come to the UK from India, the bullies teased and taunted him with

Apache-style war whoops and quizzed him as to why he wasn't wearing a feather headdress and carrying a tomahawk. 'Indie-bum' or 'Red Indian Harry' they called him, despite Cliff taking pains to try and get it into their skulls that Red Indians did not come from Calcutta.

'Right from the moment that I arrived at Stanley Park Primary School in September 1948 I was bullied and taunted mercilessly,' Cliff recalled. 'I was one month short of my eighth birthday, I'd enjoyed a wonderful childhood and then all of a sudden I was being called a wog and a nigger. The bullies would keep asking where my tepee was.

'I had a lot of fights at school,' said Cliff, who likened himself to a terrier fighting an Alsatian when he was forced to take on the bigger boys. 'When I first moved from India to England I obviously had a great tan and I got called Indie-bum and all that. It's just ridiculous really, but I fought a lot at school. I came home bruised and in tears sometimes, but I always gave as good as I got. I was little, but I always won.

'I can just remember being bullied all the time and I seemed to be fighting in every break between classes. It was a constant battle, but in spite of what picture people may have of me, I wouldn't back down.

'After a while I became very good at fighting. I remember having one child pinned to the ground, and I was so angry with him that I rubbed his wrist into the tarmac until it tore away his skin and he was bleeding quite profusely. But even after that, it didn't stop, and even the teachers would make remarks that they could never get away with today.'

Scarcely a day went by without Cliff being involved in a fight. The terrible treatment left Cliff with a lifelong hatred of discrimination.

On the way home, discretion was the wiser part of valour for Cliff. The bullies followed him, taunting him all the way, but he didn't want to be seen having fights in front of his family. However, if the clashes ended in punch-ups and he was forced to stand his ground, Cliff was always prepared to put up his fists.

The constant sniping and jeering of his tormentors made Cliff's early schooldays miserable. He decided that he hated

England, hated the nasty boys who chased him and hated trying to work out pounds, shillings and pence. Rupees had been so much easier.

It took him a long time before he was able to forget the verbal abuse he had suffered – especially when one of his teachers cruelly weighed in with an offensive remark in front of the whole class about 'Harry and his wigwam'.

Cliff was shocked and hurt by such insensitivity from an adult and a schoolteacher to boot, but he reckons the bullying, taunts and fighting pulled his family ever closer. 'It made me very sceptical of other people,' he said. 'It was like us and the rest of the world. It meant that I was never part of a group of friends. I just felt different.'

After a year, however, he was able to leave the bullies of Stanley Park Primary School behind. The Webbs decided they had been reliant for long enough on Cliff's granny and Rodger felt it would be prudent to move from Carshalton, where there was a five-year waiting list for council houses. The chance to move came when an aunt kindly offered them a room in her own home in Waltham Cross, situated in the Lea Valley on the north-east Essex outskirts of London. Importantly, Waltham Cross had only a two-year waiting list for a council house.

The one room in Carshalton next to Granny had been cramped enough for five. But the aunt's room was not much bigger, and space was soon at even more of a premium when Dorothy gave birth to Joan, a third little sister for Cliff.

It was with considerable difficulty that all six members of the Webb family now struggled to make a life for themselves within the confines of four walls. Cliff can remember that when his feet grew to be the same size as his mother's, the two of them would share one pair of Wellington boots between them in order to save buying another pair. It was one way of saving cash, but it meant that, in wet weather, either Dorothy pulled on the boots to go out and Cliff remained indoors or vice versa.

After many depressing months without employment, Rodger finally landed a factory job with Ferguson's, a well-established TV and radio manufacturer, nearby in Enfield. It was a huge relief for everyone. 'He would have died rather than go on the dole,' said Cliff of his father. 'He spent hours travelling to and from a job outside his area rather than be out of work.'

Once baby Joan was old enough not to need constant attention, Dorothy was able to take a job at a factory in Broxbourne some five miles away to help make ends meet. Like her husband, she pedalled to work on a bicycle to save a few pence rather than pay the bus fare.

The job may have added a few much-needed shillings to the family income, but it gave Dorothy a jolting insight into British trade-union practices. One day Cliff saw his mother come home in tears because she had been sent to Coventry by her fellow factory workers. They had insisted she slow her work down so they could all get overtime pay. Dorothy declared she thought that was dishonest and paid the penalty for her altruism.

But, with some money coming in, things at last were looking up for the family and their brighter circumstances were reflected in young Harry's improving work in the classroom at Kings Road School in Waltham Cross, which he had attended since their move from Carshalton. Cliff even won a prize for coming top of the class.

Now they had an income, Rodger and Dorothy put their names down for a council house, but without much real hope of decent council accommodation for some years. As newcomers they were bottom of the list, below those already living in the area.

But, unexpectedly, life for Cliff and his family took an important and heartening turn in the spring of 1951 when he was ten years old. A neighbour, appalled at the cramped and primitive conditions in which the Webbs were living, tipped off the local council about their plight. When a council housing officer duly arrived to investigate, he deemed them deserving of emergency treatment.

He assured Rodger and Dorothy they would be moved into a council house within two months. Considering there was a long waiting list, they were somewhat sceptical, but within a matter of weeks, in April 1951, a small, red-brick house on a council estate in Cheshunt, Herts, was made available to them as a priority.

To Cliff and his family, the new three-up, two-down residence felt like a palace after the claustrophobic confines of one-room multi-cohabitation. To the family's pleasure, they found that their new home even had a tiny garden, and the house went a long way to cementing Cliff's view that England, not India, was his home.

'Some people say: "Don't you feel your home is India because you were born there?" I say, "No." I remember what I remember. I have fond memories of being a child in India, but my family always considered England as home and that when we left India we were going home to Blighty. We arrived here and I felt I'd come home. So England will always be home. It is important to think of somewhere as being your grass roots. How can Britain not be that? It's the place that gave me my career, my life as a young person, my education was here. I shall be eternally grateful to this country and always consider myself British.'

Number 12 Hargreaves Close, Cheshunt, was a happy home even if it came with barely a stick of furniture and no carpets on the floor. Once again mattresses were laid down to serve as beds and Cliff's dad contrived to make two armchairs out of two packing cases he had purchased for a shilling each from the Atlas Lamp Company, where he was by now working as a clerk. The chairs would remain in the house for some while after Cliff had hit the big time as a reminder of their impoverished past and how they had come through the bad times.

Never take money for granted was the lesson Cliff learned at home. 'I was brought up in poverty, but poverty wasn't necessarily something that made us unhappy,' said Cliff years later. 'Looking back, I'm sure my mother and father could have been happier, but they never showed it.

'So many of my values come from them, because they were always so honest and even-handed. When I used to ask them for pocket money, because all the other children were given it, they'd tell me they couldn't because there wasn't any money. But they'd promise that when there was some, then I'd have some too.

'My dad impressed his values on me. I find it hard to spend money. I never take it for granted. My indulgences are my home and my clothes. I love going into garden centres and buying pots and plants. I have bursts of buying clothes, but I feel I have to justify the money I spend on stage clothes to my accountant. If my wardrobe gets too full, my secretary sends out batches of my old clothes to charities.'

In hard-up Britain in the 1950s, Rodger and Dorothy resourcefully managed what little money they had. Everywhere they looked, stores were offering furniture on hire purchase. But Cliff's parents were of the old school and preferred, if they possibly could, to save up for various items and pay for them outright rather than take up the never-never payment option.

'My father found a way to deal with poverty by himself and never expected things to be done for him. If he couldn't afford armchairs he'd get some wood and build them. He hated to be on the HP. But in the end he gave in, because there was no other way of doing it.'

Luxury items, however, had to wait, and it was not until Cliff started seeing the financial rewards of his first record that the Webbs took delivery of a television set. But thanks to a windfall, they did find the cash for a record player – the old wind-up gramophone that had given the family much musical pleasure in India had been sorely missed.

'We didn't have a record player or anything like that for ages,' Cliff said. 'I never had a TV set until I bought one with my first lot of royalties and the only way we got the record player was because my dad won about £40 on the pools. There was a big argument about what we should buy, so we had a vote on it. My mum and I voted my dad out and we said: "We'll have a record player."'

Rodger and Dorothy had learned the hard way how to survive on very little, and drew great strength from adversity as they made the most of what they had. The experience rubbed off on Cliff so that in later years when he became hugely wealthy he still lived frugally.

'My upbringing made me appreciate not only the value of money,' Cliff said, 'but so many different things. If my parents hadn't been so strong and supportive, I would not only have been a very different person, but I'm sure that my career would have all ended in tears. After all, the pop business is immensely destructive. Look at what happens to so many stars, but they gave me the strength to handle the fact that your popularity waxes and wanes and you have to deal with that, and that it's a very rough ride.'

Not long after they had settled into their new home, Cliff took his eleven-plus, a streamlining examination taken by all primary schoolchildren to determine whether they would go on to grammar school – if they were bright enough – or to a secondary modern.

Both Harry's teachers and parents were confident that he would win a place at the grammar school because he had shown real progress and had the form prize to show for it. So it came as a profound shock to everyone, not least to Cliff, when he failed his eleven-plus exam.

Cliff's parents were deeply disappointed and not a little mystified as to how he had managed to fail the exam when his previous good work in the classroom had pointed to his sailing through it.

Norman Mitham, a good friend of Cliff's throughout his schooldays and later to become a member of his first group The Drifters, may have something of an explanation – the playground bullies had been after Cliff again. 'I wouldn't say Cliff was different, but he had that Indian tinge which was unusual back in 1950s Waltham Cross,' said Norman. 'And he did stand out, so he was picked on a lot. They used to call him Sabu the Indian boy because at that time there was a popular film out about Sabu.'

Cliff said, 'It was the same thing all over again – name-calling and more fighting. My father used to say that it was all right to fight, that if they hit you, then hit back even harder, but never instigate a fight. That thought presents a dilemma for me today, as a Christian you're supposed to turn the other cheek, and that's what I do, telling myself that I'm a much stronger person for not hitting back, but I'm not always convinced that's the case.'

Cliff believes, however, that it was simply exam nerves that got the better of him and prevented him from doing his best. His failure to win a grammar-school place hit him hard: he felt he had let everyone down, including himself, and his confidence was knocked sideways.

The newly built Cheshunt Secondary School now beckoned, and Cliff was not best pleased to discover, on his very first day, that he had been placed not in the A stream but in the B stream. Fortunately, this was a mistake, and he was promptly elevated to join the other secondary-mod newcomers in the brighter bracket of pupils. Even so, Cliff managed to pass only one O-level – in English, a subject he particularly warmed to under the inspirational teaching of Mrs Jay Norris, who particularly fired Cliff's imagination when she introduced him to *Wuthering Heights* as part of his school studies.

Jay recalled: '*Wuthering Heights* was one of the set O-level texts and he took to it straight away. Unhappily, his interest in rock and roll meant that he didn't put in quite enough work and he failed the literature exam by one mark. He was very upset about it.' Both the book and Mrs Norris were, however, to figure prominently in Cliff's life many years on, when Cliff starred in the musical *Heathcliff*.

It was Jay who roped Cliff into the school's dramatic society. They were always short of boys and Jay felt Cliff had a winsome demeanour about him and a charming smile. He proved enthusiastic and a good enough actor at fifteen to play Bob Cratchit in Charles Dickens' *A Christmas Carol* at the end of the autumn term in 1956. A review in the local paper, the *Cheshunt Weekly Telegraph*, stated: 'Harry Webb acted well as Bob Cratchit, but was rather let down by the make-up team and, hard as he worked, he could not dispel the impression that he was a teenager and not a harassed father.'

A pivotal moment followed when he was offered a starring part as Ratty in another school production, *The Wind in the Willows*. The problem for Jay Norris was that Cliff was reluctant to sing. 'So I blackmailed him into it,' Jay recalled. 'I said: "No sing, no Ratty." So he sang, and he was very good.'

It prompted Cliff to ask his teacher whether she felt there might be a future for him as a singer. 'Well, I don't know about that, but I certainly think you should have a job which allows you to smile at women,' was Jay's tactful reply to the teenager with a head full of dreams. Later she qualified her reply by saying: 'I thought he was too nice for the showbusiness rat race.'

Outside school Cliff was part of a gang of youngsters typically looking to spread their wings. Like countless other British teenagers they had started to become interested in the new brand of music emanating from America, which they could hear on Radio Luxembourg. If Cliff and his gang sometimes got up to mischief, it was of a prankish nature and stayed comfortably the right side of the law. There was never any chance of Cliff going off the rails with his pals, such was the disciplined code of behaviour imposed upon him by his father.

Always closer to his mother than his father, Cliff had immense respect for his dad, whom he has described as very strong, really tough. 'He was impressive because he was a disciplinarian,' he said. 'He was pretty strict and very stubborn.' Rodger Webb set the rules in his household, and he expected his children to obey them. As the eldest child, Cliff was entrusted with growing freedom, but Rodger still liked to impose strict limits and boundaries. One night, Cliff arrived back home half an hour late after going to the cinema. He returned home to find himself locked out of the house by his furious father.

After it appeared Rodger was in no mood to lift the lock-out, Cliff resigned himself to spending the night outside and gloomily sought refuge from the cold in the coal shed. But Rodger eventually took pity on him and allowed his suitably chastened son back into the house.

When it came to imposing discipline, Rodger was uncompromising, and a clout round the ear was a not uncommon punishment. 'I remember being walloped by my dad many, many times if he felt I'd done something wrong,' said Cliff.

One day Cliff arrived back from school grumbling that he had been caned for something he hadn't done. But pleading innocence didn't wash with Rodger. Instead of receiving sympathy from his father, Cliff got another caning from his dad. 'He had a little stick and he picked it up and walloped the backs of my legs,' Cliff recalled. 'He said: "That's for letting me down. You must have done something wrong for the teacher to cane you."' Dismissing Cliff's complaint that he had been blameless, Rodger's argument was that if the school had punished him, then they must have had good reason to do so.

Rodger also drilled it into Cliff that he was letting down not just himself but his father every time he got caned. 'Remember, you're my son and they know you're my son,' he told Cliff. Thereafter Cliff refrained from telling his dad whenever he got the birch at school. 'After he'd told me off and sent me to bed, it was always Mum who would bring me my cocoa and have a chat,' Cliff said.

Of his father, Cliff recalled, 'His only fault was that he insisted on doing everything himself. If something went wrong in the house or a plug needed changing, I always had to hold things while he did it. He never shared the work.' It was only much later on, when his father became ill and died in 1961, that Cliff felt able to take over as the man of the house.

'We never had any closeness till he was too desperately ill to be stubborn, and then, just before he died, we were able at last to become close. In fact our relationship changed dramatically. Not only was I the breadwinner, I was the only one who could do anything. My mother was almost helpless with worry and my sisters were young.

'We actually had a much better time when he wasn't well, which was a shame really. Nevertheless, I'm grateful that we had that time and that we finally understood each other better, otherwise my memory would just have been of a man who was bordering on tyrannical. In fact he was just very firm and I now recognise that I actually needed that discipline.'

The Webbs were nonetheless a close-knit family, although inevitably, when they were living in such close proximity, Cliff and his sisters squabbled. Rodger tolerated the spats but, as part of a general emphasis on good manners, he was insistent that his son treat his three sisters in a gentlemanly fashion.

'They spoiled me rotten,' said Cliff of his sisters. 'I think I was fortunate that I was the eldest. I think if you're going to be the only boy you've got to be the eldest. I kind of ruled the roost, but we got on well.

'My dad always brought me up saying you never lay a finger on a woman, never ever,' Cliff recalled. 'My sister Donna – the one just younger than me – and I used to share all the jobs in the house. If she washed up one day, I did the drying up and so on. But when my granddad came to live with us, he thought the world of her, so he did all her jobs and so she'd come to me and taunt me – and that used to incense me.

'So one day I got a newspaper and rolled it up and I walloped her like mad. And when my father came home he said: "Your sister's crying, have you touched her?" And I said: "I never touched her, never laid a finger on her." I have to confess that I walloped her with a newspaper, but I didn't touch her.' Technically Cliff was right and escaped punishment on this occasion, but he was told to count to ten to control his temper in future.

As he grew older, Cliff more than pulled his weight at home. His mother cycled off for her evening factory shift in the late afternoon and it was left to Cliff to give his sisters tea and look after them for three hours until his father got home from work at 7.30 p.m. By the age of fourteen he was starting to take an interest in the opposite sex, and his settled home environment, the strength of his parents' marriage and their pride and enjoyment in family life prompted him to imagine himself happily married by the age of 27 with four children – two girls and two boys.

Cliff may not have excelled academically at Cheshunt Secondary School, but he shone on the sports field. He was good enough at football to be selected to play right-back for the county schools team and said: 'I did quite well in the sports area at school and for ages and ages I had the school record for the under-fourteens javelin of 136½ feet. Every year after I left they'd send me the sports day programme saying: "Record held by H. Webb." I also ran quite well too. I hated rugby, but I always played when they wanted me to because I was really fast. I'd run and no one caught me, so I never got walloped or anything.'

In sharp contrast to the bullying of his primary school days, Cliff's sporting prowess ensured he now enjoyed a measure of popularity among his fellow pupils. The teaching staff also thought enough of him to make him a school prefect until he was ignominiously stripped of his prefect's badge by the headmaster.

Cliff's crime? Playing truant to see in concert the son of a Michigan textile worker by the name of William John Clifton Haley Jr, who had just arrived in England to a hero's welcome.

3. ROCK

My name is Harry. I am twelve. My ambition is to be a famous star one day.

Cliff, in a letter to a pen friend in Australia

On 12 April 1954, Bill Haley, a 28-year-old country-and-western band leader, went into Decca's Pythian Temple studios in New York to record a song called '(We're Gonna) Rock Around the Clock'.

Haley had started out as a singing yodeller for a group called The Down Homers by successfully answering an ad in the US music-industry magazine *Billboard*. He went on to become a disc jockey in New Jersey before moving to Pennsylvania to form a quartet, The Four Acres of Western Swing. After disbanding them in 1949, Haley started a new band, The Saddlemen, which became The Comets in 1953. Their record 'Crazy Man, Crazy' became the first rock 'n' roll record ever to make the US Top Twenty.

Now Haley was recording 'Rock Around the Clock' as a favour to his manager, Jim Myers. The song had been part of Haley's stage act for almost a year but, due to a petty inter-rivalry in which Haley was not involved, his previous recording company, Essex, had been unwilling for him to record it.

On its release, 'Rock Around the Clock' was only mildly successful, and it was Haley's next single, a cover version of Big Joe Turner's 'Shake, Rattle and Roll' that hit the Top Ten in America and made Haley a national star.

It was not until 'Rock Around the Clock' was featured in *The Blackboard Jungle*, a film about violent school pupils, in 1955 that it became a true hit. The film was denounced as degenerate and caused riots in cinemas. 'Rock Around the Clock' was rereleased to cash in on all the hullabaloo, and in America it quickly become the number-one single in *Billboard*'s Best Sellers in Stores chart, as the singles chart was then called, as well as topping the British hit parade.

This number-one single created a dividing line between all that came before and all that followed in popular music. The rock era had begun.

In 1956, Bill Haley & His Comets were signed to star in a film entitled *Rock Around the Clock*, thus establishing a new trend in marrying rock 'n' roll with the silver screen. Again in Britain, as in America, screenings of the film caused riots in cinemas right across the country.

Police were called to cinema after cinema to eject youths who 'jived' in the aisles, clapped along and chanted to the music and ripped up the seats. The film's dialogue became virtually inaudible under excited shouts of 'We want Bill' and 'Rock, rock, rock'. Some youths took to letting off fireworks in the cinemas and many were charged and fined for 'insulting behaviour'.

On 7 February 1957, Bill Haley & His Comets sailed into Southampton on the luxury Cunard liner *Queen Elizabeth 2* for their first British tour. They transferred to a train specially hired by the *Daily Mirror*, which the newspaper dubbed the 'Rock 'n' Roll Special', and when Haley arrived at Waterloo he was greeted by some 3,000 delirious fans, all pushing and shoving to get closer to their kiss-curled idol. The resulting scuffles made perfect copy for the *Daily Mirror* and immediately invited such headlines as: 'The new battle of Waterloo'.

Haley's arrival coincided with the announcement that 'Rock Around the Clock' had sold one million copies in Great Britain – the first disc to achieve this milestone.

Caught up in the rock 'n' roll fever that was sweeping the country, Cliff decided he simply had to see Bill Haley & His Comets in concert. Their first appearance at London's Dominion Theatre was accorded rapturous reviews, with reports of the 3,000-strong audience out of their seats clapping, jiving and singing along to 'Rip it Up', 'Rockin' Through the Rye', 'Don't Knock the Rock' and, of course, 'Rock Around the Clock'.

'Its appeal is its simplicity,' Haley said of his music. 'Everyone wants to get into the act. With rock 'n' roll they can join in.' Cliff needed no second invitation. He was determined to see America's new music sensation, and on 3 March 1957, he got up at five, slipped out of the house to meet up with some like-minded school pals, all prefects like him, and set off for Kilburn in north London to join the mass of Haley fans queuing up for tickets at the vast Gaumont State cinema. Unfortunately, the box office opened later than the boys had anticipated, and by the time they had each handed over their five shillings for a ticket, it was mid-morning and they all agreed it was much too late to go back to school for the rest of the day.

That night Bill Haley went down a storm in front of 4,000 frenzied fans, among them an enthralled young Harry Webb who gasped at the energy of the band, the rhythmic beat they knocked out, and their energetic showmanship. Cliff felt exultant at being part of a largely teenage audience, all rising to acclaim this new style of music. To the teenagers, this was their music and they were only too happy to 'Shake, Rattle and Roll' and 'Razzle Dazzle'.

Haley drove the audience to fever pitch, leather-clad youngsters jived wildly in the aisles and Cliff was exhilarated at being within screaming distance of a band that had such musical sway over a vast audience. It was a never-to-be-forgotten moment for Cliff, and he knew straight away that this was what he wanted do.

Next morning, Cliff and his fellow truants were hauled before the headmaster and summarily stripped of their prefect badges. 'I bet if we'd been to the Bolshoi Ballet you'd have given us a pat on the back,' Cliff protested, but to no avail. When Jay Norris got to hear of Cliff's demotion she told him:

'In ten years' time I'll bet you won't even remember the name of Bill Haley.' Cheekily, Cliff bet her a box of chocolates that he would and, as the years went by and the teacher–pupil relationship evolved into a firm friendship, he was eventually able to collect on his bet.

Although the excitement of seeing Bill Haley made for a memorable night for Cliff, it was Elvis Presley who really got Cliff all shook up. Compared with Elvis, Haley was hardly the archetypal teen idol: by now he was thirty years old, and over his bulky frame he wore a shirt, bow tie and a smart check jacket when rocking around the clock. Youthful Memphis punk Elvis, with his slicked-back hair and pelvic gyrations, could hardly have been more excitingly different.

Cliff first heard Elvis Presley while walking through Waltham Cross with his pals one morning in the spring of 1956. He was stopped dead in his tracks by a sound like no other he had ever heard blaring from the car radio of a smart Citroën car parked outside a newsagent. As Cliff and his pals paused to admire the motor, they heard: 'Well since my baby left me . . .' sung by a vocalist in a manner that sent shockwaves through Harry Webb as he strained to catch more of the song coming from inside the car.

Cliff recalled, 'We were looking at the car and thinking: one day we're going to have one of these. By the time he'd sung a verse and a half, the guy had come out, got in the car and had gone. We didn't even know what radio station it was on. We couldn't stop talking about this.'

Cliff had found every brief note he'd heard electrifying. But what was it? Back at home Cliff desperately twiddled the dials of the family radio between Radio Luxembourg and various German stations in a bid to catch the song's title and the name of the singer.

'We didn't have phones in those days, so we just had to meet up every couple of days,' he said, 'and it was a weekend, so we had to wait till Monday and, sure enough, somebody had heard the record on American Forces Network Radio, which was beamed across from Germany.

'They said it was "Heartbreak Hotel" and it was sung by this guy called Elvis Presley. And we thought: what a funny name!

But who cares? So we went all out to try and buy the record, and did. It was the inspiration, and I think Elvis and the others inspired thousands to attempt to be like him and it was inevitable that I would try and be like that. I used to go into school trying to look as much like Elvis as possible. We really knew we'd succeeded when the dinner ladies gave us extra pudding. It was exciting times to be there at the beginning of what we now take for granted.'

By mid-May, Cliff was but one of millions transfixed enough by Elvis to send 'Heartbreak Hotel' soaring to number two in the UK hit parade.

'Heartbreak Hotel' marked Elvis's transition from a local southern American sensation to an international phenomenon and built on the foundation begun by 'Rock Around the Clock' to establish rock 'n' roll as a musical force that was simply not going to go away. The king of rock 'n' roll had just ascended to his throne, and in Cheshunt there was no keener, more enthusiastic and loyal subject than sixteen-year-old Harry Webb, who rushed off to buy Elvis's first LP (long player) from a little record shop in Cheshunt High Street as soon as he could afford it. On the way out of the shop he took it out of its wrapper so that everyone could see he was carrying an LP by the truly fantastic Elvis Presley. Cliff was an Elvis fanatic and he was desperate to show his allegiance.

At home Cliff cajoled Donna, also rapidly becoming an Elvis fan, into writing down the words of the songs so he could sing along while the King's records were on the turntable. 'He was always singing around the house,' said Cliff's youngest sister Joan. 'He always had music on, and if anything new came out, he'd sing it to me to let me know what he'd heard.'

Elvis was Cliff's idol, and soon he was also cultivating the Presley physical trademarks of long sideburns, swept-back hair and greasy quiff. When he could afford it, he bought similar clothes and practised the Elvis the Pelvis gyrations.

'I used to stand in front of the mirror in the lounge at home trying to get my lip to curl,' he said. 'That was how inspired I was. Elvis was a total inspiration. I was fourteen when I first heard him and that was it – I wanted to be a rock 'n' roll singer.

I wanted to be him. Elvis came on the scene with this animal, alien sound and I went wild. On all my early records there's this incredible American twang. I used to lay it on really thick – the Brylcreemed hair, the smouldering eyes, the folding lip. If there hadn't been an Elvis, there wouldn't have been a Cliff.'

But even before he heard Elvis, Cliff wanted to be a star. He said: 'I'd forgotten how strongly I felt about wanting to be famous until someone gave me a photocopy of a letter I'd written to a friend in Australia. I'd written: "My name is Harry. I am twelve. My ambition is to be a famous star one day."'

At school his friends were becoming just as familiar as Cliff with the hits of the day from the likes of Johnnie Ray, dubbed the Prince of Wails or the Sultan of Sob for his tear-jerking, emotional renditions of his hits, Frankie Laine, Guy Mitchell, Pat Boone and, of course, Elvis. Cliff and his schoolfriends had all read about a young man called Adrian Hill who gave up his job as a fitter in a Leeds engineering works, changed his name to Ronnie Hilton then shot to the top of the charts. Maybe I could too, thought Cliff.

Like Cliff, his pals loved to chat about the new pop stars emanating from America as well as the homegrown hit-paraders like Dickie Valentine, Jimmy Young and Alma Cogan. But Cliff set more store by this youthful musical movement than his friends did. Cliff's pals may have talked the talk about the artistes achieving stardom, the emergence of skiffle, and the rock 'n' roll explosion. But Harry Webb wanted to walk the walk. He was determined to be another Elvis, Cheshunt's Elvis, and was desperate to dive into the gathering tide of rock 'n' roll that was ready to sweep the crooners of the early 1950s into obscurity.

'When I heard Elvis, Bill Haley, Jerry Lee Lewis and the Everlys, I loved this music,' he said in an interview for *The South Bank Show*. 'I had no concept of their sexuality – I didn't even know what they looked like half the time. It was just the music. I loved the way they sounded, and I wanted to be able to stand up in front of a group of people and sing. Analysts would say that Cliff Richard had a dominant father who would never let him hold plugs and to prove himself he went and became a rock 'n' roll singer. Crap.'

Cliff's first tentative step towards fulfilling his dream was to become part of a school vocal group. They called themselves The Quintones, because there were five of them, and they nervously made their debut one Saturday night at the Holy Trinity Youth Club dance. The three girls and two boys sang mainly in unison, breaking into harmonies when they felt they could manage it. For Cliff, the high point came when he stepped up for a solo spot singing 'Heartbreak Hotel' and another Elvis hit, 'Don't Be Cruel', complete with accurate Elvis mannerisms.

The Quintones repeated their performance on Bastille Day, 14 July 1956, at an Anglo-French dance-cum-fundraiser for Holy Trinity School in front of 250 people, a performance that warranted Cliff's picture appearing in a newspaper for the very first time.

It was around this time that Rodger Webb elected to spend £2 of his hard-earned money on a guitar. Rodger had once played banjo in a jazz band and he now set about introducing his son to the most rudimentary of chord progressions. 'He taught me my first three chords,' said Cliff. 'I started playing G, C and D7 and learned how to strum.'

The gift of a guitar was perfectly timed, because in 1956 'Heartbreak Hotel' was battling for the new teenage market with British skiffle music, led by Lonnie Donegan.

Skiffle had a simple, homespun quality about it and it invited everyone to join in. Anyone, with the help of a few thimbles, could finger-tap out a rhythm on a wooden washboard, budding bass players could resonate a deep twang by slapping and plucking a taut single cord attached to a broomstick and a tea chest, and even the tone deaf could produce a sound by humming along through a comb and tissue paper or a kazoo. Add these improvised musical gadgets to more conventional musical instruments such as an acoustic guitar and a banjo, and – hey presto – you had a skiffle group.

The skiffle movement became quite a craze, and by 1956 Britain's King of Skiffle, Lonnie Donegan, had become so popular that an EP (extended-play record) called *Skiffle Session*, and an album, *Lonnie Donegan Showcase*, both reached the charts.

Lonnie explained: 'My own view of myself is as a musical stepping stone, a musical bridge between America and England. There had been no bridge. There was a musical wall up. We were not allowed to hear American musicians, nor they us. I was the little boy who kicked the first hole in that wall.'

Skiffle filled a teenage wasteland as far as music was concerned, as guitarist Joe Brown – who shot to success around the same time – confirmed: 'In the mid-fifties, the kids had no music at all. Skiffle was the best thing that ever happened. It actually started pop music in this country, and of that there's no doubt in my mind at all.'

Lonnie Donegan and Joe Brown were right. The best thing about the skiffle movement in the UK in the 1950s was that it opened the eyes of youngsters like Cliff to the idea that they could make music and that it was not completely beyond the realms of possibility that they could even have a hit record.

As luck would have it, Cliff, who had by now left school, one day found himself sitting on a bus next to a former classmate who just happened to have a boyfriend called Terry Smart, who was the drummer in a skiffle group. They were looking for a singer and, remembering Cliff's efforts at aping Elvis Presley at school, the girl suggested that Cliff might just fit the bill.

Cliff jumped at the chance, successfully auditioned, and joined Terry in The Dick Teague Skiffle Group on 19 September 1959. Within days he found himself, not entirely comfortably, singing skiffled-up versions of traditional folk songs. At least it was a start, and the musical get-togethers with the other members of the group were something to look forward to after work as, by now, Cliff had taken a job as a credit control clerk at £4 15 shillings a week at the Enfield firm where his father worked.

Thanks to an opportune piece of nepotism, Rodger Webb had negotiated the job opening for Cliff, and father and son pedalled on their bikes the eight miles to work each day, sat at either end of a large, open-plan office, and pedalled back home again at the end of the working day. Cliff was grateful to his father for engineering some employment, but he found the work anything but stimulating.

Cliff's flirtation with skiffle lasted for no more than a few months, but it gave him invaluable experience of singing in front of people at children's parties, birthday bashes and weddings. However, with Presley emerging as *the* rock 'n' roll idol and the dominant force for teenagers interested in music's new wave, Cliff found skiffle lukewarm in comparison. His heart lay in rock 'n' roll – and drummer Terry Smart felt the same way.

Together they broke away from The Dick Teague Skiffle Group intent on forming their own rock band with Cliff's long-standing friend and near neighbour Norman Mitham. 'Cliff and I were extremely good friends from early schooldays and spent all our time together,' Norman recalled. 'We also lived on the same council estate, our mums were great friends and we both came from very poor families who didn't have holidays in the summer. So Cliff and I were in each other's company almost twenty-four-seven.

'I was one of the boys who nearly went with Cliff to see Bill Haley in concert. I knew Cliff was going, but I didn't dare because I was afraid of what my father would have done if I'd missed school.

'Then, when Cliff and I heard Elvis singing "Heartbreak Hotel", we both thought: that's a bit different, and Cliff felt we should form some sort of a group purely for our own enjoyment. I'd just started work, and as I didn't smoke or drink, I spent my money on a Hofner electric guitar.'

By now Cliff had also upgraded to a decent guitar, which his father had bought for him for £27 for his sixteenth birthday. But Norman remembered that when he first plugged his guitar into his amp and the trio tried out a few numbers, the result was anything but melodious. 'We made an awful noise,' he laughed. 'In those early days Cliff was a bit quiet and I wouldn't have marked him down as ambitious. He had a mediocre job at Ferguson's and people I knew who worked there said he didn't stand out in any way. They would pass him by.'

What they lacked in musical ability, the trio more than made up for with their enthusiasm. Night after night Cliff, Norman and Terry got together, taking it in turns to host their practice sessions at their own homes. Neighbours did not take too kindly to the amplified racket that went on late into the night at Cliff's house, where he and Norman would loudly strum away in the living room to Terry's drumbeat. After an official complaint about the noise level was lodged with the local council, an official investigation was launched, which resulted in the trio being banned from playing their instruments after ten o'clock at night. In addition, Cliff was told that windows and doors must be firmly closed during practice sessions to cushion the noise.

'We used to listen to Radio Luxembourg,' Norman said, 'and when a new record came out that we didn't have and couldn't afford the sheet music, we'd listen to the radio and try to scribble down the words before the record faded and then try and work out the chords.'

Gradually the 'awful noise' improved, and Cliff's mum was particularly encouraging. In 1956 she persuaded Cliff and the boys to send in an application to appear on the newly launched TV talent show, *Opportunity Knocks*. Hosted by the indefatigable Hughie Green, who meant everything 'most sincerely, friends', *Opportunity Knocks* showed there was still a place for amateurs on television and fulfilled a vital role in bringing new artists to the small screen.

Dorothy saw no reason why her boy shouldn't be given a chance on *Opportunity Knocks*, especially when Hughie Green managed to find a place on the show for buxom Gladys Brocklehurst, a Lancashire cotton-mill girl, whose unique selling point was to grab her husband Norman by the hair and slap him while singing her number. This extraordinary act may have sent the studio 'clapometer' soaring but, despite Dorothy posting off a hopeful letter, there was no showcase for Cliff and the boys. Opportunity failed to come knocking from Hughie Green at that point in Cliff's life and by the time the application forms to appear on the show had dropped through his letterbox, Cliff was already well on the way to stardom.

* * *

Cliff and his pals never stopped trying to find a way into the pop business, even though their forays occasionally ended in abject failure and tears. 'We were told about a big talent contest at the Trocadero at Elephant and Castle,' said Norman, 'so we lugged all our equipment with us on the underground in order to get there. Then, when it was our turn to play, all our electrical stuff failed. We had no amplification at all.'

They tried every which way to trace the fault, but with no success. In the end there was nothing for it but to give up and go home, prompting Cliff to cry his eyes out on the bus on the way back to Cheshunt at this cruel twist of fate. 'Cliff was in tears,' confirms Norman, 'not at losing, but at failing even to put on a show.'

While his mum continually sought out other talent competitions, Cliff's dad was worried about his son's apparently all-consuming determination to become a pop star and warned him not to become too obsessed with his ambition.

'When I was young it was Mum who was always telling me to go for it,' said Cliff. 'My mother was the one who would push me. But my father was also one hundred per cent behind me in everything I did, even though, in the early days, he'd say to me: "Be careful – you want this so badly. If you don't get it, you've still got to get a life, you're going to have to think about getting an ordinary job." I think the balance between my dad's feelings and my mum's was very good for me.

'Dad was the counterbalance. He would ask things like: "What are you going to do if you fail?" while Mum was busy finding out where the next talent contests were. She had total belief that it was all going to work out. She had tremendous faith.'

It was Norman Mitham who came up with a name for the group. 'It sounds silly now,' he said, 'but long before we really got going as a group, we sat around designing the cover of an imaginary LP we told ourselves we'd one day make, and we were trying to tailor the design of the record sleeve to a name for the group.'

At first they thought of The Planets, but that was deemed too obvious a parallel to Bill Haley's Comets. 'Then we came up with a design which would have Terry, Cliff and myself coming down a snow slope on a toboggan,' Norman continued. 'We wanted a name that reflected that design, and we thought of The Nomads or The Wanderers until I came up with: "What about The Drifters?" It seemed to fit, as we were going into a snowdrift on the toboggan, and so that was the name we hit on.'

The trio were thrilled when they landed their first gig as The Drifters in March 1958. They played and sang rock 'n' roll at the annual dinner and dance of Enfield's Forty Hill Badminton Club, where Cliff and his parents were members and where he occasionally enjoyed a game. 'We were paid the princely sum of ten shillings,' Cliff remembered. 'But it wasn't the money that counted, it was simply performing. I was on a real high. I can remember the feeling like it was yesterday. We did "Be Bop A Lula", "Ready Teddy" and "Long Tall Sally". We whipped up twenty minutes of frenzy and people were clapping like mad. Amateurs get away with murder.'

It was around this time that a pretty, dark-haired local girl called Janice Berry started appearing at The Drifters' rehearsals. She had been head girl at Cliff's old school and he had always had an eye for her after they got to know each other in the school drama group. They started going out together but, in an age of youthful innocence, their romance comprised visits to the cinema, where they held hands, drinks at a coffee bar or being together at their respective homes, where they listened to records.

In time, The Drifters began appearing at local clubs, pubs and dances, playing the hits of the day, although neither Cliff nor Norman were good enough to play lead guitar. As they were both novices still learning and exploring a wider range of chord shapes and fingering, they tended to strum away at the same chords in unison.

'We had a very limited repertoire,' said Norman. 'Cliff was absolutely enthralled by Elvis, and so eighty per cent of what we played was Elvis. But we also did songs that were popular at the time from people like Buddy Holly, Chuck Berry and The Everly Brothers.

'Cliff had talent, but he didn't have the spark that people see today. He had a passable voice, but personally, at that stage, I wouldn't have said that he was going to go on and become famous.'

Owning a car was something the three teenagers could only dream about, and travelling to and from venues usually meant having to catch a bus. 'It seems incredible now, but we carted all our equipment around with us on the bus,' Norman recalled.

One venue that became a regular gig for The Drifters was the Five Horseshoes pub at Burford Street, Hoddesdon, in Hertfordshire. Unfortunately for Cliff, it was a long bus ride away. Any reasonably long journey was something for him to be anxious about because he was prone to travel sickness, and on one occasion he even had to hop off at a bus stop in Turnford to throw up by the roadside.

'The Five Horseshoes was basically just a regular pub,' said Norman, 'and we had to make our way past the darts players and set up our equipment on a slightly raised stage at one end of the pub near to the door to the gents toilet. Then away we'd go. We went down very well there, but then most of the punters were probably drunk.'

One night, quietly observing The Drifters through the smoky saloon-bar air while propping up the bar, was a tall, well-built young man called John Foster. When it came to closing time he approached the band as they were packing up their equipment and he had something important to say.

'I'll never forget his opening line,' said Norman. 'It was: "Do you want to play at the 2 I's coffee bar?" That certainly caught our attention.'

4. 2 I's

I was driving a tractor on a sewage farm – which I think is very good basic grounding for the rock 'n' roll business.
John Foster, first manager of Cliff Richard and The Drifters

In the late 1950s, the infamous district of Soho in the very heart of London's West End was not markedly different from the Soho of today. This colourfully cosmopolitan quarter of London perhaps had a more discreetly sinful air than today about its striptease joints, the fleapits screening erotic films to over-eighteens only, the shops selling sex aids and the girls working the streets.

But then, as now, it was also a vibrant area full of restaurants, lively bars, music dives and clubs. For teenagers like Bruce Welch, down in the Smoke from Newcastle-upon-Tyne, and Tony Meehan, two budding musicians who were soon to become members of Cliff's backing group, The Shadows, a visit to Soho for the first time was an eye-opening experience. 'It had an aura about it,' Tony recalled. 'It was a place where the hookers would be in the doorways, and there were drinking clubs, drunks, druggies, prostitutes, pimps, gangsters, musicians, bohemian artists, coffee bars, clubs, dives, jazz clubs. It was a Mecca for all the artistes in the country.'

Bruce remembered: 'The first time I saw two guys kissing was in Soho in 1958. I thought the one was trying to save the other's life. Everywhere there was a coffee bar with frothy coffee – the kind we'd never seen before in Newcastle.'

Terry Nelhams, soon to become singing sensation Adam Faith, summed it up when he said: 'It was an amazing place to be in the 1950s, so full of colour and life. I always loved the *feel* of Soho back then. The cheeses, and the ravioli, and the wine in the windows of the big Italian grocers' shops. The smell of fresh-ground beans from the Algerian coffee stores. The shops with French sausages, and Greek sweets, and Hungarian chicken livers and Swiss chocolates.'

Adam, whose skiffle group The Worried Men were to become resident for a while at the 2 I's, recalled: 'Every other doorway seemed to be a coffee bar. And into Soho every day drifted the young hopefuls with their guitars, all hoping to get a night's or a week's work from the owners of these coffee bars. They were the new employers. Everyone wanted music with their drinks, so the owners of these places were glad to take on one or other of the many young skiffle groups for a pound or two a night. If you had a group, you approached a coffee bar manager for an audition.

'Coffee bars fell into two distinct categories: beatnik – all black polo-necks and existentialism; and teeny-bop – beehive haircuts and bobby socks. We played our music to the beehives and chatted up girls dreaming of Jean-Paul Sartre.'

Soho was the music centre of the country, and so it was a natural musical hotbed in which skiffle and rock 'n' roll could take root. Soho's espresso belt had coffee-bar clubs with names like Mars, The Cat's Whiskers, Orlando's and The Skiffle Cellar. The skiffle craze was finding its voice in these bars, and far and away the best known of all the coffee bars was the 2 I's at 59 Old Compton Street.

At a casual glance, this establishment at the Wardour Street end of Old Compton Street outwardly had nothing special going for it that might have marked it out from several similar coffee bars in the vicinity.

All of them invariably had linoleum floors on which stood a jukebox – probably a Wurlitzer – and served frothy coffee, which was throatily dispensed with a mouthwatering gurgle, a loud hiss and a burst of steam from a gleaming chromium Gaggia machine. Teenagers too young to go into pubs were content to sip their coffees from see-through Pyrex cups while sitting on stools at lemon and powder-blue Formica-clad tables, listening to the jukebox and staring out of the windows into the bustling streets. 'You had to be eighteen before you were allowed in the pub, and at eighteen boys went straight into the army. So they were pubs for kids,' guitarist Joe Brown once succinctly described these coffee bars. 'And this coffee they used to serve would probably be illegal now. It was pure rocket fuel. Strong espresso coffee – three of them and you were buzzing all night.'

The 2 I's was situated between a delicatessen and a coffee lounge called Heaven and Hell, and was, in essence, no different from other coffee bars. But it was to become legendary for spawning the first wave of the UK's would-be rock 'n' rollers.

The 2 I's was the venue that encouraged these British rock pioneers to flourish, and the key to the fame the premises was eventually to enjoy was its cramped basement cellar where budding singers and musicians were given a chance to entertain the punters and show what they could do – often without being paid much more than a few shillings to take home for the electric meter.

Sometimes these rock 'n' roll trailblazers sang just for their supper, the muffled beat of their music resonating from the cellar up through the delivery hatch into Old Compton Street, where inquisitive passers-by would be drawn in, swelling the crowd jostling to get inside the door.

On hot and sticky summer evenings, condensation ran down the walls, so tightly were the teenage audience packed in. The cellar barely had room for forty people, but on some nights the crowd was reckoned to number around a hundred. They stood sweating shoulder to shoulder and the hatch door would be thrown open to allow the steam, cigarette smoke and music to filter out into the open air. Occasionally the limp body of a customer who had fainted in the heat was also passed through the grille in the pavement up into the street and fresh air.

Turning the basement into a venue to showcase untapped musical talent was the idea of Paul Lincoln, one of two Aussie wrestlers who had taken over the premises in April 1955 from the previous proprietors, two brothers called Irani – hence the name the 2 I's.

Paul, who, unknown to the majority of his customers, grappled in the ring in a eye-slit mask under the name Doctor Death, chose to keep the original name of the 2 I's. He served tea, coffee, cakes and sandwiches in the top bar and installed a jukebox, which drew in teenagers. When a youngster called Wally Whyton approached him and asked if his skiffle group, The Vipers, could play for him, Paul opened up the cellar, which had been used as a storeroom, to make space for Wally's band.

Live music went down well with the customers, and soon the place was packed out, especially at weekends. The coffee-bar kids were just as excited about hearing the new music as the groups were to be given the chance to play it.

Soon Paul brought in a friend from the film business, Tom Littlewood, to help him run the joint. At one point there were reckoned to be some 3,000 skiffle groups in greater London alone and Paul and Tom held regular auditions to pick the best of them to play in the basement. And, as the reputation of the 2 I's coffee bar grew, on the strength of unearthing several 'hit-paraders', Paul was eventually able to add the words 'Home of the Stars' to the signature sign over the premises.

It was here at the 2 I's that Terry Dene, a youngster with a job as a packer of records at HMV's Oxford Street store, jumped up to sing to his own guitar and rapidly found himself signing a recording contract with Decca and in the Top Twenty with a catchy record called 'A White Sport Coat'.

Tommy Hicks from Bermondsey was another who owed a remarkable life change to the 2 I's. A merchant seaman, he had spent time in America and taught himself the country songs of the day on the guitar. On a period of shore leave, Tommy made his way to Soho, the New Orleans of skiffle, and happened to call in at the 2 I's, fortuitously on its opening night when members of the press had been invited. He was never to appear there again, but once was enough to launch a career to last fifty years and more.

The sudden rise to stardom of Terry Dene and Tommy Steele from the basement of 59 Old Compton Street, Soho, was a very visible success for the 2 I's. It attracted not only literally hundreds of wannabe singers and musicians applying to showcase their talent but crowds of youngsters scrambling to try and get into the 2 I's to enjoy the new sound of rock 'n' roll and to see and hear stars in the making.

It was therefore little wonder that Norman Mitham was taken aback when John Foster asked Cliff, Terry Smart and him whether they'd like to play at the legendary 2 I's. If Foster was making a genuine overture, then the three Drifters would bite his hand off to appear at such a vital venue.

Foster had been quietly observing the trio over his pint as they went through their repertoire at the Five Horseshoes and he was certainly impressed, particularly by Cliff. 'He was a dark-haired kid doing an Elvis act, but there was something about him, some kind of magic,' Foster later recounted. 'Why, I'll never know, but I said to myself: "I'm going to manage that kid." I just sort of knew he had what it took to go down well with the kids, even if the beer drinkers weren't taking too much notice.' With that thought in mind, Foster proceeded to follow up his 2 I's opening gambit by offering his services as manager.

Norman, Cliff and Terry were flattered that Foster thought they were worth taking on, and it did not take the trio long to decide to place their future in Foster's hands. He was the first person to show any interest in them. Besides, they were impressed when he gave them his telephone number – none of the three had a phone at home. Moreover, they all liked his enthusiasm and his optimism. He told them they could be big stars, he seemed to mean it, and his faith in them was a welcome boost.

Cliff, Terry and Norman soon learned, however, that Foster was anything but the stereotypical, slick showbusiness manager. In fact, he was earning his living as a dumper-truck driver at a local sewage works and he had no experience whatsoever in the cut-throat world of showbusiness. What he knew about the machinations of the pop-music world could be written on a guitar string. 'I was driving a tractor on a sewage farm – which I think is very good basic grounding for the rock 'n' roll business,' Foster observed wryly.

Cliff's father was understandably less than impressed with John's lack of experience when John told him he was going to manage his son's music career. Rodger Webb was distinctly underwhelmed and Foster conceded: 'I was young and naïve and I had no idea of management.'

Foster was a self-confessed Teddy boy, but he was still impressionable enough to have travelled the 25 miles from his home in Hertford Heath into central London to drop into the 2 I's where, to his excitement, he found himself standing next to Terry Dene. John was there purely as an interested fan checking out the latest hot music scene, and he went on to become friendly with members of the management, including Tom Littlewood. His initial enquiry of Cliff and The Drifters as to whether they would like to play at the 2 I's was therefore no idle boast.

Foster was confident he could fix them up with an audition and Cliff was thrilled when he followed through by establishing a date for their try-out. But they would hardly be travelling up to London in style – Foster informed them they would be going by bus.

Norman Mitham said: 'John Foster told us that the number 715a bus went from Hertford to Guildford and stopped off outside BBC Broadcasting House. He said: "If you can be at the bus stop at Cheshunt when that bus comes through at one o'clock, get on it and I'll be on it too and I'll introduce you to the owner of the 2 I's." So the three of us with our guitars and equipment waited at the bus stop for the Green Line bus to take us to our fame and fortune in London. How naïve we were!'

For Cliff, there were the usual waves of travel sickness to overcome as the bus ground its way up to London. To cheer him up, John Foster informed Cliff that the bus would pass by the Finsbury Park Empire, at that time a big variety theatre that played host to some of the great names of showbusiness.

'One day your name will be up there in lights,' he prophesied to Cliff. Amazingly, by the end of that year, it was.

Lugging their equipment from the bus through the narrow streets of Soho, the boys felt a surge of excitement. When Cliff walked down Wardour Street carrying his guitar and saw the 2 I's sign for the first time, the nerves began to get to him. But John Foster appeared to know what he was doing and Cliff followed John in through the glass front door and walked past the serving counter towards the end of the room. Here was an entrance, usually blocked by the twenty-stone bulk of the club's bouncer, Roy Heath, leading to a narrow stairway and the basement.

'We auditioned on a Saturday afternoon because we worked during the week,' Norman remembered, 'and while we were auditioning Tommy Steele and Terry Dene walked in. We couldn't believe it.'

The audition went well enough for them to be given a booking at the 2 I's that very night. 'We played the session,' said Norman, 'and by the time I got home my parents were asleep and I had to wake them up and tell them all about it. I was so excited, of course, but they were completely disinterested. I got no response from them at all – they'd never heard of the 2 I's.'

Cliff, Norman and Terry had been hoping that Larry Parnes, best-known British rock manager of the time, or some other talent scout, influential agent or impresario might catch their performance and make all their dreams of stardom come true overnight. But they were disappointed. Parnes was away supervising a tour and, although the teenagers packed into the cellar seemed to have appreciated The Drifters and to have enjoyed their music, no one stepped up at the end of the night waving a record contract, a chequebook or a diary offering some bookings.

Watching and listening with no little interest, however, was Bruce Welch, who was sharing digs in Finsbury Park, north London, with another hopeful teenage guitarist. His name was Brian Rankin at the time, but he was on the brink of changing it to Hank B. Marvin in homage to a full-blooded Cherokee singer–songwriter called Marvin Rainwater, who had a number-one-hit in the UK in April 1958 with 'Whole Lotta Woman', which had influenced him.

Bruce and Hank had originally headed down to London together to take part in a talent contest and had stayed on to suss out the music scene. Naturally, they gravitated towards the 2 I's, where they discovered they could play their guitars, earn a few bob and chat up the girls. 'The 2 I's was a hot sweaty cellar, lots of women, hot sweaty bodies pressed together,' is Bruce's recollection. 'It was usually packed solid and people would pay just to stand on the stairs.

'On the nights we musicians weren't actually playing at the 2 I's, we'd try and get work there selling orange juice and Cokes. It was one of the nights when I was working the orange juice machine downstairs that Cliff and The Drifters came in to play.

'Cliff was electric. He looked the business. He looked like Elvis. I went back that night and said to Hank: "There was a great guy singing down there tonight called Harry." But I didn't know anything about him and I didn't speak to him. I'd never met anyone called Harry before in my whole life – except one old man.'

Cliff, Norman and Terry made enough of an impression at their audition to secure a week's engagement at the 2 I's for ten shillings (now fifty pence) each. It turned out to be a week that would change Cliff's life for ever.

On the evening of Thursday 3 April 1958, Ian 'Sammy' Samwell, a young man on leave from his RAF National Service duties, made his way to the 2 I's, squeezed his way down the stairs to the basement and managed to weave through the crush of excited teenagers to take up a vantage point perched on the ladder leading up to the delivery hatch. From there he had a perfect view of a trio whom he did not recognise pumping out more than passable rock 'n' roll.

He saw Harry Webb with his guitar strapped round his neck giving his all, the slim, upright figure of Norman Mitham strumming away on electric guitar and Terry Smart in a white James Dean-type T-shirt seated behind his rudimentary, barely adequate drum kit. They were playing numbers like 'Twenty Flight Rock', 'Milk Cow Blues' and 'Money Honey' and young Ian, known to his friends as Sammy, warmed to them instantly, particularly the singer. 'Back then Cliff was one hundred per cent, bonafide, solid gold, high energy rock 'n' roll,' was the verdict proffered in his unfinished memoirs. 'He had a vitality and an authenticity equal to Eddie Cochran, Gene Vincent or even Elvis. But he didn't sound like any of them, and what's more, no matter what anybody says, he didn't come across as an Elvis clone either.'

But as he watched and listened, Ian could not help thinking there was something missing – a lead guitar. The rock 'n' roll records he listened to generally had a lead guitar solo, whereas Cliff and Norman merely played rhythm. There was no bass guitarist either, but that was not so surprising, as bass guitars in the UK at that time were as rare as a snowflake in June.

At the end of the night, when the boys were packing up their gear and the crowd had filtered away, Ian, still wearing his RAF uniform, stayed behind to talk to John Foster. He explained he was a guitarist, that he was a couple of weeks away from being demobbed, and asked if they might consider recruiting him on lead guitar. John suggested Ian – who was playing in The Ash Valley Skiffle Group at the time and, like Cliff, preferred rock 'n' roll – should come back the following Saturday afternoon, when he could try out with the band while they were rehearsing. He would be given a chance to prove himself.

Also hovering near the group as they packed up their equipment was a young girl called Jan Vane on a rare visit to London. She had come up to the 2 I's from Rainham in Essex with her boyfriend Eddie as a treat for her sixteenth birthday. She imagined that since the boys were playing at such a legendary rock 'n' roll venue, they must be famous, and she first asked Cliff for his autograph and then ventured to ask if they had a fan club. Cliff was flattered, and by the end of the night Jan had landed herself a job as fan-club secretary. It was a post she was to hold efficiently and loyally for twenty years, regularly keeping the membership, which at one point numbered 42,000, up to date with all things Cliff.

'They were crazy nights at the 2 I's,' Adam Faith recalled. 'Something was always happening and all sorts of people were there just starting in the pop business. There were people like songwriter Lionel Bart, who used to join in the music on washboard, and Mickie Most, then a singer who became a top record producer, worked the Coca-Cola machine. Then there was Tony Sheridan, who later had The Beatles as his backing group in Hamburg, and Jim Sullivan, who became one of the very best session guitarists.

'The 2 I's attracted so many singers and musicians from all over the country and they were all out for some fun. They were exciting times, but unfortunately for Cliff, he lived quite a way out of London and had to catch the last bus down to the country at ten o'clock which was a bit of a handicap in playing a place like the 2 I's in the heart of wide-awake Soho.'

Cliff may have missed out on some wild times after he and The Drifters had finished their set each night, but he was pleased simply to be moving in such exalted musical circles. Even so, he was thoroughly dejected that his week at London's Mecca of rock 'n' roll had not brought him the overnight fame he naïvely anticipated. 'We were greeted by a tremendous round of indifference,' says Foster. 'It wasn't all of a sudden: "Here's a star." Nobody wanted to know.'

Well, not quite nobody. Chas McDevitt, one of the first of the 2 I's discoveries, remembers Cliff's impact quite differently. Chas, who had a big hit in 1957 on both sides of the Atlantic with 'Freight Train', recalls the female reaction to Cliff: 'The girls were absolutely screaming, going wild. I remember saying to Paul Lincoln: "With your money and our connections, we could manage him. He doesn't seem to have anyone looking after him." But Paul said: "No, we've had Tommy Steele. Rock 'n' roll's finished."'

On the positive side, the 2 I's engagement had at least introduced Cliff to a brand new audience and Cliff had enjoyed the experience. 'And once we'd played the 2 I's, everything escalated very quickly,' said Norman Mitham.

By mid-afternoon the following Saturday, Ian Samwell had joined The Drifters on lead guitar and was thrilled to do so.

'Cliff's renditions of rock 'n' roll songs that were hits at the time were all things by Chuck Berry, Little Richard or Elvis Presley and they were immaculate,' he enthused. 'Not just his copies, but in the spirit of the thing. He had an extraordinary vitality, terrific good looks and he was playing the music I liked anyway.'

Ian played his first gig at the 2 I's with his new bandmates that very evening, and within days he was a Drifter who no longer backed Harry Webb, but Cliff Richard.

The change of name was principally down to a promoter and ballroom manager by the name of Harry Greatorex, who had come down from the north of England to scout for new talent. He saw Cliff's group at the 2 I's and offered them their first out-of-town booking, at a dance hall in Ripley in Derbyshire.

In his trilby hat, smart raincoat, rimless glasses and with a briefcase tucked under his arm, Harry Greatorex looked more like a high-ranking civil servant than someone with a finger on the pulse of the latest teenage music craze. But Harry was not known in his area as Mr Entertainment for nothing, and he recognised the stir he could cause among Ripley's teenagers if he was able to present a London group at the Regal Ballroom, where he was manager.

John Foster almost bit his hand off when he proposed a fee of £5 plus £10 expenses. But there was one important detail Harry Greatorex wanted sorted out very quickly: how should he bill the group on posters and advertisements to promote the event locally.

He didn't favour just calling them The Drifters. The trend was for a named singer fronting a backing group, such as Gene Vincent and The Blue Caps, Tommy Steele and The Steelemen, Bill Haley and The Comets, Marty Wilde and The Wildcats.

Norman Mitham remembers that no one objected to Harry having his name up front: 'As he was obviously the centre of attraction in the group, we decided he had to be *the* name.'

Even though he himself was called Harry, the bespectacled Greatorex said he didn't care much for them to be called Harry Webb and The Drifters on his promo material. It just didn't have the right ring to it, he said, and urged them to come up with a new, trendier name that might generate a bit of excitement.

This needed some serious thought and they all repaired to the Swiss pub a few doors away to talk about it over a drink. In truth, Cliff had begun to realise that Harry Webb was not a name likely to summon up visions of a young rock 'n' roller, especially when compared with the Technicolor monikers Larry Parnes was conjuring up for his stable of singers.

Lots of names were bandied about and the talk got around to another young British singer at the time, who was called Russ Hamilton. 'I don't know why, but for some reason he particularly liked the name Clifford,' Norman Mitham recalls, 'so that evolved into Russ Clifford or Cliff Russard and then Cliff Richards.'

Finally Ian Samwell suggested Cliff Richard, stressing that the letter 's' should be knocked off the name. This was partly as a tribute to America's Little Richard who, in purely stylistic terms, was one of the most influential of the early stars of rock 'n' roll.

But the main reason for Richard singular, Ian pointed out, was that when people mistakenly called him Cliff Richards, Cliff could correct them. That way his name would be mentioned twice and was therefore likely to register more strongly. It was a clever marketing ploy that Cliff readily used in the early days whenever he could.

On making his way out of the pub, Cliff soon ran into Rick Richards, a young musician and photographer who regularly took pictures of the groups performing at the 2 I's. 'I've just stolen your name,' Cliff told him with a big grin. After Cliff hit the big time he autographed a Columbia Records publicity photo for Rick, and added: 'To Ricky, sorry I pinched your name.' Somewhat surprisingly, given that Cliff's dad was a stickler for discipline, Rodger Webb went along with his son's change of name. Cliff simply announced it as a *fait accompli* one evening and the whole family accepted it with a minimum of fuss.

Harry Greatorex, for his part, seemed satisfied with the transformation from Harry Webb to Cliff Richard and went off to telephone his local newspaper to place an advertisement.

Next day the name Cliff Richard and The Drifters appeared in print for the very first time – in the *Ripley and Heanor News*. In a single column listing forthcoming events for that week in 1958 was: Saturday 3 May, direct from the famous Soho 2 I's Coffee Bar, Cliff Richard and The Drifters plus Keith Freer and his Dixielanders.

5. DRIFTERS

As usual we were carting all our gear with us on the buses and on the train. But it was exciting times for all of us. I was with my best mate, he was now Cliff Richard, we were making music and it was all unreal at times.

Drifters guitarist Norman Mitham

Ripley, in the Amber Valley area of Derbyshire, might not be the most exciting small town in England, but it was the birthplace of the scientist and inventor Barnes Wallis, creator of the bouncing bomb used to such great effect in the Dambusters' famous raid in May 1943. Brilliant boffin Barnes had moved on from his home town long before the night some fifteen years later when Ripley qualified for its place in the history of British rock 'n' roll, as the town where Harry Webb performed as Cliff Richard for the very first time.

Some four hundred people were drawn to the Regal Ballroom that Saturday night to see the band, who were enticingly billed as 'Direct from the Famous Soho 2 I's Coffee Bar'.

Since then, of course, several thousands have claimed 'I was there' to see the seventeen-year-old Elvis idoliser running through his Presley gyrations in a white shirt and black trousers. What is beyond doubt is that Cliff was a huge hit at the Regal with an audience more accustomed to a night of sedate ballroom dancing.

As a venue, the Regal was something of a misnomer. It was a one-time snooker hall with a mock-Tudor frontage that had been converted into a drab dance hall with a scuffed and stained wooden floor. Around the walls were a number of slatted wooden benches where dance couples might perhaps sit out the Valeta and, to the right of the stage, a little side room offered for sale packets of crisps and soft drinks. No alcohol. Any rock rumpus that might occur that night certainly wouldn't be drink-fuelled.

All in all, the Regal was hardly the setting for an embryonic rock 'n' roll singer to encourage a rave-up. 'In fact, it all reminded me of a church hall,' Ian Samwell noted.

At least Cliff and the boys were impressed with the stage at the far end of the ballroom because it had deep, heavy, red velvet curtains that parted in the middle and drew back to each side. It was the first time the band had performed on a stage dressed like a theatre.

'While were setting up our gear, we kept peeping through the curtain,' said Norman Mitham. 'We wanted to see how many people were in and what kind of a crowd they were. Of course Cliff Richard and The Drifters were completely unknown then. But the fact that we were billed as from the 2 I's gave us a cachet. It was the draw of a band from London that brought a good crowd in, and that was when we had our first taste of girls screaming at us. When it first happened we were unprepared for it. Cliff and the rest of us looked around to see what on earth they were screaming at. Then we realised it was at us, but mainly at Cliff.'

The rapturous reception from the jiving teens of Ripley was all the more welcome for the four of them and Johnny Foster after a difficult journey, particularly for Cliff and Norman from Cheshunt. 'We had to get on a bus to St Pancras station to catch a train, which took about three hours, then when we got to Nottingham we had to get another bus to the venue,' said Norman.

'As usual we were carting all our gear with us on the buses and on the train. But it was exciting times for all of us. I was with my best mate, he was now Cliff Richard, we were making music and it was all unreal at times.

'We did two sets that night at the Regal with one break, so we played for around two and a half hours. We repeated our best numbers and tried to stretch out others with guitar breaks in the middle.

'It was all a very different set-up then than now. There was no sound system, so the sound was our own, it was our amp, our microphones. And there was no stage lighting. They just dimmed the lights in the hall, the curtains went back and we started playing.

'Cliff had no stage presentation to speak of at that time. He just went from one number to the next without saying barely a word. The only time he didn't sing was when we did an instrumental called "Swingin' Shepherd Blues", which was a hit for the Ted Heath Band that month. That was the only time he wasn't on the stage. Cliff was absolutely enthralled by Elvis, and so eighty per cent of what we did was Elvis. We also did some Buddy Holly and Chuck Berry numbers, but we had a very limited repertoire.'

Among the audience that night was fresh-faced schoolboy Neil West, who still lives in Derbyshire. 'It was a privilege to see Cliff that night,' said Neil. 'He was absolutely fantastic. He had such presence, he completely dominated the whole evening and the women went wild. In those days raw sex appeal was not something you got to see in public very often. Not in Ripley, anyway. But that is what Cliff demonstrated. The girl I was with that night was so turned on I still blush at the memory. The funny thing is I've completely forgotten her name, but I can remember every moment of Cliff's performance. No one who was in the Regal that night could have been at all surprised he became a star.'

Harry Greatorex showed his appreciation for the band's efforts by turning up with a bottle of whisky to share with them all once the crowd had headed for home. Everyone agreed it had been a great night, but one major problem remained for the band – where to sleep. Harry Greatorex clearly expected that a bunch of hot rock 'n' rollers from the 2 I's would have enough money to afford rooms for the night at a local hotel or a B & B. But Cliff and his bandmates had used up their entire expenses to pay for return train tickets and they had nowhere to spend the night. 'There was nothing for it,' said Norman. 'We slept on the wooden benches which lined the walls of the ballroom.'

The Ripley gig gave Cliff and his backing musicians a real glimpse of what life might be like as a pop attraction. They were a working rock 'n' roll band who had drawn in a big crowd and they had the girls screaming. Ian Samwell always maintained it was a very special milestone in the career of Cliff Richard: 'I think that night might have been the defining moment, the moment when Harry Webb truly became Cliff Richard. He in his white shirt, we in our red. We were the back-up group, he was the star . . . and we were rockin'.'

Just a few weeks later they all got the chance to meet one of America's rock 'n' roll legends, Jerry Lee Lewis from Ferriday, Louisiana, an artiste who certainly knew how to whip up an audience into a frenzy.

One of the greatest and most outrageous figures of 1950s rock 'n' roll, Jerry Lee conveyed hysterical excitement with the controlled frenzy of his playing and his whooping vocal style. Cliff Richard and The Drifters included several of his numbers in their repertoire, like 'Great Balls of Fire', 'Breathless' and 'Whole Lotta Shakin' Goin' On', and they were desperate to see him perform live.

Jerry Lee was touring Britain for the first time and his concerts had been eagerly awaited. He was, after all, a true rock original and one of the few white rock 'n' rollers of any great note who pounded a piano rather than a guitar. But Jerry Lee's popularity spectacularly and ignominiously nosedived when he encountered hostile publicity after it was revealed that the petite female he had taken as his new bride was his second cousin and was a mere thirteen years old. Suddenly Jerry Lee was not the hot attraction he might have been, and amid the furore in the press there were even calls for the singer to be deported.

As a consequence, demand for tickets for Jerry Lee Lewis's shows dropped off and became readily available, thereby allowing Cliff and his band to snap up several.

They subsequently went to see him putting his piano through its paces at the Kilburn State Theatre, and afterwards John Foster cheekily managed to wangle them all backstage by telling anyone who would listen that he had with him the UK's latest rock 'n' roll sensation.

The ploy worked. Eventually even Jerry Lee was persuaded that here were some fellow musicians he would do well to meet and greet. The boys were duly ushered into Jerry Lee's dressing room to be introduced to 'the monster' as some of the press had by now labelled him for his choice of a child-wife. And they even had their picture taken with him.

For this historic snap with one of the founding fathers of rock 'n' roll, Cliff stood right next to Jerry Lee. As Cliff well knew, Jerry Lee had begun his career at Sam Phillips's Sun Studios in Memphis, where Elvis had made his first records. He was thrilled to be pictured standing that close to one of Presley's fellow recording artistes.

Things were now starting to move fast for Cliff Richard and The Drifters, but too fast for Norman Mitham. Now that Ian Samwell had joined the band, Norman's position was becoming increasingly vulnerable.

In years to come Norman would take music lessons and become a more than proficient guitarist in successful bands. But time was not on his side in 1958. Norman, like Cliff, was still, in effect, little more than an enthusiastic beginner as a guitarist and, looking back, he admitted, 'At the time I didn't have the musical ability needed, and so I just got left behind.'

One day during a rehearsal at Terry Smart's house, Cliff was clearly on edge about something and Norman soon found out why. 'We'd got halfway through the rehearsal,' Norman remembered, 'when Cliff said: "I can't go on" and everything stopped. The reason was that Cliff's dad had something to say. He said my musical input into the group wasn't very good because I was basically playing the same chords as Cliff. Then he said that if I wasn't in the group the backing for Cliff would be just as good but the money the band made would be split three ways rather than four.

'What they were saying was correct. I had no argument with that. But I was absolutely shattered when I was told my services were no longer required. It hit me very badly.

'I had no ambition to become a rock 'n' roll star. But what hurt me was the fact that the guy I had been friends with for such a long time and been through such a lot with couldn't tell me himself. It was obvious that was the end of our close relationship. Cliff was very choked about it.'

Cliff's dislike of confrontation with a close friend was a trait to be repeated at other times in his life. And it would not be the last time he would leave it to his dad to deliver bad news to members of his immediate circle.

'So I was out of the band,' continued Norman, 'but later on Cliff was very good about it. He'd still come round to my house quite frequently and when he bought himself a scooter he'd come and take me out for rides on the back.

'I lost touch with Cliff when he eventually moved away. Then in 1981 he did a concert at Hammersmith Odeon with Phil Everly, which was being filmed for TV and the BBC sent us a couple of tickets. My wife and I had a few words on the way and so I said to her: "How about we sell these tickets and go for a meal instead?" But she said no, and when we arrived at the theatre they put us in the VIP area and we met Cliff afterwards. He came up to us and said he was taking us out for a meal, which he did. That was the last time I saw him.'

Norman stressed: 'I have no regrets,' and added with a chuckle: 'Cliff came round and sang his first record, "Move It", to me just before they recorded it. I said: "Well, yeah, it's OK, but maybe not!" But compared with Tommy Steele and Terry Dene and people like that, I always felt they didn't have the passion and the soul that Cliff had. With Cliff there was something there which comes from deep down.'

By now John Foster, who was soon to lose his job at the sewage works for taking so much time off to manage Cliff, was aware he was probably out of his depth when it came to management. He acknowledged Cliff needed proper professional guidance and, as Norman slipped out of The Drifters, he was also conscious of the fact that Cliff's dad was taking an increasing interest in the way the group was being run and the money they were making.

John was also being pressured by Larry Parnes to bring Cliff into the Parnes stable of singers. But he resisted, and Parnes's pursuit only made John redouble his own efforts to shoot Cliff into the big time.

John's next course of action was to persuade his parents to put up the £10 required to subsidise a private recording by the band, which he could then hawk around record companies. In a small studio above the HMV record shop in Oxford Street, Cliff and his band duly recorded two numbers: 'Lawdy Miss Clawdy', a popular Elvis LP track at the time, and a Jerry Lee Lewis favourite, 'Breathless'. This precious six-minute demo was eventually to provide Cliff with his breakthrough.

John's commitment, albeit amateurish due to inexperience, could hardly be faulted. He tried his utmost to get the right people at the record companies interested in Cliff and the band but, depressingly, none spotted their potential. Tommy Steele's then agent actually advised John not to let Cliff give up his day job. But John's persistence finally paid off when he managed to pull off a master stroke for which Cliff remains profoundly grateful.

John learned from a poster at the 2 I's that a Carroll Levis talent contest (Levis was a former radio announcer who became well known as a talent scout) was to be held one Saturday morning at the Gaumont Theatre at Shepherd's Bush Green, so he got in touch with the organisers to tell them about Cliff Richard and The Drifters. He cleverly told them he wasn't asking whether the band could enter the line-up of hopefuls because, after a stint at the prestigious 2 I's, they were naturally much too big for that. Instead, he said he was prepared to do the organisers a huge favour by offering a performance by the band at the talent contest for free – provided they topped the bill.

The Gaumont management couldn't resist John's seemingly generous offer of something for nothing and it was a done deal. It was also a resounding success for Cliff.

He rocked the Gaumont audience into near hysteria, was chased out of the theatre by screaming girls and took refuge in the public convenience on the corner of Shepherd's Bush Green. Cliff was thrilled by the reaction: 'I thought: wow! I'm screamable!'

For Cliff, the whole experience was a memorable one. After all the gigs at pubs, clubs and halls, it was the first time he had performed at a proper London theatre. Not only had he topped the bill, but he had sent the audience wild with excitement – just like his idol Elvis Presley.

Building on this success, Foster suggested the band return to the Gaumont to top the bill at another amateur talent contest the theatre was staging – and this time he planned to try and persuade influential showbiz agents to witness the hysteria.

In the run-up to the contest, Foster frantically phoned every agent and talent scout he knew in a bid to convince them to come along. Finally, on the day before the event, his entreaties caught the ear of George Ganjou, an agent whose name he had picked out at random from several listed in the showbiz weekly newspaper the *Stage*.

Ganjou turned out to be a strange choice. Rock 'n' roll was not his scene at all. Due to his naïvety about the workings of the showbusiness world, Foster had contacted an agent who was around sixty years old, had played flute in a Polish symphony orchestra and was mainly interested in booking speciality acts. Moreover, Warsaw-born Ganjou had only been an agent for a couple of years after spending much of his life touring the world wearing a wig, silk breeches and other finery as part of a graceful 'adagio dance presentation' act.

It was therefore asking a lot to persuade a man who was proud to describe himself as 'a square' to come down to Shepherd's Bush to check out a young would-be rock singer, especially on a Saturday morning, which Ganjou usually set aside for playing golf. But somehow John persuaded him it would be well worth his while to give up his round of golf for once. Even then it came down literally to a toss of a coin as to whether Ganjou would give Cliff Richard and The Drifters a miss. 'It was business or pleasure,' he later revealed, 'and it came down to business.'

On that following July morning, the Gaumont Theatre was buzzing with excitement as group after group went through their paces, each cheered on by the large band of faithful teenage followers they had brought along for support. Finally it was the turn of Cliff to take the stage, and he made an immediate impact in full Teddy-boy regalia – slicked-back hair, pink drape jacket, bright pink socks, tight black trousers and grey suede shoes. 'He was no Caruso,' was Ganjou's verdict. 'But he was a very beautiful young man. Vocal and visual.'

From his seat in the stalls George Ganjou could tell that here was a star in the making, especially when the teenage girls in the rows around him leaped out of their seats and started screaming and squealing with excitement whenever Cliff twitched so much as a muscle. 'They went absolutely mad,' he reflected. 'He was something new. I knew that he would become a star.'

The very next day, Sunday, George took the demo of 'Lawdy Miss Clawdy' and 'Breathless' and delivered it to his good friend Norrie Paramor, an orchestra leader and record producer with EMI.

Like Ganjou himself, Norrie Paramor was, on the face of it, not the most likely music man to approach about a promising rock singer.

Born in 1913, Norrie had been appointed recording director of the UK EMI Columbia label in 1952, after working as a pianist, bandleader, musical arranger and producer. He proved to have a priceless knack of picking hits and he turned Ruby Murray, a shy little teenage singer from Belfast, into one of the most successful female chart artists ever. By the end of 1955, Ruby had taken no less than seven songs in one year into the Top Twenty, including the chart-topper, 'Softly Softly'. Ruby's record of eighty weeks in the charts in one year was unmatched by a female singer until Madonna surpassed it in 1985, thirty years later.

Despite having produced what is thought to have been the first British rock 'n' roll single, 'Teach You To Rock' by Tony Crombie and his Rockets, Norrie was generally unsympathetic to rock 'n' roll. However, by the time he first encountered Cliff, he had edged closer to it with a series of novelty songs by The Mudlarks, the best of which were the inanely pleasing chants 'Lollipop' and 'Book of Love', both cover versions of US hits.

There was no doubting that Norrie Paramor knew a hit when he heard one, but George Ganjou recognised that Cliff's tape of two cover versions alone was unlikely to win Norrie over and he urged him to see for himself the boys in action. In addition to Cliff's tape, Ganjou took the liberty of handing Norrie a tape of a Ukrainian opera singer, Tino Valdi, whom he believed was also a star in the making.

Having taken delivery of the tapes, Norrie promptly went away on holiday, leaving Cliff to endure an agonising two weeks pondering what might be the outcome. When Norrie returned, George was more interested in hearing his reaction to Tino Valdi rather than to Cliff. Of the two, George felt that, vocally, Tino was vastly superior, and he was bitterly disappointed when Norrie informed him he had decided Tino was not for him.

The good news for George, however, was that Norrie was interested in Cliff and The Drifters, and he asked George to arrange an audition at EMI's Abbey Road studios, which, despite Cliff's nerves, they passed with ease. A three-hour recording session between seven and ten o'clock was booked for the evening of Sunday 24 July. Cliff was ecstatic, and Norrie Paramor, the hitmaker, already had a song in mind to launch him as a recording artist.

By that summer of 1958, there was growing belief in the UK that the musical storm that was rock 'n' roll had begun to blow itself out. In an article for the 14 June issue of the influential pop weekly *Melody Maker*, music aficionado Steve Race ruminated as to whether rock 'n' roll really was a fading force, as recurring reports suggested. 'So rock 'n' roll is dead, is it?' he queried. 'All right, then. My funeral oration consists of just two words: good riddance.

'What next – ballads? Some people seem to think so, but I can't help feeling that's largely wishful thinking. So many people in the profession would like ballads to return to favour.

'The fact is that up to now, as of early June 1958, there is no clear sign about what the next craze will be. Indeed there may *not* be another craze at all . . .'

The Top Twenty singles chart of 5 July reflected Steve Race's view that rock 'n' roll had had its day. Only Buddy Holly with 'Rave On' rocked the charts that week in a list of hits which featured a predominance of ballads. They included: 'On The Street Where You Live' by Vic Damone; 'Who's Sorry Now' by Connie Francis; 'Stairway Of Love' by Michael Holliday, and 'All I Have To Do Is Dream' by The Everly Brothers. A revitalised Frank Sinatra even had the satisfaction of an EP, 'The Lady Is A Tramp', jumping straight in at number nineteen. The balladeers appeared to have reclaimed nearly all the ground they had lost to the rockers.

Little did Steve Race know it at the time, but his dismissal of rock 'n' roll in print was unwittingly to inspire Ian Samwell to conjure up a spectacular musical riposte – on the top of a Green Line bus, of all places.

Ian was on his way to Cliff's house from St Albans, where he was on compassionate leave from the RAF to care for his sick mother. He clambered aboard the 715a from London Colney to Cheshunt and made his way to the top deck, which was empty. Taking a seat at the back, he took out his guitar and started playing around with a few chords, trying to work out Chuck Berry's licks.

Soon he stumbled upon a distinctive riff and, with Steve Race's article in his mind, he came up with 'Move It', a rollicking rockabilly song extolling the real country music that just drives along with a rhythm that grabs your heart and soul. Pausing only to scribble down the lyrics on a packet of guitar strings, Ian set about developing the song and composing a swaggering guitar salvo as an intro.

Once a member of a local church choir, Ian had written several hymns in a skiffle style. 'Move It' had come out of the blue, and he later reflected: 'It was truly a gift from God. So thank you, Steve Race, and God bless you. I owe it all to you.' Ian would chalk up several more hits to his name, but he would never write a better song than 'Move It', rightly revered ever since its inception as the first authentic, bona fide, truly great British rock number. It still stands up today.

By the time the bus reached Cheshunt, Ian had finished his masterpiece. When he got to Cliff's house, he calmly wrote out the lyrics afresh so Cliff could read them and proceeded to play 'Move It' to the rest of the band. Even in its rawest form, Cliff was impressed with the song and, according to Ian, it was Johnny Foster who suggested he call it 'Move It'.

As luck would have it, Ian had written 'Move It' with perfect timing. Cliff and The Drifters were due at EMI's studio number two roughly a week later for their first recording session and Norrie Paramor had just the one song lined up for them, 'Schoolboy Crush'. Another song would be needed for the 'flip side' of the record, as it was then called, so the boys could suggest 'Move It' as the filler track.

At the three-hour session the boys were swiftly made aware that time was money in the world of making records. The studios were run with strict precision. Bruce Welch, soon to become a guitarist in Cliff's new band, The Shadows, said: 'At ten p.m. you could be halfway through the greatest track of your life and the lights, everything, would go out. It was that way because the echo chambers were outside and the neighbours would complain.' Tea breaks, too, were timed to the second, with the tea ladies refusing to pour another cup once the appointed time was up.

Cliff, Terry Smart, and Ian Samwell were overawed when they had their first glimpse of Abbey Road's number two studio through the glass of the control room. They could not believe how large it was, and Ian said it reminded him of one of the aircraft hangers he had come to know so well during his days in the RAF.

As a precaution, producer Norrie Paramor had booked two fine, seasoned session musicians, bassist Frank Clarke and guitarist Ernie Shear. Norrie was far from sure The Drifters were up to the job of providing the backing required and his two skilled pros were wise insurance. Norrie had also booked The Mike Sammes Singers, a vocal group who would flesh out 'Schoolboy Crush' behind Cliff's lead voice.

Norrie had in mind some tuneful background whistling as part of the musical accompaniment, and The Mike Sammes Singers had already proved thoroughly, if unconventionally, adept in this capacity on Tommy Steele's number-one hit of 1957, 'Singing the Blues'. According to Tommy, the sound from their pursed lips gained a vital edge because they whistled through a piece of tough Bronco lavatory paper. 'Believe me, folks, if you do it through lavatory paper it's much more exciting,' chuckled Tommy.

It was customary in those days for the record companies to stick to the tried and trusted formula of using British artistes to record cover versions of American hits. Cliff's first record was to be no different. Record producers firmly believed it was the songs that the record-buying public went for, rather than a particular singer. Accordingly, Cliff and The Drifters' first recording was to be a cover of a US hit by Bobby Helms. The song had been brought to Norrie by Franklyn Boyd, a music publisher soon to take on a prominent role in Cliff's blossoming career.

'Schoolboy Crush' was recorded first after just a couple of rehearsals masterminded by Norrie. The boys had only ever seen Norrie in an executive suit, but now they were amazed to find him conducting the session wearing a colourful Hawaiian shirt and Bermuda shorts, having just returned from his holiday in Tangiers. Norrie's holiday attire at least helped to relax the tension of their first-ever recording session.

Norrie did not take much persuading to agree to 'Move It' as the flip side once the boys had played it for him. It must be stressed that this was a major departure from the norm: it was exceedingly rare in those days for a singer to record a brand-new number written by a member of his band, even if it was intended merely as a B-side filler.

'Move It' was Ian Samwell's song but, as was to be expected from a relative beginner, Ian's prowess as a guitar player fell way short of Ernie Shear's professionalism and he knew it. He therefore took no umbrage when Norrie decided that the latter should handle the more intricate guitar lines, particularly the attention-grabbing guitar rumble intro.

In his biographical account of those early days, *Let Me Tell ya Baby, it's Called Rock 'n' Roll*, Ian detailed: 'As any guitarist will know, the intro consists of a descending pattern of two notes played simultaneously. When you get to the bottom of the intro you are left with just two notes, E and B, which together form the ultra-simple rhythm chord that provides the basic foundation and rhythmic pulse of the song.'

Ernie picked up on the complexities immediately. It was agreed that Ian would play rhythm guitar, which left Cliff's guitar chords superfluous. But since Cliff felt uncomfortable singing without actually playing, Norrie agreed Cliff could simply hold his guitar as he stepped up to the microphone.

After one false start, 'Move It' was completed in two takes. The outstanding British rock record of its era, lasting all of two minutes and twenty seconds, took around twenty minutes to record. Up in the control room, Malcolm Addey, a junior engineer at EMI's studios, discreetly allowed the needle on the volume control to go beyond the stipulated limit to give the recording added punch.

' "Move It" was the first real rock 'n' roll record made outside America,' said Cliff, 'and we were very proud of that fact.' Norrie Paramor, who would go on to mastermind fifteen successive years of hit records for Cliff, was proud of it too. The partnership between record producer and singer became one of the most prolific and fruitful in recording history. Ironically, 'Brand New Song', the first record Cliff would make without Norrie, was Cliff's first miss.

Interviewed back in the 1970s by one of the authors of this book, Roy Orbison acknowledged that 'Move It' sounded so good it could well have come out of Sam Phillips's Sun Studios in Memphis, where Elvis Presley, Jerry Lee Lewis and Carl Perkins made their seminal rock recordings. 'As a rock 'n' roll record, it's just about as good as it gets,' said Roy.

Singer Vince Eager, a contemporary of Cliff's, said: 'Cliff was very fortunate in having such a great song written for him by Sammy Samwell. It really was a great song, but Cliff did it justice. The measure of it is that it's still a great song and I still include it in my set today.'

Joe Brown agrees: 'When I heard "Move It", I thought it was one of the best rock 'n' roll records. It was such a good record, the playing on it was great. On a lot of those early things you could hear the musicians reading the part, but you couldn't hear them reading it on "Move It".'

Good as it was, 'Move It' was still earmarked for the B-side, but Norrie said he would take a test pressing of the record home and play it for his teenage daughter Carolyn to get her verdict. A release date was set for 29 August and the record would be issued both on 78rpm and 45rpm. Fittingly, young Carolyn played 'Move It' so often that she virtually wore out the test pressing.

July 1958 turned out to be a remarkable few weeks for Cliff. On the strength of Cliff's impending record release, George Ganjou signed him to a sole agency agreement, which guaranteed the young singer would be earning an incredible £1,000 a week within six months. It was a huge amount of money for an as yet unknown teenage singer and a remarkable vote of confidence in Cliff from Ganjou.

George began piloting his protégé to fame by immediately securing a four-week engagement for him at a Butlins holiday camp. He had the contract to supply entertainers to the Butlins chain and booked Cliff into the holiday camp at Clacton-on-Sea, Essex. Originally the booking was just for Cliff, but the youngster put his foot down. He wasn't confident enough to fulfil the engagement on his own and insisted he needed the backing of his Drifters. Terry Smart and Ian Samwell were duly booked in, too. It was the first fully professional engagement for Cliff Richard and The Drifters, at £25 a week with board and lodging in camp chalets thrown in.

The contract stipulated the group had been hired as 'bar entertainers', so the entertainment manager kitted the boys out in the distinctive red shirts worn by Butlins staff, known as Redcoats. But John Foster wasn't happy. He felt his boys deserved better sartorial treatment. He didn't want them dressed the same way as the camp's latrine orderlies, for example, and he managed to purloin for them distinctive white shirts with, inexplicably, a large red V on the front.

At first Cliff and The Drifters were misguidedly placed in the South Sea Music Bar, a laid-back bar-cum-club where holidaymakers generally gathered for a pleasant evening to chat over a drink and lend an ear to the soft strains of lilting guitar music from a Hawaiian-style band. In such a sleepy setting, Cliff's raw, rock 'n' roll approach was not what was required.

Next morning they were informed they would be moved to the Jolly Rodger bar, an on-site contrivance of a pub, which proved equally unsatisfactory. The older holidaymakers, enjoying a pint or two, were not best pleased to find their bar suddenly swarming with teenagers ready to jive the night away.

Former Clacton Redcoat Stan Edwards recalled: 'Their repertoire was limited, and to cover the usual three-hour nightly period it was necessary for them to repeat songs they had done earlier in the evening. This did not go down well with the holidaymakers, especially as nearly all the songs were of the Elvis Presley type.'

Eventually the management recognised their mistake and installed Cliff and The Drifters in the Rock 'n' Roll Ballroom, where their style of music was warmly received. It was during his short stint at Butlins that Cliff first learned the meaning of 'being professional'. He went to bed every night knowing he had to get up in the morning fresh and ready to give a pumped, lively morning performance to keep the campers happy. This invariably lasted two hours and he was required, in addition, to give an evening show, which usually spanned three hours.

Cliff and The Drifters proved increasingly popular performers at the Rock 'n' Roll Ballroom, where they regularly performed the two songs from their debut single. They were especially pleased by the enthusiastic reaction to 'Move It'.

Their stock rose considerably in the eyes of the teenage holidaymakers when Tulah Tuke, a young actress working for the season as the DJ at the camp's radio station, played an advance pressing of the new record, thoughtfully sent by EMI, and announced: 'That was the new record by our own Cliff Richard and The Drifters. You can see them live tonight at the Rock 'n' Roll Ballroom.' Cliff was thrilled to hear his record played over the tannoy as he lay back in a deckchair and enjoyed the sun on his first seaside holiday since arriving in England.

While they were at Butlins, Norrie Paramor rang through one day to inform them that Radio Luxembourg was due to give their record its first airplay that night. In a state of feverish excitement Cliff and his bandmates gathered around a wireless in one of the chalets to hear the first radio broadcast. To the delight of them all, especially Ian Samwell, Radio Luxembourg played 'Move It', rather than 'Schoolboy Crush'.

On 31 July 1958, *Daily Mirror* showbiz writer Patrick Doncaster gave Cliff his first write-up in a national newspaper and ventured the opinion that Cliff had a personality that shone through the grooves of his first record. 'He could succeed in Discland,' Patrick predicted.

Cliff's record was one of a clutch of new September singles releases reviewed by Laurie Henshaw in *Melody Maker*. 'Cliff Richard makes a promising disc debut with "Schoolboy Crush",' he wrote. 'This follows the tortured vocal patterns that seem to be the vogue these days. "Move It" is in the Presley idiom – but it lives up to its title.'

Prophetic words, indeed.

6. LET THE GOOD TIMES ROLL

*I really think Cliff Richard is quite an alarmingly entertaining young man.
And* Oh Boy! *is simply heavenly.*

Lady Jellicoe, 1958

By 1957 more than half the homes in Britain possessed a television set, but the choice of music programming on television was desperately limited. There was, of course, only one BBC TV channel back then, and ITV was still very much in its infancy. Any teenager glancing through the TV schedules found nothing in the way of music to suit his or her tastes, and their mums and dads fared little better. There was Eric Robinson's *Music For You*, a programme that had been running for seven years and that prided itself on inviting major overseas operatic stars to take part, and the old-time section on *Come Dancing*. And that was just about the sum of it.

But, in February 1957, the Toddlers' Truce, the television shutdown between six and seven o'clock in the evening, aimed at tricking children into believing TV had finished for the night and it was time for bed, had ended. Bowing to the inevitable, the BBC saw the chance to fill that particular timeslot on Saturday evenings with a show catering for teenagers. They launched *Six-Five Special*, a programme teens could enjoy before they went out to the cinema to see Elvis in *Jailhouse Rock*, or to the youth clubs or to the dance halls.

On Saturday 16 February 1957, *Six-Five Special* – so called because it was screened at five minutes past six – came over the points and down the line for the first time with an opening sequence of a speeding train to Johnny Johnson's theme music.

It was a show blatantly aimed to reflect the changes in musical tastes, and in youngsters generally, and co-presenter Pete Murray welcomed viewers by saying: 'We've got almost a hundred cats jumping here, some real characters to give us a gas! So let's get on with it and have us a ball!'

The first show included the Bob Cort Skiffle Group, Pouishnoff the classical pianist, modern jazz trumpeter Kenny Baker and a film clip of Little Richard from the movie *Don't Stop the Rock*. A studio audience of a hundred and fifty kids were kept in order by regimental Sergeant Major Brittain and boxer Freddie Mills.

In the coming weeks, the teenagers were encouraged to jive and clap along to music from the likes of Tommy Steele and his Steelmen, who became regulars on the show, and Adam Faith, who made his TV debut on the programme.

These new 'stars of discland' were introduced by Pete Murray and Josephine Douglas with Don Lang and his Frantic Five, and the programme soon built up a huge following of over eight million viewers and led to a film, two stage shows and a concert version.

Producer of this innovative show was Jack Good, a bespectacled and erudite Oxford graduate in his late twenties with a degree in philosophy and English language. Like many of his contemporaries, Jack developed a burning passion for rock 'n' roll after seeing the film *Rock Around the Clock* at the cinema. Up to that point he had never taken much interest in pop music – he was much more of a Bach and Mozart man. But, as he sat in the stalls and all around him teenagers got up from their seats to dance in the aisles to the music, he was gripped by the pulsating atmosphere and resolved to try and bring this high-energy participation to television. *Six-Five Special* was his first attempt to project the excitement of rock through the TV screen.

His brief as a BBC light entertainment producer was to make a programme to appeal to adolescents, 'something with mountain climbing for boys, fashion for girls, that sort of thing'. But Jack was always a maverick, and he trod a tricky tightrope with his BBC bosses. Good's full-on, innovative approach was at odds with the view of the staid BBC 'suits', who felt *Six-Five Special* should have something of a message.

In March 1957, after a handful of shows, executive producer Jo Douglas felt compelled to write a memo to the head of religious broadcasting that read: 'I do hope you don't still feel that we are corrupting the morals of the youth of this country. This is far from our intent.'

In the event, incredibly, a priest in a dog collar was actually brought in to do the hand-jive to show the church was 'with it'.

Despite early appearances by rocker Tommy Steele, skiffle king Lonnie Donegan and jazzman Johnny Dankworth, Good soon became fed up with the BBC's restrictions and his bosses' demands that the programme reflect a teenage magazine format. Jack wanted to focus more on music, correctly believing this was what the youthful audience really wanted from *Six-Five Special*. In exasperation, he resigned from the BBC at the start of 1958 and took his talents and his programme concept off to the independent television company ABC, where his verve, enthusiasm, imagination and groundbreaking ideas could be given full rein.

ABC welcomed him with open arms and gave him the chance to make two pilot rock 'n' roll shows at the Wood Green Empire in the summer of 1958 with Marty Wilde, by now an established regular in the charts, as the major star.

Good gave the programmes the title *Oh Boy!* after the popular Buddy Holly hit. Jazz critic Tony Hall, who eventually alternated as *Oh Boy!*'s presenter with Jimmy Henney, told *TV Times* in 1958: 'I saw the two trial shows and thought they were the most exciting things I've ever seen on television. The lighting, the camera work was great, and I thought the music was swinging more than most of TV's attempts to present jazz.' With unbridled enthusiasm for the music, Jack had created a musical montage bursting with energy.

The pilot shows were deemed enough of a success for ABC to give the go-ahead for a series of half-hour *Oh Boy!*

programmes in an early Saturday evening slot on the ITV network.

At a time when it was a generally held view that rock 'n' roll was a passing craze that simply could not last, Good was way ahead of the game. He recognised it as a major cultural and social phenomenon, and he even dared to state on the radio that Elvis Presley was a genius and that he would go down as one of the twentieth century's great artistic figures. In the mood of the times, that was tantamount to anarchy, but Jack Good knew exactly what he was saying. Moreover, he knew precisely what he was doing, especially when it came to packaging rock 'n' roll for TV. Like Dick Clark in the US with his *American Bandstand*, Good had discovered a successful formula for televising rock 'n' roll.

He said: 'I was interested in *Oh Boy!* as a half-hour score, so it was an opera in a sense. Theatrical performance was the first thing that mattered to me, and the music, of course, was the guts of it. If the music wasn't right, then all the theatrical effects of the lighting, hair, and twitching and all of the gimmicks would have been meaningless.'

It was Cliff's good fortune that he turned out to be Good's golden boy in the revolutionary musical extravaganza that was *Oh Boy!*.

Jack was devising *Oh Boy!* as Britain's first truly visual pop show at a time when Cliff was playing at Butlins during that August of 1958. Jack wanted exciting, hip young singers, groups and dancers, plus a lively, jiving and screaming audience, and he planned to punch home the rock beat with snappy camera cuts from his singing stars to the dancing teenagers 'getting hep' to the music. With music arranger Harry Robinson he put together a rocking house band and, with tongue firmly in cheek, he named them Lord Rockingham's XI as a play on the words 'rocking 'em'– bizarrely, the band's members actually numbered thirteen.

Before confirming his line-up of musicians, Robinson took himself off to a seaside caravan and locked himself in with a pile of American hit records in an effort to understand fully how their sound was achieved so he could replicate it.

It was time well spent: Lord Rockingham's XI sounded authentic and even went on to have a novelty chart-topping hit in their own right with 'Hoots Mon'.

With the resident band in place, now the search was on for a bright new star – and Cliff happened to be the right singer in the right place with the right looks and the right record at the right time. He was absolutely right for the show.

Ironically, Cliff had failed a BBC audition for *Six-Five Special* but, fortunately for him, it was after Jack Good had jumped ship to commercial television. He was therefore not tainted by this failure when he came to Jack's attention via Norrie Paramor and music publisher Franklyn Boyd.

Norrie knew about Jack's upcoming TV show *Oh Boy!* and urged Franklyn to get in touch with Jack and play him Cliff's debut single. Jack liked the production and the singer's voice on 'Schoolboy Crush', but otherwise it left him cold. 'Just the sort of drivel I hated,' was Jack's verdict. 'No guts.' But he was completely knocked out when he turned the record over and played 'Move It'. 'I was amazed,' he said. 'It was a genuine rock 'n' roll record, it was British, and the singer sounded like a rock 'n' roll singer.' Was this Cliff Richard boy really British? Jack asked Franklyn incredulously.

In his excitement Jack sought out Marty Wilde, then a rising hit parade singer whom Jack had persuaded to join him on *Oh Boy!* from *Six-Five Special*, and asked him to give 'Move It' a listen. Marty, too, could hardly believe it was a home-grown effort.

In a column he later wrote for the music paper *Disc*, Jack expressed his enthusiasm in a feature headlined 'Just another beginner? No – this boy is really terrific'. Explaining his feelings on hearing 'Move It' for the first time, Jack wrote: 'Wham! This disc could sell 50,000 on its first eight bars alone. It kicks off with a forceful, dramatic guitar phrase that runs an electric shock down the spine. In comes the drum, driving a vicious beat through the heart of the number. Then the voice rides confidently over this glorious backing – a voice with an amazingly non-imitative style, considering that this kind of music ought to be foreign to anyone who is not a native of the southern States . . . when one considers that this is the product of a seventeen-year-old boy from Cheshunt, Hertfordshire, the mind just boggles.'

Fittingly, this glowing endorsement found its way into newsagents on 9 August, Cliff's last day as an employee of Atlas Lamps.

Jack Good may have waxed lyrical over 'Move It', but he had no idea what Cliff looked like in person. Before he signed Cliff up for an appearance on *Oh Boy!* Jack wanted to see for himself whether Cliff had the right kind of looks to go with 'Move It'. He didn't dare hope Cliff looked as good as he sounded. There was no doubting the record had made a big impact on Jack and he was praying that its singer wasn't an overweight youth with buck teeth, a squint, and a face covered in acne.

Looks would be vital in a show aiming to be visually cool, and Jack also wanted to find out whether Cliff and The Drifters were capable of performing on a live TV show. An audition was therefore quickly arranged at a rehearsal room close to Leicester Square tube station.

Jack was relieved when he met Cliff and The Drifters for the first time. 'They were practising, I opened the door and there they were. I couldn't believe my luck – this guy looked great. He wasn't doing anything spectacular, but he certainly looked fine.'

Jack was first struck by how dark Cliff was, how shy and how young – an authentic, immature teenager. Cliff was still growing and was no more than five feet nine, but Jack Good knew immediately that with Cliff's looks he could package him perfectly for *Oh Boy!*. 'He was malleable,' Jack said of that first meeting. 'I thought: something could be done with this boy.'

'Cliff had Harry Belafonte's shirt on, Elvis's sideburns, something from Jerry Lee Lewis, a bit from somebody else – but he looked a good possibility. He looked like somebody who could compel attention when I saw him and he was perfect. There was a magic in his eyes – they were definitely not your average English eyes – his whole face was fascinating. Nothing was irregular except his teeth when he opened his mouth. His teeth were ragged and he had sharp canines. I realised the effect there could be when he rolled back his top lip. The angel could draw blood.

'But he was no use to me the way he was. He was just a seventeen-year-old boy who'd come up from the sticks and didn't quite know what was happening.

'At the audition he did a Jerry Lee Lewis number and was strumming away on his guitar. He didn't really play it very well. I thought: yes, we've got to have this guy. But he looked too cornily Elvis, a bit of a Teddy boy with the sideburns.'

Cliff's working relationship with Jack got off to an un-promising start. Jack wanted a brand new star, not an Elvis lookalike, and insisted Cliff's Presley-style long sideburns must go. Naturally Cliff was devastated – Elvis was his idol and the sideburns were an important part of Cliff's personal look. Jack insisted, and shocked Cliff still further by telling him he would be divesting him of his guitar when he sang, to distance him still further from Elvis.

'When I said: "Shave off your sideburns," there was an argument,' Jack recounted. 'He was very nice, not self-assured, but he knew his mind. And there was this stubborn streak: his sideburns and his guitar were props because he felt so insecure. Without them he felt he would be revealed and just look like Harry Webb making an idiot of himself. But he actually looked tremendously exciting.'

Very reluctantly Cliff agreed to let go of the guitar and took a razor to his sideburns. He was young, grateful even to be considered for a TV appearance, and he felt it wasn't his place to argue with the man who had put *Six-Five Special* on the map and seemed so sure of what he was doing.

Cliff was booked to appear on *Oh Boy!* on 13 September, which gave Jack a week of rehearsals at the Four Provinces of Ireland Club in Canonbury Lane, near Highbury in north London, in which to mould Cliff, minus guitar and sideburns, into a brand new British teen idol. Fellow singer Vince Eager, who was at the rehearsals, remembered Cliff changing before his very eyes: 'Cliff had great star quality and Jack was a genius. He took singers like Cliff, Marty Wilde, Billy Fury and Gene Vincent and produced them, moulded them, directed them and created them into something they never thought they could be.'

'He had amazing persuasive powers,' Marty Wilde concurred. 'He was like a high priest because whatever he said, you had to listen, because he was intelligent – and it was said in such a wonderful accent.'

Those who witnessed it still chuckle at Jack's remoulding of Gene Vincent when the American rocker appeared on *Boy Meets Girl*, Jack's follow-up TV show to *Oh Boy!*. A shipyard worker's son from Norfolk, Virginia, Vincent's left leg had been shattered in a road accident in 1955 but, undeterred, he pressed on with a singing career.

Jack had Vincent flown over to Britain and went out to Heathrow to meet the man he imagined to be 'the ultimate dangerous dagger boy'. To his surprise, Jack found himself greeting not the rough, tough, menacing rocker he expected, but a thoroughly pleasant, polite young Southern gentleman who even called him 'Sir'.

Equally disappointing for Jack was that Gene was dressed in a red felt ice-hockey jacket, which didn't fit in at all with the image Jack planned for him of an evil, malformed, limping Richard III figure. So for *Boy Meets Girl* Jack made him wear a large black pendant, black gauntlets, black high-heeled boots and black leather trousers with his leg-irons to give Gene a sinister appearance and to further intensify his original greasy, working-class image.

To emphasise Gene's limp on his first television appearance, Jack built a series of steps for him to climb. But the singer was adept at concealing his disability, which left Jack resorting to desperate measures. As Gene made his way to the microphone to take up his awkward stance, Jack famously shouted four words of encouragement: 'Limp, you bugger, limp!' The overall visual effect created by Jack Good, however, was evil enough for Gene Vincent to trade for many years to come.

The moulding of Cliff was less dramatic but no less considered. Jack's method was to start off by sitting Cliff in a chair with his hands folded and then build up elements of his performances. He told Cliff not to hold his hands in front of his body and to stand with his feet spread a foot apart because it would relax him. Good also told him to tilt his head downwards and look up at the camera with his big, dark, soulful eyes, and urged him not to stand square on to the microphone. He even instructed Cliff to grab his elbow at one point while he was singing, as if he had been suddenly jabbed by a hypodermic needle. It would add dramatic effect and give special impact to a particular line, Jack told his eager pupil. 'He even had Cliff have a sort of sneer, which the girls thought was sexy,' said Joe Brown, then a brilliant young guitarist with Lord Rockingham's XI before being singled out for solo stardom.

Jack groomed Cliff to be 'the quiet smoulderer', the boy idol almost innocently unaware of the flames of passion he could ignite among the opposite sex. 'I told him not to smile, but to look smouldery – and it worked,' said Jack. 'He was very slim, very innocent-looking, but he couldn't help being a smoulderer! We presented it as if it was beyond him not to be a smoulderer – yet he didn't mean to be! That was the excitement.'

Cliff happily went along with it: 'One of my front teeth was capped and the shadow from the TV lighting made it look as though I had a tooth missing. So instead of smiling, I smouldered!

'He gave me this image, and I became this sultry person, because that's what he told me to do. And it caught on. I had reviews saying I had sexy eyes. Of course, when I read them I thought: oh have I? So of course I played on it more. I didn't know what to do, I was still fumbling and trying to find myself, but Jack was that strong.'

Watching the transformation was Vince Eager. 'We could see Jack doing all the movements himself and coaching Cliff in how to do them,' said Vince. 'He listened, and he learned fast.'

Hours before he was due to go in front of the TV cameras for the first time, Cliff told a writer from the *New Musical Express*: 'I feel so nervous I don't know what to do. I mean, I only turned professional five weeks ago, and before that I was working as a clerk and only playing at local dances and things in my spare time. I wore sideburns then, but I shaved them off last night – Jack thought it would make me look more original. I think he's right.'

Dressed in an outfit, approved by his mentor, of pink jacket, black shirt, pink tie and pink socks, Cliff made his first appearance on *Oh Boy!* with Marty Wilde, Ronnie Carroll, the John Barry Seven and Lord Rockingham's XI.

Jack had it all figured out to give Cliff's entrance a big build-up. 'I had the curtains closed, the lights on the curtains, then at the signal, the spotlight would hit the curtains, the curtains would whip aside and the band would rock into a great number. Then the vocal groups would come on, then The Vernon Girls would come on, and then the spotlight would hit the microphone with nobody there and I'd dash forward and say: "Here's the boy who's going to rock the world – Cliff Richard!"'

Of all the performers, however, Marty Wilde was the one who had the girls squealing in excitement. Nobody screamed at Cliff on his TV debut but, as Jack Good explained: 'It was only because they were sucking in their breath . . . The audience were quivering. On screen he was so lithe it was as if he could leap out at you like a panther.'

Not all the critics agreed. One reviewer wrote that *Oh Boy!* burst on to TV screens and consisted mainly of shots of a young man seemingly chewing gum. 'That was me!' laughs Cliff.

Unusually, Jack allowed his new discovery to sing not one but two songs on his TV debut, 'Move It' and 'Don't Bug Me Baby'. It was a generous gesture on Good's part, since an average of at least ten different acts had to be squeezed into a show lasting just 25 minutes. Cliff also joined the rest of the cast for the show's finale of 'Hoots Mon', the signature hit for Lord Rockinghham's XI.

The following week Cliff was back on the show to sing 'Schoolboy Crush', and by the time he was due to make his third consecutive appearance, 'Move It' had gone straight into *Melody Maker's* Top Twenty chart at number twelve. All of EMI's marketing and publicity plans had been switched from 'Schoolboy Crush' to 'Move It' as the A-side of the single the minute Jack had decided to plump for it.

The fact that Cliff now had a big hit triggered a very different reaction from the studio audience when he made his third consecutive appearance. They looked upon him as a very real star now he had a record shooting up the charts.

'I was quite outrageous the first time I was on *Oh Boy!* and got no reaction at all,' he said. 'Three weeks later, "Move It" entered the charts and I did the same number, in the same clothes, in the same way and I got screamed off the stage. Not because of me. I didn't change anything. But I became the thing to scream at.'

Jack Good commented: 'After "Move It", the audience reaction was such that he couldn't help but be exciting because he didn't have to do anything. The spotlight came on him and the whole audience went wild.

'He used to get a fortune in pennies when a penny used to be a real-sized penny – thrown at him on the stage by angry boys. There would be girls falling about and going into hysterics and foaming at the mouth and these furious boys chucking these great pennies at Cliff. Poor fellow! They didn't know it wasn't his fault that he had to wear this pink jacket and smoulder!'

Cliff later jokily reflected: 'Physically I was a greasy slob. I was probably the first bad-taste dresser in this country. I wore pink socks and a pink jacket. I used to fluoresce!'

'Move It' eventually peaked at number two in the charts, with sales sustained by his *Oh Boy!* appearances. Cliff was able to scan the charts with pride and see his name sandwiched in the best-seller lists between those of his idols, Elvis Presley with 'King Creole' and The Everly Brothers with 'Bird Dog'.

'Our first recording contract gave us an old penny for each record sold,' Cliff later revealed many years later, 'and I remember saying to the boys: "Hey! I'm rich! I can buy a TV set for my mum and dad."' And he did just that.

'Move It's success was matched by Cliff's rapid rise to undisputed number-one star of *Oh Boy!*, but a slice of luck was required to elevate him to top attraction on the show.

Vince Eager explains: 'Larry Parnes, who managed Marty Wilde and myself, had a row with Jack about what Marty should wear on the show. Larry wanted Marty to wear the grey mohair suit Marty had turned up in, but Jack said it wasn't suitable because it wouldn't go with the lighting. He told him: "I'm the producer and what I say goes." '

A major row blew up, Vince remembers, and Jack Good actually had Larry escorted from the theatre after summoning security. Marty eventually did go on stage in his shiny suit on the 18 October show, but afterwards an enraged Larry Parnes carried out his threat to pull Marty out of the series. 'Once Marty dropped out,' said Vince, 'Cliff had it to himself as resident singer. I always thought he would be a big rock 'n' roll star but I didn't think it would happen so quickly.'

Cliff and Marty were by now good friends and wisely stayed out of the row. But that didn't stop the press from drumming up a story that the two singers were at each other's throats, much to their annoyance. 'I hope people realise that Marty and I stayed pals throughout,' Cliff protested. 'There was something which irritated us both while the row was on, however, and that was a big newspaper's headline that said "Richard versus Wilde row". Millions of readers must have thought we were out to knock each other to pieces. It wouldn't have been so bad if a few more people had looked on us as human beings, instead of just as names.'

Marty was nevertheless acutely aware of the consequences of his enforced absences, said Vince. 'Marty told me he was worried that Cliff could become so big he might not even get back on to *Oh Boy!*' Marty did eventually return to the show early in February 1959.

Marty's non-appearance meant the opportunity was there for Cliff to be built up week by week as the unquestioned star of the show and the singer to set female pulses racing. Cliff appeared in thirteen of the sixteen *Oh Boy!* shows broadcast in 1958 and, with Marty sidelined, Cliff was promoted to sing no less than seven tracks on the official *Oh Boy!* LP, many of which had been earmarked for Marty.

When he found the time, Cliff would join other *Oh Boy!* regulars for a bite to eat at the Lotus House restaurant on the Edgware Road, a popular showbiz haunt. One evening Cliff's youthful good looks caught the eye of another diner by the name of Ronnie Kray, a Lotus House regular who liked to mingle with celebrities. The notorious East End gangster did not recognise Cliff as the rising singer on *Oh Boy!*, but he had other designs on the good-looking teenager. Kray sent over one of his aides to invite Cliff to join him at his table. Fortunately for Cliff, there were others around him who knew the score and urged him to decline the invitation.

Jack Good is of the opinion that Cliff found the adulation he received on *Oh Boy!* to be more of an embarrassment than a turn-on. 'All the cast loved him,' he said. 'Nobody felt resentment when in three weeks he became the star of the show, as it were – which is an amazing achievement in itself. It would have cracked up some people, but it didn't even begin to dent him. He continued being shy and nice and turning up on time.'

He may have appeared shy and nice to those who knew him but, under Jack's tutelage, there was no denying that Cliff performed in a sexual way as a young man – something viewers had previously only seen in female performers. As one observer put it: 'It wasn't effeminate. He was overtly projecting sexuality and trying to draw you into him.'

But not everyone believed it was within the bounds of decency, and Cliff's TV gyrations as he sang were soon sparking controversy. The *New Musical Express* described Cliff's TV performance as 'the most crude exhibitionism ever seen on British TV'. It labelled Cliff's 'violent hip-swinging' as 'revolting' and 'hardly the kind of performance any parent could wish his children to witness.'

It added: 'If we are expected to believe that Cliff Richard was acting "naturally", then consideration for medical treatment before it's too late may be advisable.

'While firmly believing that Cliff Richard can emerge into a top star and enjoy a lengthy musical career, it will only be accomplished by dispensing with short-sighted, vulgar tactics.' (Cliff later had a copy of the article framed to hang in his home.)

The teenage readers of the *New Musical Express* weren't overly bothered by the stinging comments about their idol, but the tabloid *Daily Sketch* picked up on the debate and followed up with a headline that asked: 'Is This Boy TV Star Too Sexy?'

Elvis the Pelvis had received similar castigation in America, where his hip-swaying was initially considered too vulgar for TV, resulting in his being filmed only from the waist up. Now Cliff, similarly, was suddenly considered to be a corrupting influence on teenagers and definitely too hot for television.

Cliff was hurt by the attacks in the press. Incurring parental disapproval and being painted as the *enfant terrible* of British rock 'n' roll was not what he had expected, but it was all priceless publicity for *Oh Boy!*. The furore prompted a surge in the TV audience as parents in homes across the country tuned in to see what the fuss was all about.

Happily for Cliff, there were many who disagreed with the opinion of the *New Musical Express*, and support for the singer came from some of the unlikeliest quarters. No less than the distinguished Lady Jellicoe, wife of a high-ranking Foreign Office minister, gave him a ringing endorsement by saying: 'I really think Cliff Richard is quite an alarmingly entertaining young man. And *Oh Boy!* is simply heavenly.'

And Elfrida Eden, the aristocratic eighteen-year-old niece of former Prime Minister Sir Anthony Eden, proved that Cliff's appeal was far from limited to secretaries in the typing pool by drooling: 'I think Cliff's action is incredible. My mother doesn't approve, but give me *Oh Boy!* every time instead of all that debbery nonsense.'

Cliff was adamant he was not a corrupting influence on teenagers. 'When I stood on stage and people thought my movements were sexy, I was never flaunting sexuality and it was never contrived,' he has said. 'I just tried to adopt an Elvis pose like all rock singers did at that time.'

With every appearance on *Oh Boy!* Cliff's fame spread. He was still living at home and now fans had found out the location and address, they were turning up on his doorstep or hanging about outside.

One week, a train-load of six hundred teenagers came in from Birmingham and thronged the back entrance of the *Oh Boy!* studios in Hackney, thereby preventing Cliff from leaving.

He was due to proceed straight to an appearance in Hammersmith, and there was no way through the crowd to the tour coach until police managed to clear a path for him. But once he made a dash for it, the escape route disappeared into a melée as the crowd surged forward. With hands frantically tearing at his hair and clothes, Cliff took refuge in a public convenience over the road. He was stuck there for fully half an hour wondering how he was going to get out. 'Then three or four boys came in. They looked like roughs. They stared at me. "Are you Cliff Richard?" they asked. I said: "Yes." "Can I shake hands with you?" I said: "With pleasure." Then they went out and got their friends and made a big archway and got us to the coach.'

Oh Boy!'s dynamic weekly half-hour parade of non-stop rockers attracted several top acts from America, including The Inkspots, Conway Twitty and Brenda Lee. Their appearances gave the show extra credibility for an audience becoming increasingly interested in and familiar with American popular music. US stars on the bill also helped to gain *Oh Boy!* a screening, albeit limited, on American TV.

To Good's great satisfaction, *Oh Boy!* made its rival, *Six-Five Special*, screened in direct opposition, look positively 'square'. His show crackled with energy and Barbara Mitchell, the blonde bombshell of *Oh Boy!*'s ever-present and glamorous vocal trio, The Vernon Girls, put much of it down to Jack's own pumped-up presence: 'Jack would jump up and down like a child and run wild, gesticulating like some mad Russian composer. But his infectious enthusiasm and brilliance worked wonders.'

Marty Wilde recalled in a BBC interview in 1981: 'He would get the audience so buzzed up on the night itself, you could have sent on a milk float and that would have got applause. It was the most exciting television show ever. Nothing will ever take its place.'

Cliff's admiration for Jack was just as unstinting, and he particularly recalls a remarkable screening of Lord Rockingham's XI with their chart-topper, 'Hoots Mon'.

'He made a camera cut on every single bar – a camera shot up the nostrils of the guitarist, on the fingers of the saxophonist, on the haircut of the keyboard player, on the dog that sat on

Cherry Wainer's organ. Watching it, you'd think: "This is impossible. It's unbelievable!" That's how good it was.'

Jack Good and *Oh Boy!* were vastly influential in launching Cliff to stardom. Joe Brown goes so far as to say: 'Jack Good was the guru. He was the guy who invented Cliff.'

Cliff himself has never shied away from acknowledging how important the TV rock impresario was in shaping his early career. 'By making me cut my sideburns off and throw my guitar away, he immediately made me unlike Elvis,' he said. 'He got me to think about performing in a way that wasn't like Elvis and it took me a while to find out how to do it without actually being a copy.

'My great fantasy was to have a photograph taken where I did have the Elvis look, the lip curled, the hair looking good and smouldering eyes. I wanted to look like him. Then I realised you can't have a good individual specific career as somebody else because they've already done it.

'When Jack Good wanted "Move It" rather than "Schoolboy Crush", EMI swung their whole campaign around. They changed all the posters and the advertising to "Cliff Richard sings his new single 'Move It'". It was the right thing and I had TV behind me when the record happened. It was great to be able to sing it on *Oh Boy!* when it was 28 in the charts and then sing it as the record went up to number two, its highest position.' Cliff added: 'Jack was a tremendous help to me, particularly as I was just an idiot kid at the time. He helped me find Cliff Richard.'

It was also Jack's idea that Cliff should not speak on screen for the first six months of the programme in order to maintain a mystique.

During the second series of *Oh Boy!* Cliff's appearances on the show became less frequent as his fee and his star status grew. In all, he made just seven appearances in 1959, which irritated Jack Good no end. 'There was Cliff going off into the sticks making a few hundred pounds for himself singing "Living Doll" or whatever, when he should have been on my show,' Good said ruefully. 'I thought these evil thoughts: "There is no greater show than *Oh Boy!* to appear on, no greater producer than Jack Good, what is this guy walking off into the sticks for, doing all these shows, wearing himself out just to earn a few thousands pounds?"'

Cliff says he was all too aware that Jack really hated it when he went off into 'Living Doll' mode. 'But as much as I love him dearly, I couldn't give two hoots what Jack thinks,' Cliff explained, 'because I wanted more.'

By the time he was making his final *Oh Boy!* appearances, Cliff had seen 'Move It' peak at number two in the charts, his follow-up single, 'High Class Baby', at number seven, and third single, 'Livin' Lovin' Doll', at number twenty. It was a downward graph in terms of chart positions, which was then arrested by 'Living Doll' reaching number one. 'I didn't want my career to end-dead. I wanted a career, and I liked what I was getting out of my life at that stage and I wasn't going to relinquish my hold on it. It seemed to me that the only way I could advance myself was by moving into other areas that rock 'n' roll afforded.'

The very process of filming *Oh Boy!* was of priceless benefit to Cliff. It was a huge learning curve for him at such a young age, not least the discipline needed to build up through the week to a live TV performance. Five days a week he was required to be at rehearsals at 9.30 in the morning, ready to be put through his paces immediately by Jack Good. That meant getting up very early to make the journey from his home. On Saturdays, when the show was transmitted live at 6 p.m. from the Hackney Empire, Cliff was required to be ready at 8.30 a.m. for a day of final intensive rehearsals.

'Looking back on some of the film footage of my early career, I sometimes cringe,' Cliff has admitted. 'In those days I used to stand in front of a mirror and practise twitching my lips. One reason I never used to smile was that peculiar small tooth, which I tried to hide by glowering.'

Amateurish he may have been in those early days, but it was nonetheless thrilling for Cliff to find himself right there at the birth of British rock 'n' roll. And he believes a vibrant, credible UK rock scene was just what the country needed to help pierce through the post-war gloom.

'There was a kind of drabness, and I guess that's inevitable given what people went through here. Maybe that's why some of us were so keen that we should make something of ourselves, not just rock 'n' roll singers, but all sorts of artistes. The whole of England was wanting to pull itself up by its bootlaces. That's where rock 'n' roll fits in – certainly there was this blast of light from America and we had Elvis, Jerry Lee, The Everly Brothers, Buddy Holly, Ricky Nelson, Little Richard. That was just fantastic and was part of the regrowth, the rejuvenation of Britain. Rock 'n' roll played a major role.'

While Jack Good must take immense credit for putting Cliff on the map as a rock 'n' roll singer, he was not surprised at how quickly Cliff moved on to become an all-round entertainer. Elvis Presley had swiftly managed to change from threatening, swaggering sex symbol to patriotic soldier and movie star, and yet Elvis still managed to maintain a dangerous edge and continued to be a keeper of the rock 'n' roll flame. Not so Cliff, thought Jack Good.

'He was always destined to be a nice chap, almost bound not to keep up that tough rock 'n' roll image. He was always too nice and too sensible.

'I don't think you can be a good Christian, like Cliff, and a rock 'n' roller. I regard rock as music with its pants down.'

7. ROCKING THE UK

I wouldn't call it a great incident, after all nobody has been killed or seriously hurt. Our rock 'n' roll nights sometimes do get a bit rough.
George Anderson, manager of the London Lyceum,
after a Teddy-boy riot halted Cliff's concert in 1959

The sudden success of 'Move It' and some scream-worthy appearances on TV were quickly turning Cliff into hot showbiz property. His meteoric rise had attracted the attention of leading promoter Arthur Howes, and soon John Foster was able to tell Cliff that he had secured a spot for him on a UK theatre tour in October at £200 a week – a huge fee compared with the usual rates of Cliff Richard and The Drifters.

Headlining the tour would be The Kalin Twins, an American vocal duo discovered by Clint Ballard Jr, writer of several hits, including 'Good Timin'' for Jimmy Jones and 'I'm Alive', which became a UK chart-topper for The Hollies. Hal and Herbie Kalin, who were genuine twins, were booked on the strength of their catchy record 'When' which proved to be a big hit on both sides of the Atlantic.

The tour represented a welcome chance for Cliff to take his brand of rock 'n' roll to fans around the country at major venues, but this significant step up the ladder created its own set of problems for Cliff and The Drifters. At Butlins, a guitarist by the name of Ken Pavey had made a number of fill-in appearances as one of The Drifters, which in turn allowed Ian Samwell to switch to bass. Pavey, however, was unavailable for the tour with The Kalin Twins, which left the band without the services of a regular lead guitarist. It was a problem for John Foster and he set out to solve it in the only way he knew how at the time – by looking for a replacement at the 2 I's.

Foster had in mind Tony Sheridan, who had a reputation at the time as the best rock 'n' roll performer and lead guitarist in Britain. Sheridan was a regular visitor and performer at Soho's most famous coffee bar and music cellar, and Foster set out for Soho to meet Sheridan at the 2 I's, ready to offer him a job. On his arrival, Foster was delighted to be told Sheridan would soon be there. But hour after hour went by and Foster became increasingly impatient when there was no sign of him.

While he was waiting, he saw a slim young man with glasses walk in with a guitar case, unpack it and begin to play a few licks. Foster watched and listened with growing interest as the youngster ran through some Buddy Holly numbers, complete with guitar solos true to Buddy's rendition on his hit records, and then produced what Foster recognised as a perfect replica of a guitar solo by James Burton, noted guitarist for American star Rick Nelson.

With Sheridan still nowhere to be seen and Foster beginning to fret that he was in danger of missing his last bus home, he went up to the teenager and introduced himself as Cliff Richard's manager. Rock 'n' roll history was about to be made. Without beating about the bush, Foster asked the youngster straight out if he would like to tour as lead guitar in Cliff's backing group. The young man said his name was Hank B. Marvin and that he knew of Cliff from hearing 'Move It' on the radio and from his TV appearances on *Oh Boy!*. He really liked 'Move It', he said, and once the tour details were outlined to him, he told Foster he would be happy to back Cliff on tour, but on one condition. 'I'll do it only if my mate Bruce can come along,' he said of his fellow 2 I's rhythm guitarist.

Foster agreed, and immediately took Hank and Bruce Welch round to a Soho tailor's, where Cliff was in the process of being fitted for a luridly bright pink jacket as part of his stage outfit for the tour. Although he didn't say as much, being much too polite and well mannered, the singer's initial reaction to his new bandmates was that he felt they looked like a couple of yobs. The two teenagers standing in front of him with their scruffy clothes, greasy hair and pimples looked anything but cool guitarists. But Cliff was swayed by Foster's assurance that Hank could play Buddy Holly's guitar solos note perfect and that there was a touch of the revered James Burton about his playing too. The fact that the bespectacled and wiry-framed Hank also had a look of Buddy Holly about him was another definite plus.

It was Tony Sheridan's ill fortune that due to his unreliable timekeeping that he missed out on becoming a prominent part of Cliff Richard's success. But it was not his last flirtation with fame. He later came to prominence when performing in the nightclubs of Hamburg with a backing group called The Silver Beatles, which happened to number among its members John Lennon, George Harrison and Paul McCartney.

Hank Marvin, whose real name was Brian Rankin, and Bruce Welch, whose birth certificate has him down as Brian Cripps, were both Geordies and had been close pals since they became pupils at Rutherford Grammar School, in Newcastle-upon-Tyne, on the same day. Both shared a passionate interest in the music of the day and both had begun to play instruments when very young. Bruce started out on the ukulele when he was just five years old, and Hank was fourteen when he was given a Windsor five-string banjo bought from one of his schoolmasters for £2 10 shillings (£2.50).

Like Bruce, Hank's path to rock 'n' roll was via skiffle. He formed a group with his brother Joe, while Bruce played in a group called The Railroaders. Like so many other teenagers of his generation, Bruce first became hooked on rock 'n' roll thanks to Bill Haley. 'Haley always gets overlooked,' he says. 'As kids of fourteen we'd go and see *The Blackboard Jungle* with older boys who became Teddy boys and I'd see them literally ripping up the seats. We loved the music because it was totally new. So we mustn't forget the huge influence Haley had.

"Rock Around the Clock" was the international record of all time. It still sounds fantastic today.'

Playing music took a more serious turn for both Hank and Bruce when Hank acquired an American National guitar, and Bruce was given a Hofner guitar with electric pick-up by his father for his sixteenth birthday. As well as playing guitar together, the two pals blended their voices harmoniously for Everly Brothers-style vocals.

Hoping to further their careers together, they headed down to London to take part in a talent contest, and while they were in the capital they were inevitably drawn, like so many other budding musicians, to the 2 I's. Unlike the vast majority, it had paid off – these two sixteen-year-olds had now been recruited to back the hottest young singer in Britain, just by being in the right place at the right time.

'I used to work at the 2 I's at the same time as Hank and Bruce,' says Vince Eager, 'and these two lads told everybody they were going to become The Drifters with Cliff. But I always remember somebody saying to the two of them: "*He*'ll never make it, but as long as you're a good band you'll get work with other people!"'

Just a few days before the tour started, Cliff went back into the Abbey Road recording studios to record his second single, 'High Class Baby'. Again it was an Ian Samwell composition, written this time not on top of a bus, but while standing at a rainy bus stop shelter in Barnet, north London while Ian was imagining he was playing Jerry Lee Lewis's piano.

For the recording, Norrie Paramor once more brought in Frank Clarke and Ernie Shear to give the backing added impetus. But, as a song, 'High Class Baby' paled in comparison with 'Move It', and Cliff knew it as soon as he had put the finishing touches to it. He was so despondent about *his* follow-up that when he got back home after the recording session, he actually broke down and cried. He seriously thought he was going to be a one-hit wonder and that he was heading for oblivion.

Fortunately for Cliff, he was quickly lifted out of his despondency by the incredible audience reaction to him at every venue on the tour. It kicked off at the Victoria Hall, Hanley, Stoke-on-Trent, on 5 October, with a bill offering a mixed bag of music. It included The Most Brothers, two singers who weren't brothers at all. And, in the honest opinion of Mickie Most, one half of the duo, who went on to become a hugely successful record producer: 'We were a poor man's Everly Brothers.' Also on the bill were a jazzy trio, The Londonaires, and Eddie Calvert, the trumpeter Norrie Paramor had so successfully steered into the charts.

Cliff opened the second half of the show, and Hank Marvin and Bruce Welch standing behind him watched the fans go crazy over him. 'He'd just come into the hit parade,' Hank recalled, 'and we'd thought: maybe he's just another singer; he's exceptionally good-looking, he carries himself well, he's got this natural dignity thing, but not much more. Well, we got made up and turned up for the first show. And then Cliff came in wearing a pink suit, pink tie, shirt, socks, shoes. It looked fantastic. We went on stage and tore the place apart.'

Cliff's set was based around six numbers he had rehearsed with Hank, Bruce, Ian and Terry at his home shortly after the two new guitarists had been recruited. It comprised 'Baby I Don't Care', 'Don't Bug Me Baby', 'Move It', 'Blueberry Hill', 'Whole Lotta Shakin' Goin' On' and 'King Creole'. The set effectively gave the fans a home-grown flavour of Elvis, Buddy Holly, Jerry Lee Lewis and Fats Domino, and the teenagers went for it with wild abandon.

Observing Cliff from the wings, Mickie Most could not help but stand and admire. 'I knew I was watching Cliff become a huge star before my eyes,' Mickie said in an interview many years later, when he himself became a TV favourite as a plain-speaking judge on the ITV talent show *New Faces* in the 1970s. 'He was just terrific. He drove the audience wild, and it was the same wherever we went.

'You had to feel sorry for The Kalin Twins, who had to follow him. They had to go on stage with the crowd yelling for more from Cliff. Hal and Herbie Kalin were nice guys, but they were just one-hit wonders and you couldn't call them rock 'n' rollers. It was a nightmare scenario for them – Cliff had brought the audience to its feet with rock 'n' roll and The Kalin Twins just couldn't follow him.'

Despite the fact they had been groomed as two Presleys for the price of one and sported gravity-defying quiffs, Hal and Herbie Kalin in truth were not rock 'n' rollers. Their big hit, 'When', was a catchy, feelgood, finger-clicking number, which they sang jauntily on American TV while dressed in open-neck shirts and striped blazers. It was hardly a Presley-esque performance.

Hal and Herbie Kalin knew the writing was pretty much on the wall for them from the very first show. They watched Cliff's performance and were left in no doubt that he would be a hard act to follow. Cliff was rock 'n' roll, The Kalin Twins were not, and Cliff was blowing the audience away.

'The Kalin Twins had a real hard time,' said Bruce Welch. '"When" was a great record – still is – and they were two lovely Jewish twins from New York, but they looked like young bankers in their suits and ties compared with Cliff in his pink jacket, being sexy, purposely being like Elvis, and wiggling his hips.

'The girls went nuts about him. He celebrated his eighteenth birthday at the De Montfort Hall in Leicester and the whole audience of 2,500 stood up and sang "Happy Birthday" to him and threw flowers and presents on the stage.'

Vince Eager, who caught one of Cliff's early shows, can also testify to the extraordinary effect Cliff had on his audiences. He says: 'I'd seen Marty Wilde, Tommy Steele, and Johnny Ray live in concert, but when I saw Cliff there was nothing to compare with the reaction to him. He'd taken it to another level.'

The Kalin Twins had the misfortune to start the tour just as their chart-topper 'When' had reached its peak. It was still top of the hit parade on opening night and Hal and Bobbie's live rendition inevitably generated some excited yells from the audience. But thereafter 'When' slid down the charts as the tour progressed, while Cliff's 'Move It' went in the opposite direction.

By mid-November Cliff's second single, 'High Class Baby', was also in the Top Ten. Cliff was the rising star of the show in every way, aided by Hank and Bruce rocking up a storm with their guitar riffs behind him. 'I can still remember Bruce coming up to me and saying: "OK, let's wreck the place" – that meant go frantic, have people rush the stage, have a riot,' said Cliff. 'I liked being there, being screamed at and having my shirt torn off.'

Just two nights into the tour, the manager of The Kalin Twins felt it necessary to ask for Cliff and The Drifters to move their set to the first half in order to give the twins a chance. They were desperate to avoid having to walk out on to the stage when the entire audience was on its feet demanding to see and hear more of Cliff.

It was suggested that Cliff should close the first half of the show, which would allow The Kalin Twins to take the stage without having to counter the insistent chants of 'We want Cliff!' But Cliff dug his heels in. Opening the second half was what he and his band were contracted to do and he was happy to abide by it. There was also the quiet satisfaction of experiencing the audience go ape for him rather than a chart-topping act from America. He was getting great reviews, partly by stealing The Kalin Twins' thunder, 'And we knew that if we moved we wouldn't be stealing the thunder as much,' said Cliff.

He may have blown Hal and Herbie off the stage, but Cliff forged a lasting friendship with The Kalin Twins, and in 1989 he invited them to join him on stage for a re-creation of the *Oh Boy!* section of his two shows at Wembley stadium, which he called *The Event*. He said: 'Although I was influenced by Presley a lot at the start of my career, there were two other people to whom I owe a great deal – The Kalin Twins. That may sound strange, but they were great guys who taught me a lot about stagecraft on that first tour.'

Mickie Most's highly proficient bass player on that first tour was a nineteen-year-old called Terry Harris who, while working with Tony Crombie's Rockets, had managed to acquire one of the very first bass guitars ever to be imported into England. By part-exchanging his string bass and shelling out a further £40 at a music shop in London's Charing Cross Road, the rarely seen 'new invention' was his.

It was customary for artists to share their backing musicians around on tour to cut down the costs, and Mickie had no objections when Cliff asked if he was happy for the bass guitarist to join The Drifters on stage on occasion to augment the sound. The addition of Terry Harris not only gave The Drifters a more balanced, fuller sound, but his striking blond good looks also gave the girls something extra to scream at. Terry was known to all and sundry as Jet Harris, Jet being a moniker he had acquired at college. 'I was a great sprinter,' he explained, 'winning races all over the shop. My friends said: "You go like a jet," so it became my nickname. I had no say in the matter.'

A first tour at the tender age of seventeen was an exciting adventure in every way for Cliff and his band. And, as Bruce pointed out: 'That three-week tour was the only time in his life when Cliff wasn't top of the bill. After that he was always the star, always top of the bill. The tour was fantastic for Cliff and for all of us. Hank and I had left Newcastle in the first week of April, and by October we were back there at City Hall playing for Cliff with all the girls screaming and all our old schoolmates were there in the audience.

'We all just kept going and that three weeks turned into years and years with Cliff. We were very lucky.'

Not every aspect of the tour was magical for Cliff. The £200 a week for himself and the band soon disappeared on travelling expenses and accommodation. He says: 'The band got paid more than I did. Out of the £50 a week I got paid to do the tour, after paying all the musicians a fiver each a week, it left me about £2.50.'

Overnight accommodation also frequently left a lot to be desired. Cliff said: 'At first we couldn't afford hotels and whenever we were asked where we were staying, we'd say: "At the Bedford." But it wasn't an hotel, it was the Bedford van we travelled in!'

At each new town, Cliff and the band would pile out of the bus and disperse to seek out the best deals at the bed and breakfasts. Then they would all meet back at an appointed time and share the information about which digs offered the best prices and the best breakfast deals.

'Stars weren't pampered in luxury accommodation then,' Cliff stressed. 'Pre-motorways, London to York would be an overnight trek. You'd get on the coach and sleep as best as you can, get there and doze during the day and play at night.

'In those days we were on the road for about ten months of the year. We pushed ourselves hard and missed sleep, but we were only eighteen years old and we had age on our side.

'We didn't have a lot of money, and out of that you had to pay for your digs at fifteen shillings and sixpence a night. We'd all run in different directions and report back. Sometimes we had to share rooms and occasionally share beds. But we were young, remember, and you can do this when you're young.

'But after little while it gets tiring and as your fame spreads and you start to earn some money, you say to yourself: "I can afford a hotel." I remember the first hotel wasn't very good, but boy! it felt like the Dorchester compared with some of the places we stayed. They were great days, exciting days, but I prefer it now. I can make better music now, I can live better now, and everything about today is better.'

A triumphant tour ended on a sour note on the very last night when the much-treasured guitar Cliff's dad had given him for his sixteenth birthday was stolen from backstage at the Colston Hall, Bristol.

The tour had established Cliff as Britain's foremost rock 'n' roller by some distance and the only one who could come anywhere near matching the American rock idols. Within his immediate circle it also became apparent to everyone that Cliff and The Drifters had progressed to a level of musical professionalism that Ian Samwell and Terry Smart were struggling to reach.

Cliff realised that Jet Harris was a far better bet as a bass guitarist than Ian Samwell, both in musicianship and in his on-stage image. Slim and enigmatic, with his dyed blond hair swept into an outrageous quiff, Jet looked the coolest of rock 'n' roll cats on stage as he played his then unique electric bass.

Bruce says: 'Cliff would stand at the side of the stage and watch Jet play bass for The Most Brothers and think: "We've got to have him." Jet looked fantastic. He was James Dean. He looked perfect, and Hank was so far ahead of anybody as a guitarist, even at that age. Ian Samwell couldn't play like Hank and Terry Smart couldn't play like Tony Meehan, who was being considered as his replacement. By then Cliff was not ruthless, but he was ambitious, so they both had to go.'

Cliff's dislike of confrontation was again in evidence when it came to the act of replacing Ian Samwell with Jet. Ian was given the bad news not by Cliff, but by John Foster when Ian turned up for a rehearsal ready to offer Cliff a new song he had written. There he discovered The Drifters had been rehearsing without him. Ian, whose wonderful composition 'Move It' had propelled Cliff to stardom, was out in the cold.

The official version was that Ian was stepping down to devote more time to songwriting. But in reality, Ian was less than happy at being ousted from the band. He knew his limitations on bass guitar, but he believed that, given time, he could have reached the standard required. Time, however, was not on Ian's side. Cliff was a young man in a hurry, Hank and Bruce had given Cliff's musical backing a big kick forward and Jet was their unanimous choice to augment the band. 'There was nothing I could do,' Ian sadly explained to friends. 'It was a *fait accompli*. Everybody wanted Jet in, so I was out.'

Ian's connections with Cliff and The Drifters were not severed completely. He was briefly to act as their manager and continued to write songs for Cliff, including his 1959 Top Twenty hit 'Dynamite', as well as contributing songs after the group became The Shadows. Ian later went on to enjoy a distinguished career in the music business, both as songwriter and producer, working with a host of major stars including Frank Zappa, Joni Mitchell, Al Jarreau, John Sebastian and The Grateful Dead. He also, in effect, launched The Small Faces by co-writing their 1965 debut hit, 'Whatcha Gonna Do About It?'

For Christmas 2006, with the help of Brian May and Brian Bennett, a percussionist and arranger whose long working relationship with Cliff began in 1961, Cliff breathed new life into the remarkable 'Move It' by releasing it as the extra track on his hit single '21st Century Christmas'. 'I don't think I'll ever stop singing it,' said Cliff of the number which first put him on the map. When Ian Samwell died in March 2003, one obituary writer commented: 'Without him, Cliff Richard might still be Harry Webb, retired clerk.'

The enforced change of name from The Drifters to The Shadows came about to avoid confusion with a group bearing the same name in America. The US-based Drifters were the first black vocal group of the rock 'n' roll era to have continued success – although their very existence was unknown to Bruce, Hank and Jet at the time. The clash of names was revealed when Cliff's Drifters attempted to have a single in their own right released in America and the USA's Drifters threatened legal action. The soul group had been using the name The Drifters for far longer and Cliff's boys willingly bowed to them rather than become embroiled in what might have become a costly lawsuit.

The backing group's debut record, an instrumental written by Jet called 'Jet Black', was released under the name The Four Jets instead. But soon afterwards Jet thought up a new name for the group over a drink at a Ruislip pub. 'We were mulling around Zephyrs, Zodiacs – all the Ford cars of the time,' he said. 'Nothing sounded right and then we started going off at tangents. The Plastic Armadillos was one of those. After about half an hour, I came up with The Shadows. I thought it summed up our place in the Cliff Richard organisation,' Jet concluded. 'Always in the background.'

Ian Samwell was not the only casualty in the increasing need for a better standard of musicianship. Cliff, Hank and Bruce had come to the conclusion that Terry Smart also needed replacing. During the tour Terry had begun to realise his limitations and that he was failing to keep up to the level reached by the three professional guitarists. In the event, Terry solved the problem for everyone by deciding to quit to fulfil a long-held ambition to join the merchant navy when he was eighteen. His decision signalled the departure of the last original member of The Drifters.

Swiftly installed behind the drums in Terry's place was Tony Meehan, whom Cliff, Hank, Bruce and Jet had all encountered at the 2 I's. Tony was a mere fifteen years old when he replaced Terry Smart, but he was brimming with precocious talent.

Tony was only ten when he was given his first drum kit one Christmas, and by the time he joined Cliff he had played in various combos in north London as well as drumming alongside Hank and Bruce in The Vipers. He joined up with his old guitarist buddies and backed Cliff for the first time at Free Trade Hall, Manchester, in January 1959. 'It all worked,' said Bruce. 'Jet was James Dean, Hank was Buddy Holly, I wanted to be Elvis and Tony Meehan was fifteen! People always link Cliff and The Shadows together, but that bit lasted ten years – from October 1958 to October 1968. It was an amazing time with hit records backing Cliff, hit records for ourselves, performing in panto with Cliff and making films with him.'

For young Tony Meehan, wielding his drumsticks behind a teen idol creating mass hysteria was a strange experience. 'It used to annoy us a little bit because we used to rehearse for hours and hours and hours doing elaborate arrangements and things that we felt were really worth listening to and then we'd go on with Cliff and the whole place would break down and there'd just be screaming.'

New personnel among the backing group wasn't the only change afoot within Cliff's immediate circle. Around the time he was touring with The Kalin Twins, Cliff found himself with a new manager. Although John Foster was by now getting a fair grasp of the business, he also knew he had taken Cliff as far as he could and that the singer needed a manager with a wider knowledge of the machinations of showbusiness now Cliff was suddenly in huge demand. Because Cliff was under 21, Foster had never been able to secure a legitimate contract with him and he was therefore vulnerable when it came to claiming any legal rights over guiding Cliff's career. He could easily be ousted.

Norrie Paramor instigated the change after suggesting to Cliff's father that it would be to everyone's benefit if Cliff had experienced, professional management now he was such hot property. Rodger Webb was by now starting to take much more interest in the business side of Cliff's career and he went along with Norrie's suggestion that Franklyn Boyd, the music publisher who had brought Norrie the song 'Schoolboy Crush', should take over. Franklyn had himself been a singer and John Foster was man enough to see the logic of the switch.

Foster took his demotion graciously and was retained, as Cliff's personal road manager, at £18 a week. His relegation to the lower ranks from his exalted role as manager came at a time when Cliff secured a week's engagement at Finsbury Park Empire – just as Foster had prophesied a mere few months before.

Franklyn's stint as Cliff's manager was even more short-lived. He lasted just three months and was then dismissed in a letter he received from Cliff's father a few days before Christmas. His crime, it seems, had been to work Cliff too hard for Rodger Webb's liking.

Matters came to a head at the end of a hectic week for Cliff. He was getting up very early each weekday morning to film a small part in his first movie, *Serious Charge*, as well as performing two shows a night for a week at the Finsbury Park Empire. In addition he was due to rehearse for an *Oh Boy!* show on the Sunday. It was a crippling workload and it all got too much for him.

On the Saturday night, the final night of his Finsbury Park engagement, Cliff's voice was completely shot through and, backstage, Foster resorted to melting butter on a hot spoon to try to ease his vocal chords. As with all good showbusiness pros, the show had to go on, and Cliff proceeded to give what must surely be the most remarkable performance of his career. He went on stage and 'sang' while his old 2 I's pal Wee Willie Harris provided the vocals, hidden in the wings out of sight of the fans.

Cliff merely mimed his way through his songs and the crowd were none the wiser. Wee Willie did a credible job of copying Cliff's singing and the screams from the girls in the audience prevented even the most ardent fan from detecting that Cliff's vocals were not entirely his own.

After the show Cliff was taken back to Cheshunt, where he was immediately put to bed. Next day, still exhausted, he failed to make the *Oh Boy!* rehearsal after waking up and telling his mother that he couldn't stand the showbusiness life a moment longer.

Dorothy and Rodger Webb were shocked at Cliff's heavy workload and were naturally concerned for his welfare. They felt their boy wasn't being looked after properly and Rodger duly sent off a letter to Franklyn Boyd dispensing with his services as manager. 'I've never been so stunned or hurt in all my life as the day I opened that letter,' Franklyn was quoted as saying in the *People*, the red-top Sunday newspaper. 'At the time my wife and I were living in town and for six weeks Cliff stayed with us because his home was too far out for convenience. I spent days with him during those early recording sessions, guiding him, trying to inject some professionalism into his act.'

Franklyn's sacking also made headlines in the Christmas edition of *Melody Maker* and carried his explanation that he had never had a proper contract with Cliff, merely a verbal agreement and a letter that authorised him to sign contracts. 'I got him the *Oh Boy!* series and his film work,' he said ruefully.

Within weeks John Foster also found a letter from Cliff's dad waiting for him when he came home one night. Rodger Webb had given him a fortnight's notice as well.

In a heated meeting, Rodger Webb accused Foster of not looking after his boy and of not ensuring he ate adequately. A furious row developed and Cliff, once again shrinking from confrontation, walked out. Foster later told Cliff he had had enough anyway and packed his bags. The *Daily Sketch* deemed the parting of the ways to be worthy of a story and quoted Cliff as saying of John: 'He's pulled me out of a few jams, especially with fans in the north, but now he is to try to do better for himself. I'll miss him.'

To his credit, John Foster harboured no real bitterness at the turn of events and later went on to have a successful career in public relations. And there was one thing no one could ever take away from him – he would forever hold the title of The Man Who Discovered Cliff Richard.

John had enjoyed some fun times with Cliff, not least when they had shared a London flat for a while above Sainsbury's at

100 Marylebone Road in the centre of town. Having a bolthole in town had made sense for Cliff, rather than having to trek back to Cheshunt every evening and it was the first time he had lived away from home.

Cliff covered the walls of one of the spare bedrooms in the six-roomed apartment with photographs of his favourite rock 'n' roll stars. His own bedroom was dominated by a lucky mascot called Lord Rockingham – a three-foot-tall soft toy rabbit presented to him by his fans. The rabbit was too big to cart around as his mascot on tour, but Cliff was fond enough of it to keep a photo of it in his wallet.

Naturally, the flat quickly became a convenient place for The Shadows to lay their heads. They soon moved in, too, and helped share the twelve guineas a week rent. Inevitably, there was no shortage of female visitors, and on his way to make a cup of tea in the morning, Cliff often found himself stepping over unfamiliar female forms curled up asleep in the lounge. 'Some mornings the living room would be littered with bodies,' he recalled. 'You never knew who was going to be there, but they were good times.'

The flat also became a magnet for Cliff's contemporaries. Singers such as Billy Fury, Marty Wilde, Dickie Pride and Vince Eager were among the regular visitors.

A cheeky comic from Liverpool by the name of Jimmy Tarbuck, then the compère on Cliff's early concert tours, was another friend who frequently availed himself of Cliff's hospitality and the offer of a bed for the night in one of Cliff's spare bedrooms. And Jet Harris also regularly made use of another spare bedroom after he had started going steady with Carol Costa, a sexy young girl he had met at the Chiswick Empire.

Inevitably, Cliff's fans eventually discovered where he was living and they all had to move out rather than bear the constant siege. With the prospect of some handsome royalties coming his way before too long, Cliff was advised to look to buying a place of his own.

While John Foster's influence over Cliff was now coming to an end, Cherry Wainer, a friend from Cliff's days on *Oh Boy!*, suggested that her manager, ex-bandleader Tito Burns, should take over the job of guiding Cliff's career. After several meetings with Cliff's father – Cliff was still under age when it came to contractual matters – Tito got the job. 'He seems just right for my boy,' Rodger Webb declared. Shrewdly, Rodger engineered a contract with Tito that would expire on Cliff's 21st birthday, by which time the singer would be able to negotiate and sign in his own right. Cliff later revealed that the agreement with Tito included a clause to ensure he was not overworked: 'In my new contract I've insisted on a week off every month. Even then I'll have to do television and records, but that's fairly easy.'

Tito was tough, experienced and knew a showbiz hot property when he saw one. 'I had a good look at Cliff and I liked what I saw,' he said. 'I could see so much potential.' Another pleasing aspect for Tito was Cliff's willingness to take advice and do what he was told. 'He was so receptive. I mean, you only had to tell him something once,' Tito enthused about the young singer.

Like many of the established showbusiness agents and managers of the day, Tito was not convinced rock 'n' roll was here to stay and he envisaged his new charge taking the well-tried route to sustained success: records, television, films and concerts where he would be presented as an all-round entertainer.

'I wanted to further him as a solo person because I didn't want him to live and die just leading a rock 'n' roll band, which was very possible,' Tito explained in what, in essence, was a thinly veiled declaration of his intention to distance Cliff from The Shadows and soften his rock-singer image.

Cliff's loyalty to his backing group ensured, however, that Tito would not have an easy job prising him away from Hank, Bruce, Jet and Tony in order to groom the singer as a family favourite. Before long, Cliff had demonstrated this loyalty by arranging for The Shadows to audition for Norrie Paramor, which led to their landing a recording contract as a group in their own right and the release on 9 January 1959 of their first single.

Ironically, Tito's plans for Cliff were to be given their biggest boost by one of The Shadows. Rhythm guitarist Bruce Welch would unwittingly broaden Cliff's appeal to mums and dads by coming up with an instantly catchy arrangement of a Lionel Bart song, 'Living Doll'. But first there were concert commitments to fulfil, the audiences were clamouring for Cliff the rock 'n' roller and he was not about to disappoint.

Cliff-mania in general and the excitement generated by Cliff at his concerts convinced Norrie Paramor to record Cliff's first LP, simply called *Cliff*, live. But, instead of taking all the necessary recording equipment to one of Cliff's shows, Norrie chose to try and re-create the atmosphere of a live Cliff Richard concert in front of a specially chosen audience at EMI's Abbey Road studios. Around three hundred Cliff fans were given tickets to the recording sessions conducted over two nights and, after being provided with a buffet, they were urged to unleash as much fan fervour as they wished as Cliff went through a dozen numbers. The venture proved not to be the smoothest of operations because on the first night the crush barriers aimed at keeping the fans at bay had been installed too close to the studios, which resulted in too much screaming erroneously being picked up by the microphones.

The following night Cliff was suffering from laryngitis and his vocals were not his best. The fans didn't seem to care, however, when the album was released in April 1959, and they bought it in large enough quantities to propel the album to number four in the LP charts. It consisted largely of versions of hits of the day, such as 'Donna', 'Ready Teddy', and Buddy Holly's 'That'll Be The Day', and finished with 'Whole Lotta Shakin' Goin' On', the number Cliff usually chose as a frantic finale to his concerts. *Cliff* stayed in the album chart for 31 weeks.

Few live albums have ever fully captured the exciting atmosphere of a rock gig, and Cliff's fell well short. But the fans did not have to wait long to experience the real thing once the promoter Arthur Howes decided to send Cliff out on a series of concert dates where he would be given top billing.

In those days there was no blueprint for how a rock 'n' roll singer should be presented live. Rock was still very much in its infancy and had yet to set the pattern of one-night pop package tours. In showbusiness circles there were still suspicions about rock 'n' roll's longevity and, rather than put together a line-up consisting solely of rock and pop acts, Arthur Howes chose to tack Cliff on to the end of variety shows as the main attraction of a bill which might include jugglers, conjurers, classical dancers, comedians and ventriloquists. 'These days people talk about the music business,' says Bruce Welch. 'It wasn't a music business back then – when we came in it was variety, showbusiness.'

Still in its formative years, rock had yet to establish a circuit of its own and, although three years had passed since Tommy Steele had first taken rock 'n' roll to UK venues, lessons had still to be learned.

Tommy was bewildered, for example, when he first joined a variety package in the north of England in November 1956. On the bill were comedians Mike and Bernie Winters, a soprano, the Ballet Montmartre, and a Welshman called Thunderclap Jones, a former classical pianist. 'He had absolutely no idea why he was there,' Tommy remembered. 'He complained that when he went on, he had to put his leg up on the piano and take his coat off because it sent everyone mad. But it doesn't go very well with Tchaikovsky and Shostakovich.'

When Tommy himself went on stage he was greeted with screams. He said: 'Nobody had screamed in England at a performer for real – we'd seen it in the newsreels with Sinatra. But suddenly these kids were part of the show.'

Unlike Cliff, Tommy resented the wild reaction. 'I came off afterwards and I thought: "I'd come to sing my music and they were screaming and not clapping in tempo." There were ushers running up and own the aisles with torches in complete fear that maybe the kids were going to tear up the seats like the hooligans had done at "Rock Around the Clock" the year before. They were kids enjoying the evening doing what they felt was part of the evening, which was to scream at the performers.'

Instead of realising that Cliff and The Shadows were entirely capable of filling a theatre and providing a full evening's entertainment on their own, they were booked for the closing spot on the bill. Cliff said: 'You'd arrive and you'd be expected to do the last half an hour, but on the show there would be fire-eaters and jugglers, lots of comedians, all sorts of singers and I'd be the rock 'n' roll end to the evening. It was a strange mixture, but it seemed to work.

'When people came to see me in those variety shows, the house was jammed from the beginning, so there were people there who would enjoy a juggler or another type of singer or a violinist. It really was a family thing, and what happened was that we became entertainers as opposed to rock singers. It's all the same as far as I'm concerned. The minute you go on stage, you are presenting yourself as an object to be looked at, derided or applauded. So, either way, folks, welcome to showbusiness!'

Unfortunately for Cliff, his appearances also attracted an unruly element, and in Burnley he was shocked to witness a nasty fight breaking out between rival gangs in the front row of the stalls. There were similar rucks when he and The Shadows performed in Manchester, Birmingham and Nottingham. In Manchester Cliff was horrified when police resorted to turning hoses on the fans. He feared for their safety and, when one girl fought her way through the water jets and stood before him dripping wet, demanding he give her something for her perseverance, he tore off the chain and crucifix he was wearing around his neck and handed it to her.

At the Trocadero at the Elephant and Castle, scene just a few months previously of Cliff's fruitless entry into the talent contest, he was showered with coins. Screaming girls fought a Teddy-boy gang as Cliff was pelted and his road manager ordered the safety curtains to be closed while he was in the middle of his last number.

Cliff was also forced off stage at London's Lyceum in the Strand after being pelted with fruit, eggs, tomatoes, bottles, cigarette packets, coins and even lampshades and strips of lino torn from the floor.

Trouble flared the minute the revolving stage brought Cliff into view in front of a densely packed, swaying crowd of two thousand on the dance floor. The mere sight of him elicited excited screams from girls in the audience, which in turn prompted loud hissing, catcalls and angry stamping of feet from their jealous Teddy-boy boyfriends.

After the barracking came the barrage, leaving a visibly shocked Cliff desperately dodging the flying missiles while trying to sing. Fights broke out all over the hall and in the melée several girls fainted. Cliff watched with mounting concern as stewards in evening dress heaved the limp bodies of the swooning females on to the stage to escape the crush.

The event turned even uglier when scores of troublemakers attempted to storm the stage. Some managed to barge their way to within a few feet of the band and one tried to swing a punch at Cliff. With the help of several attendants, the Lyceum's manager George Anderson managed to drag Cliff's would-be assailant away before he could land a blow. It was a chaotic scene and Anderson frantically signalled to his staff to continue to revolve the stage. In what seemed agonisingly slow motion, Cliff and his band were gradually rotated to safety out of reach of the hostile, baying crowd.

Backstage, in the safety of the dressing room, Cliff was shaking, partly with fear, but partly with anger that his show had been wrecked so violently before it had barely begun. He was also worried and concerned for the girls who had been hurt in the crush. Meanwhile, outside the Lyceum, several hundred disappointed teenagers crowded around the dance hall booing and holding up the traffic as running scuffles continued down the Strand.

The incident brought Cliff unwanted headlines about inciting rock 'n' roll riots. In his defence Cliff said: 'It was jealousy that started the trouble. When we begin to play, the girls start screaming with delight. They love it, but their boyfriends don't. They get jealous because their girls are forgetting about them and going for us in a big way. That's when the trouble starts – the boys try to stop us playing. It's nothing personal, just jealousy.'

Lyceum manager George Anderson tried to play down the fracas. 'I wouldn't call it a great incident, after all nobody has been killed or seriously hurt,' he said, but conceded: 'Our rock 'n' roll nights sometimes do get a bit rough.'

Cliff's mum Dorothy was quoted in the national press as saying: 'I never realised how dreadful it was. I came all the way up to London to see him and Dad had to go to work as usual. I'm so worried I'm trying to persuade him to give up.'

After the disgraceful scenes at the Lyceum, Cliff cancelled his act at the venue, said to be worth £300 for five nightly performances. He cited a troublesome voice for the cancellation and he had a doctor's certificate to prove it. 'I just can't go on. I will not be able to complete my week's contract,' he said. It was left to Tito Burns to explain to the press: 'When you're hurt bad, it goes through the most vulnerable part of your body. In Cliff's case it's his voice and he's upset.'

Following the Lyceum rumpus, it was not uncommon to find helmeted policemen at Cliff Richard concerts, ambulance men patrolling the aisles and nurses ready to care for fainting adolescents. Despite theatres reassessing their security procedures, the fan fervour was too much for some. At Blackpool's Opera House, hundreds of fans smashed down a side door in their determined efforts to get in.

Pat McDonald, Cliff's personal secretary for four years, never forgot her first experience of how terrifying it could be when violence erupted at a Cliff Richard concert and what courage it took for him to go on with the show.

Pat had taken along a girlfriend, Mavis, to the Chiswick Empire one night but, unfortunately for them both, they picked the Friday night, when two rival gangs of Teddy boys were out to settle some scores. The gangs, from Hackney and Hammersmith, had been feuding for some time and they had pinpointed a Cliff Richard appearance in a variety show at the Chiswick Empire as the perfect excuse to meet up for the decisive rumble.

Prior to Cliff's spot, Pat went backstage to introduce Mavis to him before he went on. Cliff was his usual polite self and chatted away to the girls, but he became tense when word came back that the audience were getting rowdy and had begun throwing objects on to the stage. Pat wouldn't have blamed Cliff if he had refused to go on stage, but she remembers him turning to The Shadows and saying quietly: 'Let's go, fellows, after all, they can't kill us.'

Pat was appalled at what happened next. 'A shower of eggs, tomatoes and vegetables of all descriptions met them as they launched into their first number,' she recounted. 'The music was almost drowned by the noise from the gallery. Within seconds, the stage looked like a miniature Covent Garden.

'Throughout it all, Cliff and the boys kept on playing. As they played, Cliff had to move back and forwards, his body shaking to the rhythm, following a pattern carefully worked out during rehearsals. The debris at his feet, including banana skins, threatened to bring him crashing down. With one eye on the missiles coming thick and fast, and another on what was on the stage, Cliff kept kicking the stuff out of his way.'

Out front there was mayhem as the Teds flew at each other with fists flying. Chillingly, one yob in the balcony wrenched a heavy fire extinguisher off the wall and hurled it downwards towards the stalls. It bounced off the brass balcony rail then dropped with sickening force on to two young girls below. One of the girls suffered a broken collarbone and the other was concussed. Des O'Connor, one of the stars on the bill, tried to calm the mob with some humorous observations but it had the opposite effect. He, too, had to retreat, and ventriloquist Ray Alan wisely brought down the safety curtain to protect the performers.

Pat shared Cliff's utter relief when he reached the safety of his dressing room. 'Did you see anything like that?' he asked her. 'I thought they were going to lynch us.'

When word of the fire extinguisher injuries to two fans reached Cliff, he turned white with horror. He immediately instructed Pat to find out to which hospital they had been taken and ordered her to send flowers to them with a note of apology, which he wrote out himself.

Pat McDonald saw for herself how personally Cliff always took the rioting at his concerts: 'I've seen him sit down in his dressing room after a show and cover his face with his hands in shame and embarrassment,' she said. 'Yet the fault rarely lay with the real fans.'

At a concert in Romford, another ugly scene developed when hundreds of fans clamouring for tickets were locked out. Cliff and his entourage were trapped for more than an hour inside the theatre after the gig as fans surrounded the exits shouting: 'We want Cliff!' Eventually the tour bus was drawn up outside the stage door and everyone made a run for it. But the bus proved to be no sanctuary as its windows shattered under a hail of stones and lumps of wood.

Bruce Welch took a sickening blow to the head from a brick thrown through a broken window, and a firework landed dangerously close to Hank's face as he tried to take cover behind an amp. Police were called to give Cliff protection and he eventually made good his escape through a lavatory window and was driven away.

Similar mayhem greeted Cliff and The Shadows on their concert forays into Europe. In Kiel, Germany, they were besieged in their dressing rooms as fans went berserk, prompting police to use water hoses and smoke bombs to try and clear the auditorium. These tactics simply made matters worse, forcing fans to cram into the corridors backstage in dangerously tightly packed numbers to evade the water and smoke. A tragedy was only avoided when police reverted to common sense to restore order and rescue the stars of the show. By the end of 1959, Cliff and The Shadows decided they would no longer accept engagements at ballrooms. The risk of the gigs descending into chaos was too great and prevented the boys from developing an act.

Not all Cliff's concerts were marred by violence, and there were moments of humour, too, notably at Birmingham's Hippodrome, when Cliff managed to split his trousers. At first Cliff thought that the zip had merely come apart and he just turned his back to the audience to effect what he thought would be simple repairs. In fact, there was a sizeable tear showing too much of Cliff's anatomy for decorum and he finished singing his number sideways on to the audience before disappearing into the wings to change while The Shadows filled in with an instrumental.

Bruce Welch noted: 'Cliff was mobbed every night of the tour. The stage door at every theatre we played at was besieged by girls waiting for him after every show.'

Speaking in a 1981 TV documentary, Cliff said he was aware he was a desirable sex object and thus a temptation to others. 'I haven't gone out of my way to provide sexual fantasy,' he said, 'but some people don't know where fantasy stops. Girls sometimes arrive at my door with their overnight bags ready to stay the weekend. Others float up to me and say: "The Lord has meant us for each other."'

Particularly in Cliff's early rock 'n' roll days, the fans tried every conceivable ruse to try to reach their idol. At Bradford, two fifteen-year-old girls managed to get into the number-one dressing room and shut themselves into the tiny, almost airless clothes closet. It was four hours before Cliff got the closet door open and found the girls in a state of exhaustion. 'They want to make sure of seeing me, but why half kill themselves?' he protested. 'Once a girl sort of posted herself to me,' said Cliff. 'She put herself in a box and got someone to deliver her. I thought someone had given me a television set and I was so excited. I ripped the box open and this girl popped out and went: "Can I have your autograph?"'

The Shadows, too, of course, had their quota of female fans. Bruce admitted: 'With so many girls around, groupies became a thriving and very pleasant distraction for some of us. And why not? We were young and single and very willing. We each had our fair share.'

In his fascinating autobiography, *Rock 'n' Roll, I Gave You The Best Years Of My Life: A Life In The Shadows*, Bruce recounted: 'On one visit to Bradford, no less than eight of us from the show had the same girl – not all at once, I hasten to add – under the stage at St George's Hall because it had been rumoured that she had slept with Buddy Holly during his British tour the year before.'

In Bournemouth, says Bruce, a buxom girl who announced she would do anything to get into showbusiness arrived at the stage door with a portfolio of nude modelling photos. 'She was game for anything, and in the interval we took her into one of the dressing rooms where she stripped naked and lay on top of a table. Then in turn almost every male member of the company except Cliff attempted to make love to her, while the others roared on their encouragement.'

Bruce maintains that Cliff was largely oblivious to the sexual shenanigans that went on. 'Half the time he didn't know,' he says. 'He was so cosseted at that time because he was so famous. He would be smuggled into the theatre and smuggled out straight from the stage.

'It was the screaming time, it was Beatlemania long before Beatlemania. Sinatra had it in the 1940s with the bobby-soxers, and now Cliff had it. He just couldn't go anywhere, he couldn't walk down the street without being mobbed. He was almost trapped in a way – it's the same price that Elvis paid. Cliff didn't go nuts, but it's a fact of life that he simply couldn't walk down the street at that time.

'So we were the ones who tended to have more fun. None of us did drugs or anything like that. I had a shandy when I was 21 – I genuinely didn't drink till I was 21. It may be hard to imagine now, but back then Cliff Richard was a serious sex symbol. Some of us were weak of the flesh. Cliff wasn't – which left more for us.'

Despite Bruce's assertion that Cliff didn't know what was going on with the groupies, the singer has maintained exactly the opposite. 'I knew what was going on, I wasn't a naïve person. But if I had four women throwing themselves at me I'd say: "This is not right." Old-fashioned maybe, but not right. Therefore I was able to do that.'

Pursuing his point in an interview for *The South Bank Show*, Cliff said he was fed up at the notion that he was considered conformist when, in point of fact, he was the only one with a lifestyle completely different from any other rock star. 'Who's the one who's different?' he asked. 'Who's the one who said: "No, I don't want to do that." And I happen to believe that's the right way of doing it. If you show me someone who's slept around, I'll show you someone who's guilty or feels bad about it if they've ever got married.'

When Tito Burns was once asked whether Cliff had ever become caught up in the hedonistic lifestyle of sex, drugs and rock and roll, Cliff's manager said protectively: 'That wasn't Cliff at all. No way sex and drugs. Nothing like that at all. It wasn't that he was consciously saying: "I'm going to be a goodie-goodie." He just wasn't that way. He'd much prefer a good curry. He never had a girlfriend. He was not concerned with any of that. He's not concerned about women – he never was.'

While The Shadows made merry, they may have felt that Cliff was sacrificing his youth to his career. But his extraordinary fame and the hysteria that accompanied his every move at that point prevented him from going out and enjoying the kind of fun other teenage boys could have.

The nearest Cliff came to bad behaviour was his tendency to swear frequently. 'When I first came into showbusiness, I used to cuss and swear a lot, and every other word was an f,' he once confessed. 'But effing and blinding was just part of the scene. Everyone did it and it didn't mean anything.

'Then I suddenly thought: "How ridiculous!" So I got Jet Harris and my road manager to tell me every time I swore. I always think that if there's something you can't say in front of people you love, like your mother or your sister, then it's basically something you don't want to do. So I just stopped swearing because I found it embarrassing that I couldn't do it at home.'

In an interview with *Melody Maker* in the autumn of 1959, Cliff was clearly starting to think long and hard about the effect he was having on his female fans. He said: 'I started off in the business just for fun. Then suddenly I'm a "teenage idol" – or so the papers say. I honestly can't say I enjoy it much. Sure it's great to be a success. But it gets really complicated. Take Ardwick Green Hippodrome in Manchester. We always go big there with a number of young girls who come six and seven times a week to the front rows of the stalls. It must cost them pounds.

'I've met these kids and there's a sort of innocent faithfulness about them that really frightens me stiff. And they do the craziest things – stay too late and miss their transport, follow us all over the place regardless of the hour. Of course I feel responsible. Their parents must think I'm to blame. I'm flattered, naturally, but I worry about them like mad.'

Cliff also bemoaned the fact that since he had shot to fame he had lost nearly all the friends he had grown up with. 'When I was at school I had lots of pals. Now I've only got one real one from those days. But I'm no different. My house is still there and any of my old mates are welcome to come anytime and my mother takes care of us all. But it isn't like that any more. Suddenly these old friends, my one-time gang, are all peculiar and stiff and strange. And they take the mickey, too, and try and impersonate me.'

While she was working for Cliff, Pat McDonald saw for herself what an ordeal it was for him to meet strangers. 'When he begins talking to them, he generally loses this self-consciousness and appears calm and poised. No one would ever dream that a few minutes earlier he may well have been a bundle of nerves,' she revealed.

Pat noticed that while waiting to be introduced to Prince Philip and Princess Alexandra at a Royal Film Command Performance in March 1960, it looked as though Cliff might not be able to go ahead with it. Cliff's personal telltale signs of feeling ill at ease were all there – little coughs, biting his lower lip and unnecessarily combing and recombing his hair. Standing in the line-up of stars he was fidgeting so much that actress Mai Zetterling took him aside and said calmly: 'Don't worry, Cliff. Just relax and let them take you as they find you.'

At difficult times, Cliff always had his family to turn to for loyal and unwavering support, even if his fame wasn't always entirely welcome. Cliff's little sister Joan was eight when his career began, and at first it was exciting for her to stay up late and watch him on TV. 'Friends' reaction wasn't too bad,' she told Gloria Hunniford, one of Cliff's close pals. 'It was when I went to senior school that the trouble started. Nobody had cars except for us, and Mum would send the chauffeur and I'd say: "If he gets out of the car I'm not going to get in it." In those days it wasn't nice to have money or someone famous as a relative. I'd get in many fights because of that.'

Cliff's mother, in particular, attended many of her son's concerts and Pat McDonald noted that he was always a tender and adoring son. 'Mrs Webb visited Tito Burns's office quite often and Cliff treated her like a queen. Whatever he was doing, whoever he was seeing, everything stopped while he saw to his mother's comfort.

'Even when he was performing at one-night stands all over the country, Cliff kept constantly in touch with her, writing to her at least three times a week.'

As his fame spread and he consistently began notching up hits all over the world, with the notable exception of America, overseas tours became more frequent and Cliff was delighted to find the reception he was accorded was just as warm as at home. 'We went to Australia, New Zealand and South Africa,' said Bruce Welch. 'This was the first time these countries had seen a big-name rock 'n' roll star come to their country. It was all fresh and new to them.'

In the spring of 1961 Cliff and The Shadows visited South Africa for the first time amid extraordinary scenes. There they were, enjoying unprecedented record success, with no less than eight records between them in South Africa's Top Ten at the time. Many thousands of fans greeted them at Johannesburg airport, and South African golfer Gary Player, whom Cliff had never met, generously lent Cliff his beautiful red convertible Lincoln Continental to transport him and The Shadows from the airport to their hotel.

Their journey resembled a presidential open-top motorcade as thousands turned out in the streets to line the route, while others hung out of the windows of office buildings or climbed lamp posts to cheer the boys every inch of the way into the city centre. At the end of Eloff Street, in the heart of the city's busy shopping area, they were greeted by a huge banner strung from one side of the road to the other proclaiming: 'Welcome Cliff and The Shadows.' There an excited crowd numbering ten thousand completely disrupted the traffic as they waited to catch a glimpse of Cliff arriving at the Carlton Hotel.

A heavy police presence helped him make it safely inside, and he was urged to go out on to the hotel balcony to wave to the fans massed below, chanting: 'We want Cliff!' The sight that greeted him has remained etched in his memory.

'I waved and thousands and thousands of arms and handkerchiefs waved back,' Cliff remembered in his autobiography *Which One's Cliff?*. 'It's hard to describe the sensation. Every adjective, every superlative would work. It was total elation – an unbelievable, once-in-a-lifetime experience.'

Cliff revealed that among his proudest possessions was a black-and-white newsreel shot at Johannesburg airport and at Eloff Street. Not many of his friends had seen it, he said, but occasionally he ran it through just to convince himself that it had really happened and to prove to any doubting Thomases that The Beatles and The Rolling Stones did not have the monopoly on screaming crowds.

On his return to England in April, Cliff was at pains to explain in the press that when they were first offered the contract to go to South Africa, he and The Shadows were unaware their shows had been arranged for whites only, in accordance with South Africa's apartheid policies. 'We didn't realise there would be those problems,' he said, 'and when they arose, we found ourselves in rather an awkward position. We overcame this position to the best of our ability by offering to do a couple of shows especially for the non-Europeans, with the proceeds going to charity. Those shows took place in Cape Town and Salisbury.'

Cliff had been appalled by the segregation he had witnessed for himself in America's deep south when touring the United States, and now he stressed that he was firmly against apartheid and that he wanted to entertain everybody, no matter what the colour of their skin.

Despite his obvious and very public rejection of apartheid, Cliff was later to earn a blacklisting from the United Nations for touring South Africa.

Of far greater concern, however, was a death threat he received in 1985 from political extremists over his South African appearances. Chillingly, he was warned he would be shot while he was visiting Norway and the threat was real enough for the police to treat it most seriously.

'Anti-apartheid extremists got the wrong idea about why I'd been to South Africa,' he revealed in 1989, 'and they decided they would shoot me while I was in Norway for a concert. I tried to explain by issuing a statement to them, but it was no good.

'The police sealed off an entire hotel top floor and held me there for safety. It was the worst moment of my life. Although I'm not afraid of dying, because of my belief in God, the way I die is important to me. I didn't want to die from a bullet, just as I don't want to get run over.' With obvious relief, Cliff was able to add: 'I'm no longer on their hit list because I satisfied them that I'm not against them. But it shows we have to fear extremists even when they are fighting for a good cause.'

8. STATESIDE

Elvis Presley was my idol, but there must have been something missing in his life for him to go the way he did – a sad, sick man.

Cliff Richard

On the strength of the hysteria he had generated on the UK tour while upstaging America's Kalin Twins, Cliff, together with The Shadows, was swiftly booked into an American package tour due to start in January 1960. While Cliff had been appearing in *Babes in the Wood* in pantomime, 'Living Doll' had been released in America and was starting to make a minor impact on the US charts. The tour would be an ideal opportunity for Cliff to promote the record in person.

By 11 February, 'Living Doll' was at number 30 in the *Billboard* singles chart and for Cliff the dream was coming true. Less than eighteen months earlier he had been pen-pushing at work, and now he suddenly had a record rubbing shoulders in the US hit parade with hits by top American singers, including his idol Elvis Presley. And, to top it all, now he would be performing in the very country whose music had originally inspired him. 'Maybe I might even get to meet Elvis,' he told Tito Burns, more in hope than real expectation.

The US tour comprised 33 one-nighter dates and was enticingly billed as *The Biggest Show of Stars – 1960 Winter*

Edition. While grateful even to be setting foot in America, Cliff was still disappointed to learn that he would be bottom of the bill, but he understood why when he learned the full line-up of artistes. Between them, the roster of Americans on the bill could boast more than forty major hit records. To Cliff, they were all massive stars.

Top of the bill were three good-looking American teen idols of Italian extraction, Frankie Avalon (born Francis Avallone), then 21, Bobby Rydell (Robert Ridarelli), then 20, and Freddy Cannon (Frederick Picariello), also 21, who had all risen to fame via regular appearances on Dick Clark's hugely popular US TV show *American Bandstand.*

Avalon had notched up seven hits in two years, including the teen ballads 'Venus' and 'Why?'. Both reached number one in America and were Top Twenty hits in England. Like Avalon, Rydell was also riding on a crest of a wave with a trio of million-sellers in the US, including 'Wild One', which also reached number seven in the UK charts. Freddy Cannon, one of the more talented rock 'n' rollers, had also enjoyed a big hit on both sides of the Atlantic with 'Tallahassee Lassie'.

In addition to these three hot favourites with American teenagers, the bill included R & B singer Clyde McPhatter, described by Jerry Wexler, architect of the legendary Atlantic record company, as 'the great, unique singer of all time'. Of particular interest to The Shadows was the fact that Clyde had been a founding member of The Drifters, the American band that had forced Cliff's Drifters to change their name.

The rest of the supporting stars were no amateurs either: the gimmick-laden instrumental group Johnny and The Hurricanes, whom Cliff knew from their two huge 1959 UK hits, 'Red River Rock' and 'Reveille Rock'; The Isley Brothers, pioneers of gospel-influenced soul music; The Crests, a New York doo-wop vocal group who had made it big with their first record 'Sixteen Candles', a paean to teenagedom; The Clovers, an influential vocal group who had seventeen consecutive R & B hits before uncharacteristically registering a smash on the pop charts with the ballad 'Blue Velvet'; and Sammy Turner, a rock 'n' roll balladeer whose speciality was recycled pop songs of the past, notably a remake ten years on of a 1949 hit, 'Lavender Blue'.

It was an impressive array of talent and, almost as an afterthought, the promotional posters for the tour would proclaim: 'Extra Added Attraction: England's No. 1 singing sensation Cliff Richards'. At least it was another chance for Cliff to put Ian Samwell's publicity ploy into action yet again. 'No, it's Cliff Richard,' he would say.

Faced with taking his place in such a formidable line-up, Cliff realised he would have his work cut out to make any sort of impression, and the day before he was due to fly out for the tour, he arrived at Tito Burns's offices around lunchtime to show everyone the outfit he planned to wear for his performances – a white sharkskin suit, black shirt, white tie, black socks and white shoes.

Cliff's personal secretary Pat McDonald later recounted: 'With almost one voice Tito, Ann Davison – the receptionist – and I exclaimed: "Ghastly!" When he put on his full rig, we almost had to shade our eyes to avoid being dazzled. When the light fell on him he shone like the headlamps of a motorcar.

'We thought it was far too rock 'n' roll, almost going back to the days when Cliff wore sideburns and, with some justice, was accused of aping Presley. But Cliff wouldn't listen to us. He argued that the gear was absolutely right for American audiences and that it was no good going over there and looking like a wallflower. You had to be flamboyant, he said, flamboyant and exciting. He was right, of course.'

Cliff was in good spirits when he flew out with his father and Tito for the start of the tour, which kicked off in Montreal, Canada, on 22 January. From there it crisscrossed the States, taking in sizeable venues in major cities where the audiences numbered between five and seven thousand.

Cliff and The Shadows opened the second half of each show and were permitted by the terms of their contract to play just five numbers, which amounted to barely fifteen minutes on stage. They began with 'Forty Days', and followed up with 'My Babe', 'Voice in the Wilderness' and 'Living Doll' before signing off with the Jerry Lee Lewis classic 'Whole Lotta

Shakin' Goin' On'. This generally brought the crowd to their feet and screams from some of the girls, but way short of the decibels Cliff induced from girls at his British gigs.

Cliff wore his gleaming sharkskin suit every night, and he was so desperate to keep it clean that he kept a white handkerchief in his pocket, which he pulled out and surreptitiously placed on the stage so he could drop dramatically to one knee during his final barnstorming number without the trouser leg getting dirty.

As the tour rolled on, Cliff and The Shadows were able to gauge the reaction of American fans and tailored their all-too-brief twice-nightly performances accordingly. They replaced 'My Babe' with the more punchy 'Dynamite' to give their short set more energy, and they tried to put on more of a show as opposed to the American artistes, who seemed content to walk on and simply sing the hits the audience had paid their money to hear.

'Cliff went down really well with the American audiences,' Bruce Welch said. 'They really liked him and all the American artists on the bill liked him too. Where Cliff scored with the audience was the fact that we were doing rock 'n' roll. We were a singer with a group playing guitars, whereas the rest of them on the bill, including Frankie Avalon, were singing with a big band backing.

'Avalon was a gigantic star then, almost manufactured – a good-looking Italian boy who had all the gear. He had his eyebrows plucked and a make-up artist before he went on. He looked a million dollars – he couldn't sing, bless him, but he was huge. He had some very big hits.'

Cliff and The Shadows quickly accepted that life on the road meant they would not see nearly as much of America as they had hoped. The police in each city were anxious to avoid any possibility of rock 'n' roll-inspired riots, so at the end of each show all the artistes were immediately escorted at speed from the venue to their Greyhound coach, waiting with its engine running, ready to make a quick getaway.

Cliff would settle into a seat with all the other singers and musicians to be driven sometimes five hundred miles through the night to the next arena. They all essentially lived on the coach, and fifteen more or less continuous hours on the road was not uncommon. They would arrive at their hotel and sink thankfully into bed to sleep before being woken in time to eat and prepare for the next show.

The Greyhound coach transporting them all was at least very different from the Green Line bus Cliff had become accustomed to boarding to gigs from his Cheshunt home in his early days. Now there was air-conditioning and better upholstered, comfortable seats that reclined. There was even a lavatory at the back of the coach to avoid stop-offs, which could steal precious minutes from what was a tight venue-to-venue schedule. In between taking naps or eating, hour after monotonous hour on the road travelling through the night meant there was plenty of time for Cliff to chat to the other artistes, to swap stories, talk music and forge friendships. But he couldn't help noticing that the more the American audiences took a shine to him at the concerts, the less friendly the established stars of the show appeared to be towards him.

In an intense five weeks with barely a single day off, one town seemed to merge into the next, with little chance to sightsee. At least Cliff and The Shadows could tick off visits to cities that they knew to be the hometowns or birthplaces of their idols: Norfolk, Virginia, where Gene Vincent had his roots; Kentucky, from where The Everly Brothers originated; Memphis, where Elvis lived; Lubbock, the Texas town forever associated musically with Buddy Holly.

Lubbock was a particularly poignant stop, because Buddy was a singer they had all admired so much, particularly Bruce and Hank, and his tragic death in a plane crash less than a year before was still fresh in the memory. Cliff was touched that members of Buddy's family, including his father, came to their concert at Lubbock's Coliseum. The family, in turn, were moved to hear that Cliff and The Shadows held Buddy in such high regard and that he had been such an influence upon them.

'It was a seven-thousand-seater venue and there was an incredible hush when we came on,' said Bruce. 'Like Buddy, Hank was slim, he was dark, he was wearing the same kind of

National Health glasses, and by then he had the same guitar, a Fender Stratocaster. To some people in the audience it must have seemed as though it was Buddy standing there. We were Holly fanatics and I can remember when we first played the London Palladium in the days when the microphone came up through a hole in the stage, I went over to Hank and said: "Do you realise Buddy Holly was standing right here?" We were Holly fanatics and we all would have loved to have gone to pay our respects at his grave on that first US trip, but there just wasn't time.'

Hank had acquired his much-coveted Fender Stratocaster in April 1959, thanks to Cliff's generosity and his determination to give his ace guitarist the instrument he desperately wanted. Hank and Bruce had first fallen in love with the look of the Strat when they saw a picture of Buddy Holly holding one on the front of the album sleeve of Buddy's LP *The Chirping Crickets*.

Bruce said: 'We were all sitting around going through various albums by Gene Vincent and The Blue Caps, Ricky Nelson and Buddy Holly, and when we saw the sleeve cover of Buddy holding this fabulous guitar we said: "We've got to have one of those." No one had seen one before and, to us, who had been playing acoustic guitars, this one looked like a spaceship, especially to me, as I was still playing the guitar I'd had at school. In fact, I've got pictures of me at the London Palladium playing that £5 guitar I'd had at school.

'We found out it was a Fender Stratocaster and that Ricky Nelson's guitarist also played a Fender. So Cliff sent off to California for the Fender catalogue and when it arrived we all went through this little catalogue and on the centre pages there were these guitars that looked like spaceships, including one that was pink with a gold-plated maple neck.

'Cliff sent off for the guitar for Hank. It was 140 guineas and, of course, he was the only one of us who could afford it – we were on £20 a week. So Cliff imported the first Fender Strat into this country. It was flamingo pink and it contributed greatly to the sound of The Shadows. So Cliff was the fairy godmother, or godfather – one of the two!'

Oh Boy! Rocking up a storm with The Shadows
on TV (© Dezo Hoffmann / Rex Features)

Topping the
bill at the London
Palladium in 1960
(© Dezo Hoffmann / Rex Features)

An early glimpse of Cliff recording at EMI's
Abbey Road studios (© McCabe / Getty Images)

Thumbs up from Cliff after laying down another hit
track with The Shadows (© McCabe / Getty Images)

A warm US welcome for Cliff, but lasting success in America has eluded him (© Bettmann / Corbis)

Just 19 years old and Cliff has already enjoyed two years as a major star (© Hulton Archive / Getty Images)

Beating out a rhythm on screen in the movie *Expresso Bongo* (© George Konig / Rex Features)

Cliff and co-star Carole Grey take a break from dance rehearsals on the set of *The Young Ones* (© Keystone Features / Getty Images)

A tug of love with Una Stubbs in the movie *Wonderful Life*
(© McCabe / Getty Images)

Jackie Irving, the beautiful dancer Cliff considered marrying, weds Adam Faith in 1967 (© Rex Features)

A kiss for mum on arriving back at Heathrow from America in 1960 (© George Stroud / Getty Images)

Man about the house: Cliff with his mother and three sisters at home in 1964 (© Peter Hustler / Getty Images)

Cheers! Cliff celebrates his early string of hits (© Bob Haswell / Getty Images)

Kisses from fellow chart-toppers Cilla Black (left) and Lulu at a
pop awards ceremony (© Keystone Features / Getty Images)

No romance, but a
lasting friendship with
singer Olivia Newton-John
(© Doug McKenzie / Getty Images)

Cliff in concert in 1978 to raise money
for the Christian charity TEAR Fund
(© Evening Standard / Getty Images)

Cliff meets the Queen after one of his many Royal Variety
Show performances (© Tim Graham / Getty Images)

Vintage Shadows: Brian Bennett, Hank Marvin
and Bruce Welch with Cliff (© Allstar)

Cliff with Sue Barker
during their romance
(© Peter Brooker / Rex Features)

Cliff with Bill Latham, a long-time mentor (© Stephen Barker / Rex Features)

A proud Sir Cliff with his family at Buckingham Palace after receiving his knighthood (© Rex Features)

Serve up! Cliff on court in Birmingham, 2004, during the
annual tournament he staged to raise money for the Cliff
Richard Tennis Foundation (© MJ Kim / Getty Images)

Still rocking: Cliff on stage at The Point Theatre, Dublin
in December 2006 (© ShowBizIreland / Getty Images)

Cliff's impromptu sing-along brightened a wet Wimbledon washout in 1996. Joining in with the applause is champion Martina Navratilova, right
(© Clive Brunskill / Getty Images)

A hug for Una Stubbs at the after-show party following filming of the TV show *An Audience with Cliff Richard* in 1999
(© Ken McKay / Rex Features)

Cliff at home on his farm in the Algarve (© Cliff Kent / Rex Features)

Two years later Fender gave Hank and Bruce matching Strats. 'It's the old story,' said Bruce. 'When you're struggling to make it, you can't afford one, and then when you're famous, they give you one!'

The US tour was a sharp learning curve for Cliff in every way. He and The Shadows were appalled at the 'Whites Only' signs they saw outside diners and bars in some of the southern states. The shocking irony was not lost on Cliff – he was travelling across America and virtually living cheek by jowl on the coach with black musicians and singers like Clyde McPhatter and Sammy Turner, and yet on stopovers in some cities the law dictated they sit down to eat in separate restaurants.

The day before the tour started, Cliff was able to make his carefully selected debut on American TV as a guest on Pat Boone's show for the giant ABC network. Pat was the clean-cut all-American boy of popular music who, after Elvis Presley, had become America's most successful teenage singer of the 1950s. Whereas Presley's greased hair, swivelling hips and pink Cadillacs seemed to threaten, Pat's white buck shoes, polite manner, university background, happy family image, and his series of soft, tuneful cover versions of songs plundered from black artistes went a long way to diluting the explosive power of rock 'n' roll for those 'twixt twelve and twenty' in 1950s America.

Pat's deep, rich voice on ballads like 'April Love' and 'Love Letters in the Sand' established him as the acceptable alternative to the rebellious Elvis Presley. 'Hearing a record of mine on the radio for the first time was the closest I ever came to being drunk,' commented the clean-living Pat. His scrubbed looks and boy-next-door manner made the songs much more palatable to millions who couldn't get Elvis and Little Richard.

After he topped the US and UK charts with a soft version of The Flamingos' rhythm and blues hit 'I'll Be Home', Pat's general popularity and super-wholesome demeanour earned him his own TV series, where guests tended to be the 'nicer' popular singers, such as Johnny Mathis or Nat 'King' Cole, together with such pleasant and hearty acts as The Texas Boys'

Choir. Pat's was therefore deemed a safe show in which Cliff should make his US TV debut.

On 21 January 1960, Pat introduced Cliff as: 'Britain's most important singing and record star – a young British lad – terribly young, terribly rich, who tonight makes his American television debut . . . welcome Cliff Richard.'

Cliff sang 'Living Doll' before indulging in some pre-rehearsed cringeworthy banter worked out by a team of staff writers, which included a young Woody Allen trying to make a name for himself.

'Wizard! Smashing! Top-ho,' Pat volunteered at the end of Cliff's number, which had Cliff replying: 'Excuse me a moment please,' before consulting an American dictionary and adding: 'Oh, you mean crazy!'

When Pat informed viewers Cliff had been born in India and enquired why he had left, Cliff replied: 'Frankly, Pat, when you've shot one elephant you've shot them all. Besides I was getting to be quite a burden on the family. A year old and I hadn't had a single hit record yet.'

Cliff was allocated a significant portion of the show, which ended with his duetting with Pat on 'Pretty Blue Eyes'. As an exercise in introducing the unknown Cliff to American TV viewers, his appearance on such a well-watched show was deemed an important first step in the process of trying to launch him to stardom in America. Pat Boone was impressed enough to say: 'Cliff should have a long and impressive showbusiness career.'

After a month on tour, a four-day break allowed Cliff to fly back to London from Wichita in Kansas via New York. The purpose of the flying 24-hour visit back home was twofold: to collect an award at the *New Musical Express* Poll Winners' Concert at the Empire Pool, Wembley, and to appear on the top-rated TV entertainment show, *Sunday Night at the London Palladium*.

Conspicuous by their absence at both events were The Shadows. They remained in America and they were none too pleased to be left behind. They rightly suspected it was all part of a Tito Burns plan to prise Cliff away from his backing group, who were becoming far too permanently attached to Cliff professionally for Tito's liking.

'It was the management, never Cliff, who tried to imply we were just Cliff's backing musicians,' Bruce Welch confirms. 'Certainly that was Tito Burns's view. Cliff never looked at us like that. With Cliff it was five guys, very much the five of us. He was obviously the singer, he was the star and he was making all of the money, but it was very much a five-piece group and very exciting for the five of us.'

Because of the time difference, a jet-lagged Cliff arrived back in England at midnight and went straight into rehearsals until four in the morning with The Parker Royal Four, who had been hired to back him both at the *NME* Poll Winners' Concert and on the TV show.

Later that afternoon a bleary-eyed Cliff was driven to Wembley, managing to grab some fish and chips at a dingy café on the way. After he had put in a singing appearance at the Poll Winners' Concert, where *New Musical Express* readers had voted him Top British Male Singer, he fell into a deep sleep, so deep that he needed water splashed in his face to rouse him prior to being driven to the London Palladium. On the go for some 36 hours without proper rest, Cliff put in a thoroughly lacklustre performance on the TV show, for which he later apologised to his fans, admitting he was not at his best.

Cliff's mum, Dorothy, nervously taking her first-ever plane trip, accompanied Cliff back to America, where he rejoined the tour for its final three dates. Cliff confessed he had been homesick and it was his mum he had missed the most.

During the US tour, which ended at the end of February, Cliff never did get around to meeting Elvis Presley, although he did encounter Presley's manager, Colonel Tom Parker, who was in New York waiting for 'my boy' to return from Germany, where he had been doing his Army national service. The colonel was staying at the Warwick Hotel and Cliff and his parents went to see him for an informal chat. When Parker invited them to have lunch with him, Cliff, Dorothy and Rodger imagined the great Colonel Parker would take them out for a meal or invite them to dine with him at the hotel restaurant. Instead, the famously hard-nosed colonel cannily opened a drawer and produced packets of sandwiches, which he proceeded to hand round to them all.

While Cliff was in the States, 'Living Doll' managed to stay in the US singles charts for just four weeks, but the record company never seriously got behind it and their contact with Cliff was minimal, much to Cliff's frustration. Company-generated promotion of the record was almost non-existent and a glorious opportunity to put Cliff on the map in America was lost.

With the certainty of hindsight, however, it was hardly surprising that Cliff's US record bosses showed little appetite for promoting him. Up to that point only two British singers had ever topped the US charts – Vera Lynn with 'Auf Wiederseh'n Sweetheart' in 1952, and fourteen-year-old Laurie London with 'He's Got the Whole World In His Hands' in 1958.

Bruce Welch explained: 'As far as the American record companies were concerned, we were, in effect, taking coals to Newcastle. Why should they bother with releasing foreign rock 'n' roll records when they had the originals? In those days, you could count the rock 'n' roll industry on both hands: Elvis, Bill Haley, Jerry Lee Lewis, Buddy Holly, The Everlys, Little Richard, Fats Domino and that was it. They were all Americans and we were copying them in those days. So why should they bother when they had the genuine thing?

'Back then, the record companies in America used to do what they called token releases – if you had a number-one hit in the UK, it meant you had to have it released in America. But very often it was just a token release, with no promotion behind it. Like Cliff, we, The Shadows, suffered in 1960 when our number-one UK hit "Apache" went out on EMI America two months before a rival version went out on the Atlantic label. The other record went to number one and ours didn't get promoted at all.

'Bear in mind, this is four years before The Beatles cracked it, and when they did, the British invasion then followed and almost everybody had a hit – The Dave Clark Five, Herman's Hermits, The Animals, and so on. Cliff and The Shadows were too early to catch that wave in America. It was a shame for us. Who knows what would have happened if we and Cliff had really cracked the US market?'

One trip to America for Cliff and The Shadows did at least produce another hit single for the UK. On the flight back to London a pretty air hostess enquired of the group how they went about writing a hit single. Their instant practical demonstration was to come up with 'Gee Whiz it's You' which Cliff took to number four in the charts in March 1961.

Cliff was eventually to enjoy Top Ten hit records in America, but it seems that all his efforts to establish himself as a major star in the United States were dogged by ill fortune.

When he returned to the States for another tour, the timing of it could hardly have been worse. Cliff and The Shadows went back hoping to establish a significant US footing, but it was bad luck on Cliff that it took place in October 1962, when the world, and in particular everyone in America, was holding its breath as the Cuban missile crisis escalated to the very brink of World War Three.

On 28 October, American President John F. Kennedy and Russia's Nikita Khrushchev played what amounted to nuclear poker over the Soviet Union's installation of nuclear weapons in Cuba. Kennedy raised the stakes to issue a 'Back off, or else' ultimatum to the Russian leader and, in a climate of such acute fear and alarm, Americans were not in the mood to venture out to enjoy themselves and be entertained by a little-known British singer. They were far too busy buying up tins of food and anxiously preparing to barricade themselves inside their homes and hastily made nuclear shelters. An Elvis copycat from England and his backing group were not going to entice them out in their hordes for an evening in such a moment of global crisis. As a result, many of the large arenas Cliff and The Shadows were booked into were sparsely attended, at best.

The trips to America did, however, provide Cliff with a memorable visit to Elvis Presley's Memphis mansion, Graceland, even though the King himself wasn't at home. While they were playing Memphis, there was a knock on the dressing-room door and the message came back to Cliff and The Shadows that there was a Mr Presley asking to see them. That sent a shiver down the spine, but it turned out to be Elvis's father, Vernon, who said he knew all about Cliff, and was fully aware that he was 'the British Elvis'. Vernon told Cliff that if his son had been in town he would most certainly have invited them all back to his home. He was therefore extending the same invitation.

Vernon was courteous, polite and hospitable and took Cliff and the boys on a guided tour of Graceland and its grounds. Cliff marvelled at the gold discs framed on the walls and gasped at the sheer opulence of the mansion, which included a carpet with Elvis's image stitched into it. 'Vernon showed us everywhere except Elvis's mother's room,' said Bruce. 'We saw Elvis's bedroom with its big circular bed, and also the bathroom where, of course, eventually Elvis was to be found dead.'

Cliff – who just months before had been living with his family in a council house – and The Shadows almost had to pinch themselves to believe that they were actually being royally entertained at the legendary Graceland. 'Hank and I shared a flat in Marylebone High Street paying £4 a week each,' said Bruce, 'and then suddenly we were in Graceland. We couldn't believe it.'

That visit to the King's Memphis palace was as near as Cliff would ever get to his idol, although there was a near miss when Cliff was on holiday in Germany with some pals at a time when Presley was doing his stint in the US Army.

Cliff knew exactly where Elvis was stationed in Germany, and he and his friends boldly drove up to the barracks and managed to wheedle out of a guard Presley's exact address by telling him that Cliff was the English equivalent of Elvis. The guard on duty helpfully directed them to Elvis Presley's house, and when Cliff and his pals drew up at the location there was no doubting they were in the right place – the walls were covered in lipstick messages scribbled by adoring fans. Nervously Cliff got out of the car and knocked on Presley's door. He waited until it became clear no one was going to answer, then returned to the car and they drove away.

'Sadly I missed him by twenty minutes,' he said. 'But I had a chance to meet him once. It was in the States, he was not well and he'd put on a lot of weight, and I decided to keep my earlier memories of him intact. The Elvis I remember was the Elvis of "Heartbreak Hotel" and "All Shook Up", classic hit after classic hit. I wasn't interested in Elvis's music from "Crying in the Chapel" onwards. He lost me after that. But he was the best, the prototype. I don't suppose there will ever be anyone like him again.

'In the beginning all we did was copy American music. America is still the fatherland of rock 'n' roll. I don't think America has control of rock 'n' roll. Nobody does. It belongs to the world now. But America gave it to the world and therefore holds pride of place.

'This is why I've always desperately wanted something to happen for me in the States. I've cracked it everywhere else but where it started, and it irks me. The Shadows and I always seemed to represent the rest of the world, and it was the rest of the world versus America.

'In 1965, a poll taken in the American trade magazine *Billboard* showed that The Beatles were the biggest record-sellers in the world. And who was the biggest solo artist in the world? Me. And I didn't sell a record in America.'

Another golden opportunity to make a big impact on the American public was lost when Cliff was booked to appear on *The Ed Sullivan Show*. If any programme in the history of American television could be called an institution, it was this one. Every Sunday night for more than two decades this homely former newspaper columnist with strange diction, deadpan delivery, stiff neck, hunched shoulders, and awkward gestures introduced an incredible variety of entertainment into American homes via the TV screen.

Numerous top performers made their American TV debuts on the programme, including Bob Hope, Lena Horne, Eddie Fisher, Dinah Shore and even Walt Disney. Virtually every 'name' act in American music, comedy, theatre and film appeared over the years between 1948 and 1971, and to a man they were always pleased to do so, because *The Ed Sullivan Show* was a fantastic showcase watched by most of America.

Cliff's invitation to appear on the programme was not only a feather in his cap, but an ideal opportunity to demonstrate to a vast American audience just why he was being hailed as 'England's Elvis'. He was eagerly looking forward to his appearance, especially as he was to be given the closing spot on the show. He planned to sing 'Move It' and 'Living Doll', two very different numbers that would show 45 million Americans tuning in that the UK possessed a credible rock 'n' roll singer.

But to his bewilderment, Cliff was given a Charlie Chaplin cane and a straw boater and ordered to perform 'What Do You Know, We Have A Show', a music-hall sequence from his film *The Young Ones* instead. This was the elaborate production number Cliff and The Shadows performed in the film when they 'broke into' Finsbury Park Empire and tried on a series of theatrical costumes.

Cliff was far from happy at being presented to the American public as a young vaudeville singer, assisted for the show by chorus girls, some in clown costumes and others dressed as magicians. He was dumbfounded at the sudden change of plans, but he was not about to argue his case with one of the most powerful men in TV in America at the time.

Sullivan was not a man to be crossed – he once exploded with anger and cut Bo Diddley off in the middle of a number after Bo played his repetitive big-riff hit, 'Bo Diddley', live on the show despite expressly being told not to do so during rehearsals. Sullivan was so enraged that he then cornered the singer backstage and verbally tore into him. Later, when Diddley received his cheque for $700, he was ordered to endorse it and hand it back.

Sullivan always enjoyed putting together a strange collection of acts – grand opera and the latest rock stars, classical ballet and long-legged Broadway showgirls, slapstick comedy and recitations from great dramatic writings frequently juxtaposed on a single show. That very variety made Sullivan's shows a resounding success, even though he was criticised in some quarters for presenting a format that appeared to be that of an old-fashioned vaudeville revue.

In Cliff's case, however, the sudden U-turn was surprising, and baffling. Never a great fan of rock 'n' roll, Sullivan had nevertheless introduced rock stars on his show before and simply allowed them to be themselves. So why did he insist on a vaudevillian Cliff Richard?

The answer is Elvis Presley or, to be precise, Presley's manager, the irrepressible Colonel Tom Parker. He got wind of Cliff's appearance and personally telephoned Sullivan to tell him in no uncertain terms that he did not want to turn on his TV on Sunday night and see Cliff given the big build-up as England's Elvis. 'There's only one Elvis,' he growled, and Sullivan should not forget it.

Parker was able to exert his influence because Presley had given *The Talk of the Town*, as Sullivan's show was originally called, priceless publicity when Elvis the Pelvis, the nation's hottest new singing sensation, was filmed just from the waist up during his TV performance to avoid scandalising home viewers with his goading crotch and heaving hips. Sullivan, a newspaperman who knew controversy in the press meant an increase in TV ratings, remained in Colonel Parker's debt and did a deal with the colonel to have Presley on his show three times in the next six months.

A few weeks later Cliff appeared on *The Dick Clark Show* before flying back to London to deliver a despondent view of his chances in the United States. 'In America nobody knows us at all,' he said shortly after stepping off the plane. 'You've got to fight a bit to make yourself known, you're up against so much. It's a bit strange but true – you're up against so much.'

In the midst of expressing his disappointment, Cliff couldn't resist taking a swipe at Americans: 'Everyone there was amazed I was wearing pointed shoes. They're so square over there – no idea of clothes,' he said.

Over a decade was to elapse before Cliff attempted, in 1976, to show Americans that he was a very different kind of singer. He set out on a 35-concert North American tour to last six weeks, but it got off to a disastrous start before Cliff was even able to sing a note.

A truck containing £40,000 worth of guitars and sound equipment was stolen from outside a Hollywood hotel just three days before he went to Seattle for the opening show.

The theft itself was catastrophic enough, but the thieves also left a little note for Cliff. It read: 'Have a nice day.'

'I'm sure it irks Cliff that he's never really cracked America,' said Bruce Welch. 'Many times they wanted Cliff to go and spend six months in America, because that's how you break America – you have to do the rounds of radio, TV, and concerts. America's so massive that you can be a star in New York and nobody's heard of you in Los Angeles. But Cliff didn't care to go and spend that amount of time. He's had his home at St George's Hill in Weybridge, Surrey, and his religion, and so he's said: "I don't want to leave home and schlep around the States for six to nine months."

'He's said it, and he meant it. Besides, Cliff Richard is massive everywhere else in the world.

'He's had chart success in America with "Devil Woman", "We Don't Talk Anymore" and "A Little in Love". But you can have two, three, four or five hits in America and they're just records – not a career.'

Any hopes Cliff might originally have harboured of being hailed as the English Elvis in the rock 'n' roll king's own backyard were never fulfilled. Cliff's admiration for Elvis's early music is unstinting today, but it's tempered with sadness at Presley's terrible decline into a bloated, drug-ravaged wreck.

Speaking in 1981 at a preview of the BBC's four-part series, *Cliff*, about his life, Cliff said: 'I was modelled on Elvis, and I faced all the same temptations. I was young and single and there were girls and drink. Before I found Christianity, I sometimes got terribly drunk. And I'm ashamed to say I have been drunk a couple of times since.

'Without my faith, there is no doubt I could have gone down the same road as Elvis.

'The media and others tried to build me up as Britain's answer to Elvis, which I never was. I admired him and I still do, but I think of that magical man who came from nowhere and changed the world. The sick and sad man who died full of drugs is something else.

'Elvis was the best, the greatest. He had material success, but there must have been something missing. I think the difference between us was that I had the genuine love and support of friends and family, not to mention my Christianity, whereas no one really loved Elvis. He had nothing to sustain him.

'Elvis was undoubtedly religious. He came from a religious background. But unless you discover how to find God, which I have discovered, it's a pointless exercise.

'A friend of mine knew someone who worked with Elvis close to his death and they said he was like a lost soul. I find that very, very sad. The love of fans is very different from that of family and friends – which is what I've got. The trouble was, Elvis had no one close enough to take him to one side and blow a raspberry at him when he was in the wrong.'

9. BONGO

I wrote the song 'Living Doll' in about ten minutes flat.

Lionel Bart on the song that changed Cliff from
rock 'n' roller to family entertainer

Cliff Richard might never have made his film debut in *Serious Charge* and crossed over from rocker to family entertainer if it hadn't been for songwriter Lionel Bart.

Bart, who went on to grand acclaim for a string of compositions, notably the score for the phenomenally successful musical *Oliver!*, had been hired to write the music for a screen version of a play which, at that time, was considered sensational because it dealt with hints of homosexuality.

Serious Charge, which was released in 1959, was all about a small-town nineteen-year-old troublemaker, who is accused by his parish priest of being responsible for the death of a young girl, and who proceeds to amuse himself by accusing the priest of making homosexual advances.

Bart, who had seen Cliff perform just once, suggested him for the role of Curley Thompson, a young rock 'n' roll singer, brother of the leader of an unsavoury gang of youngsters just living for kicks. Cliff was screen-tested at Elstree Studios and, drawing on his experiences in front of the *Oh Boy!* cameras, showed enough acting potential to quickly land the part of

Curley. Bart then travelled down to Cheshunt to pay Cliff a visit at his home, as he was still living with his family at this time, met Cliff's mum, and told Cliff he would be writing three songs for him to sing in the movie.

It was the start of a working relationship rather than a great friendship between the two. 'Let's face it, we had different lifestyles,' said Lionel. 'I was living dangerously and pretty close to the flame, while Cliff was a good boy!'

One Sunday morning Lionel was thumbing through the *Sunday Pictorial* red-top newspaper when an advertisement for a child's doll caught his eye. It was for 'The new improved Darling Doll' and went on to proclaim: 'She kneels, walks, sits and sings.' And that was all the inspiration he needed to get composing. 'I thought: that'll do,' said Bart, 'and I wrote the song "Living Doll" in about ten minutes flat.'

Cliff was far from impressed when he was first given 'Living Doll' to sing in the film. 'I went into the movie thinking: I *can* sing that. It's not my idea of great rock 'n' roll, but if it's necessary for the movie I'll do it. So we didn't like that song, but we did it because we were doing a movie – anything to be in a movie – and we did it the way Lionel wrote it.'

For the purposes of the film soundtrack, Cliff recorded 'Living Doll' not with The Drifters, as they then were, but with a group of musicians engaged by the film studios. They interpreted the song as an up-tempo quasi-rock song, but Cliff disliked their musical treatment of the number intensely and said: 'It was pseudo-rock, English rock 'n' roll, and we were trying to move away from that. "Move It" was the first real rock 'n' roll record made outside America and we were very proud of that fact.'

While preparing for a concert at Sheffield City Hall, word came through to Cliff that a line in his *Serious Charge* contract stipulated that he must release a single from the film and the obvious choice was 'Living Doll'. Cliff was shocked and far from pleased. 'We hadn't read the small print,' he said.

Cliff was adamant that 'Living Doll' should not be released as a single in its soundtrack form. And The Drifters were equally unimpressed when they heard the movie version. 'It was pretty awful,' said Bruce. 'It was like a big-band version. Cliff had recorded it for the soundtrack with this orchestra and brass and it sounded like a BBC session. It was essentially a great song, especially for Cliff's image. You could see all the women fainting already because of the message of the song. But you couldn't release it the way it was.'

It was Bruce who quickly came to Cliff's rescue. Cliff recalled: 'At Sheffield City Hall there used to be two magnificent lions right in the middle of the stage – we used to make our entry up the steps to the left and right of them. And I remember we sat on those steps in rehearsals and Bruce said: "Look, I don't know what we're going to do about this. It's not going to work as a rock song." And he then strummed a bit and said: "How about we do it like a country song?" We thought, yeah, it's crap, but let's do it.'

Cliff was granted permission to rerecord 'Living Doll', this time with The Drifters backing him, and a very different, Bruce Welch-inspired version was the result. 'Honestly, we thought it was horrible,' Cliff laughed. 'But Bruce tried it like a country song with jangling guitar and Hank played a great guitar solo and we had a hit. It went to number one – and we grew to love it!'

Lionel Bart was amazed, not just by Bruce's treatment, but by the reaction of Cliff's fans. He said: 'When the film came out, public demand from Cliff's fans was such that they had to release an EP of the four numbers from the film, and it was the first EP into the Top Twenty charts. Then public demand was such that a few weeks later they had to put "Living Doll" out as a single as well, so it went into the charts again.'

'Living Doll' shot to number one on 31 July 1959, and in the process knocked no less a star than Bobby Darin and his 'Dream Lover' off the top spot, staying there for an impressive six weeks. It also reached number one a second time, 27 years later when Cliff rerecorded the song with the comedy quartet the Young Ones in aid of Comic Relief. But, first time round, it won an Ivor Novello award, and earned Cliff his first gold disc for sales of one million copies.

The actual presentation was made by Bruce Forsyth on *Sunday Night at the London Palladium*, in front of millions of

TV viewers, and it came as a huge surprise to Cliff. It had been kept a closely guarded secret from the singer, and viewers could see he was genuinely startled by the sudden appearance of Bruce clutching his surprise award. Caught unawares, Cliff was in a quandary as to what to do with the gold disc itself once the show was over. In the end he entrusted it to Pat, his personal secretary, and at the end of the night Pat slipped away from the Palladium and travelled home on the tube to Romford with Cliff's precious gold disc wrapped up and hidden under her coat.

Back in 1959, 'Living Doll' did so much more for Cliff than bring him a gold disc. 'It's funny,' he said, 'because when I set out all those years ago, I thought I'd last a couple of weeks and then I'd have to get a proper job. It never occurred to me that it might last. "Move It" got to number two, the next four records didn't do so well and it seemed to be slipping away from me. Today a record company would probably dump you and that would be it. One failure and you're out. As it was, my next single, "Living Doll", went to number one, and everything was fine. But it wasn't until 1968 and I realised that I'd been in the business ten years that I really accepted that I wasn't just a one-hit wonder, here today, forgotten tomorrow.'

'Living Doll' also brought Cliff to a whole new audience, as Bruce Welch explained: 'It's weird. For six months we considered ourselves rock 'n' roll – or Cliff did – but when we made "Living Doll" together that changed everything.

'That record broke him to the mums and dads. Suddenly they were saying: "Ah, that Cliff, isn't he a lovely boy?" It broke him to a family audience. He started to tone down his leg movements and he was like a family entertainer. That was only six months after we'd started.

'That one record broadened his career from being a sexy rock 'n' roll star to almost being a family entertainer. The mums and dads loved it, and somehow the raw rock 'n' roll image smoothed out.

'Cliff and The Shadows became very quickly the Establishment instead of the rat pack of rock 'n' roll. We aged before our time, not in years but in outlook – we had to look smart, had to look bow-tied. So by the time The Beatles arrived, we were those lovely, nice, clean-living boys with nice short-back-and-sides haircuts: Cliff and The Shads. We were family entertainers. We were in the zoot suits, we were the Establishment of showbiz. We'd be doing the Royal Variety shows in bow ties with Bob Hope and Sammy Davis Junior.'

Cliff may have initially disliked 'Living Doll', but it was a considerable stroke of luck that the song that transformed his career ever found his way to him at all. It was originally destined for Russ Sainty, a singer and guitarist in a skiffle group in Leyton, east London.

Like so many other hopefuls, Russ had gone along to the 2 I's with his guitar and successfully passed an audition, which earned him regular appearances at the famous coffee bar. One night in December 1958, Lionel Bart dropped into the 2 I's and took Russ over the road for a chat at another coffee bar called Act 1 Scene 1.

Russ recalled: 'He said: "I think I've got a song that would be perfect for you. Would you like to come back to my place and let me play it for you?" I was so bloody naïve in those days. But I was working a shift for Leyton Borough Council, so I said: "I'd rather not go back. I've got work in the morning."

'The song I was going to get was "Living Doll". Cliff had a massive hit with it in the spring of 1959 and I missed it.'

Despite earnest performances from Anthony Quayle as the maligned parson and Sarah Churchill as a spurned woman furious that the vicar has rejected her advances, *Serious Charge* turned out to be a dour film version of what at the time was a highly controversial play.

In the film – directed by Terence Young, who went on to direct the early James Bond movies – Cliff's role called for him to do little other than sulk, look moody and sing, and he was given a first taste of the strange methods by which film-makers create make-believe.

As the name of his screen character was Curley, Cliff was subjected to the complex and painful process of having his hair curled with hot tongs every morning before shooting began. He thought it was daft, when simply changing Curley's name would have been so much simpler and less time-consuming.

Cliff's film debut may not have set the box office alight, but *Serious Charge* and its catchy Lionel Bart song changed his life.

Cliff's first four singles had all been in the rock 'n' roll vein, but having switched tack with 'Living Doll', he followed up with another easy-paced song with a country feel, 'Travellin' Light'. This also shot to the top of the charts at the end of October 1959, once again deposing Bobby Darin, this time his 'Mack the Knife', and stayed in pole position for five weeks.

The transformation to family entertainer was so sudden that by the end of 1959 Cliff and The Shadows found themselves appearing in the pantomime *Babes in the Wood* at the Stockton-on-Tees Globe Theatre. The seemingly dangerous rocker of just a few months earlier was now to be seen in the role of the Sheriff's troubadour. Instead of being pelted with fruit and vegetables by yobs, it was cheers that now came raining down upon Cliff from over the footlights from mums and dads with excited youngsters perched on their knees.

Pantomime initially did not appeal to Cliff, and there was an obvious danger that they might alienate Cliff's hard core of rock fans. They saw Cliff as Britain's Elvis, not as a yuletide panto star in fancy dress. But, as Marty Wilde pointed out, for pop singers like himself and Cliff: 'The showbiz route was the only way to avoid obsolescence. I remember doing pantomimes and it was laughable, really. I thought: it isn't me, but maybe it'll help my career in some shape or form. There you were being Robin Hood one minute and trying to be a sexy singer the next. To me it was stupid.'

Cliff saw it differently. He was happy to follow in the direction his fans chose to lead him. In a TV interview he was asked what direction his career was taking and he replied: 'I don't really know. It's hard to say, because in this business, whether you're a rock 'n' roll singer or a straight singer, you can be up one day and down the next, and I think the main thing is to do exactly what they want. In say two years, if they don't want rock 'n' roll, then I shall try and do whatever they want.'

Was he a servant to the people? 'They mould my career,' Cliff conceded. 'Everyone knows that the fans are the ones that make you do what you want to do. I can't get over at the moment that I'm earning money doing the stuff that I really like to do. I don't know how long it'll last and how long my fans will go on wanting rock 'n' roll, but as long as they do, I'll give it to them.'

When it came to adapting from rock 'n' roller to pantomime attraction, Cliff had a priceless advantage over pop rivals like Marty Wilde. He had The Shadows as his backing group on record and on stage. And not only were they becoming stars in their own right, but Cliff's two guitarists Hank and Bruce were turning out to be prolific songwriters. They were capable of knocking out – to order – collections of new songs suitable for Cliff's pantomimes.

Cliff said of the pantomimes: 'They were absolutely fresh scores, so when people came to see and hear them, they came to a brand new show. The Shadows and I treated them as such. The pantos I did were not just pantos, they were musicals. The thing that appealed to me was that *Aladdin* is all right – but I want to play Aladdin! It's all very well women playing it, women's lib and all that, but I think I must have been one of the first males to play the leading female part. Legitimately!'

Hank's and Bruce's versatility as songwriters was invaluable for Cliff, as he has happily testified. 'You could say to them, for instance: "We want an opening number, and it need not be pop and it need not necessarily be a hit," and they would come through with a real sort of show-type song.'

Inevitably, the panto scores produced hit singles for Cliff. 'I Could Easily Fall (in Love with You)', for example, was a Top Ten record in 1964 from *Aladdin and his Wonderful Lamp*. And 'In the Country', which emanated from *Cinderella*, in which Cliff played Buttons, reached number six in the charts in December 1966.

Both these pantomime productions played to packed houses at the London Palladium with the entire scores written by The Shadows. *Aladdin and his Wonderful Lamp* ran twice daily for three and a half months and included Arthur Askey and Una Stubbs in the cast.

After his small role in *Serious Charge*, Cliff was soon back in front of the film cameras again at Shepperton Studios in a new movie, *Expresso Bongo*, in a role that appeared tailor-made for him.

Expresso Bongo had first surfaced as a cynical play by Wolf Mankowitz about London's Tin Pan Alley in 1958, and it reached the West End at the Savile Theatre in the spring of 1959, where it earned a description as 'one of the first of the hard-nosed British musicals'.

Loosely based on the rise of Tommy Steele, the story was set in and around the coffee bars of Soho frequented by showbiz agents, managers, would-be music stars, ad men, gossip writers, strippers and hustlers. His central character is Johnny Jackson, an unscrupulous and exploitative talent agent who discovers in a coffee house a rock 'n' roll bongo player and singer called Herbert 'Bongo' Rudge. Making use of his contacts in the record business and in radio, Johnny fast-tracks Bongo to stardom by making his first single a smash hit. But just when Johnny feels he has hit the jackpot with Bongo, he finds out his discovery is a minor and therefore his contract with him is null and void. It leaves Bongo to enjoy his success without his crafty creator.

Unlike the Broadway musicals of the 1950s, it was exceedingly rare for a British musical to be regarded as worthy of development into a film. But *Expresso Bongo* proved an exception, and thereby an enticing vehicle for Cliff, who was signed up after being preferred to Marty Wilde for the role.

Cliff was cast as the unknown Cockney teenager, 'Bongo' Herbert, with Laurence Harvey as Johnny Jackson, his fast-talking manager, and Yolande Donlan as Dixie Collins, a fading American female singer, who tries to use the youngster to revive her own flagging career by having him guest on her London show. Sylvia Syms, as stripper Maisie King, Johnny's girlfriend, completed the leading cast. Only Susan Hampshire, as an empty-headed debutante, managed to survive from the original West End stage line-up.

Apart from the drastic recasting, the major change from stage play to movie was the retention of just two of the original seventeen musical numbers, which allowed room for Norrie Paramor to write a number specially for Cliff so the film-makers could cash in on the singer's massive popularity.

Norrie's 'Voice in the Wilderness', first released in January 1960, took Cliff to number two in the charts at a time when, incredibly, the EP from the movie – also offering 'Voice in the Wilderness' – was at number fourteen in the very same singles chart. A slow, tuneful, sentimental ballad, 'Voice in the Wilderness' continued Cliff's drift away from hard rock 'n' roll. It was never particularly one of Cliff's favourite songs and he rarely included it in his concert repertoire. But it has proved to be an enduring favourite with Cliff's loyal fans down the years. He was genuinely surprised when it came in ranked number eighteen, as voted for by 20,000 of his fans, in a BBC Radio 2 poll of their ultimate Top Twenty Cliff records in the summer of 2006.

For the Cliff Richard faithful who flocked to see their idol on screen in *Expresso Bongo*, it was left to Susan Hampshire as dishy deb Cynthia to utter the most memorable line in the film. 'Isn't he sweet, isn't he pure heaven?' is Cynthia's summation of Bongo/Cliff when she goes backstage to meet him after his TV appearance. Susan would later go on to star with Cliff in *Wonderful Life*.

In the stage version of *Expresso Bongo*, the satire relied heavily on Bongo being painted as a youngster who cared precious little for the music that was turning him into an overnight sensation. But Cliff insisted his movie portrayal should allow Bongo to project genuine enjoyment in his singing. Cliff pointed out to the producers he would find it nigh on impossible to sing with accentuated apathy. It simply wasn't in his nature, he stressed. 'I shall be dead serious,' he said when speaking of his role. 'I won't be a party to anything which mocks rock.'

Cliff was duly granted the concession to do it his way, and his own singing talent was allowed to shine without seriously diminishing the satire. When the film was released, there was some speculation as to whether it in any way reflected Cliff's own career and meteoric rise to stardom. The answer was that there was no comparison – Cliff had made it big in his own right, whereas Bongo was artfully manufactured.

At one point in the film, Laurence Harvey's Johnny Jackson enthusiastically maps out his strategy for shooting Bongo to stardom and says: 'For a few days you become sort of anti-national hero. You've got a chip on your shoulder and an H-bomb in your pants, a sneer and a twitch. It's you against the world, baby, and the world loves you by hating it.'

The movie enabled Cliff to show a degree of acting ability and, although he was playing a character very far removed from himself, it was noticeable that Bongo displayed one or two hints of the real Cliff Richard. Bongo appears unconcerned to the point of disinterest when the all-knowing, love-starved Dixie seductively turns her eyes on the innocent teenager. And when she enquires of her toy-boy as to whether he has a girlfriend, Bongo says: 'Girlfriends just pin you down. They're always wanting things.' Dixie's vampish response is to purr: 'Sometimes the feeling is mutual, you know.'

At one point, Bongo is advised to think of his future: 'You can't go on being a teenage singer for very far beyond your teenage years, you know,' he is told. 'Yeah that's right,' Bongo agrees. 'What am I going to do when I hit twenty?'

Another scene finds the hyperactive Johnny desperately trying to think of new ways to broaden the appeal of his shooting star. 'So far, what have we got?' asks Johnny of Bongo. 'Sex, beat, violence – we've got it all. We've got it all except for one thing – religion. We've got to get religion!'

Cliff was reasonably pleased with his own performance. 'I don't know whether I meant to do it, but I did it really well,' he said. 'I do come across as a really naïve young singer who doesn't quite know what's happening and I've got a feeling it was natural for me to do that.'

Ironically, of course, *Expresso Bongo*'s singing star did go on to 'get religion' in 1966 – but totally of his own volition and conviction. The movie had nothing do with spurring Cliff into becoming a committed Christian.

And, whereas for Bongo it was seen as a gimmick to enhance his career, many of Cliff's fans and close associates viewed the singer's public declaration that he had found God as the kiss of death for his career.

10. LOVE TRIANGLE

The first thing I knew was when Bruce and Hank said: 'Hey, I should watch your wife if I were you.'

Jet Harris

Carol Costa from Hounslow was just one of thousands of pretty teenage girls who was eager to see Britain's latest singing sensation, Cliff Richard, live, in person and in concert. Like so many girls of her age, she had quickly become a big fan of the singer she had seen on *Oh Boy!* and whose record 'Move It' had taken the music world by storm.

She got her wish to see Cliff and The Shadows when they topped the bill at Finsbury Park Empire, and by the end of the night Carol had, to her surprise, also landed herself a date with a member of Cliff's backing band, the handsome bass guitarist, who seemed cool personified in his tight, black, high-buttoned shiny suit, his dyed blond hair slicked back, and a cigarette dangling from his mouth.

Although only sixteen, Carol had the kind of blossoming beauty and a natural sex appeal that turned male heads wherever she went.

'She was the epitome of a British Brigitte Bardot,' said Bruce Welch, referring to the French actress with the famously curvy figure, tumbling blonde hair and sexy pout who became one of the great screen sex sirens of the 1960s. 'Carol modelled herself on that look. She was a great-looking girl and had all the attributes – big tits and everything else.'

Jet Harris was instantly struck by Carol's youthful beauty the minute he set eyes on her in the bar of the Finsbury Park Empire, and before long he strolled over to chat to her, eventually asking her for a date the following night, which Carol accepted.

Soon Jet and Carol were dating regularly, although it was obvious to everyone in their circle that Cliff had an eye for her as well. Carol had exactly the kind of dream-girl looks Cliff admired – a magazine picture of Brigitte Bardot had adorned his bedroom wall when he was younger.

At parties there were mild flirtations between Cliff and Carol and, although she was going out with Jet, she was flattered that Britain's top teenage sex symbol had clearly taken a shine to her. And she knew she had feelings for Cliff, too.

But Jet's affair with Carol soon led to marriage for the couple and they were wed at Hounslow West Church with hundreds of screaming teenagers scrambling to catch a glimpse of the famous Shadows guitarist and his bride as they arrived at the church. Cliff missed the ceremony because he was on holiday in Spain at the time, but Bruce Welch and Hank Marvin were among the guests who saw the bass guitarist tie the knot before the newly-weds headed off for a couple of days in Grimsby by way of a honeymoon.

Jet and Carol were very young when they married, and Jet's frantic schedule with The Shadows, his roving eye for the girls, and his over-fondness for a drink were hardly conducive to a settled, harmonious life of domesticity. Within less than a year the marriage was in trouble, and even the arrival of a son, Ricky, named after the American singer Ricky Nelson, failed to mend the differences between them.

Without his really knowing it himself, Jet's excessive drinking was starting to cause serious problems. 'Cliff's father was the first to notice,' he said. 'He could see that I liked a tipple, and he used to say: "I should take it easy if I were you, Jet." But I didn't give it a second thought, not for a long time.

'What I didn't realise or know at the time was that I was in the perfect social setting for an alcoholic – the pop business. No one notices you drinking there. It goes with the job. It's just that I would always have a few more than the others. I was the first in and last out, even in the early days of The Shadows. I used to get up around eleven a.m. and the first thing I'd do was pour myself a beer. I wasn't aware that I had a problem. I thought that was how people with money lived.'

Cliff, meanwhile, almost certainly aware that Jet was playing around with other girls and neglecting his wife, found himself drawn to Carol, partly out of sympathy for the way Jet was treating her and partly because he still found her enormously attractive.

Setting the record straight in a TV interview, Cliff said: 'I loved her. Jet had personal problems. It was obvious that he and Carol weren't hysterically happy together.

'We had a mutual attraction. She was a very attractive girl, and even now when you see photographs of her in those days, the strange thing was I didn't realise how much like Brigitte Bardot she looked. I had this great thing about BB and we had a physical attraction, there was no doubt about it whatsoever.'

On an overnight train journey back to London from Black-pool after a concert by Cliff and The Shadows, Cliff was due to share a sleeping car with Tony Meehan, but Tony offered his berth to Carol instead, which allowed the couple to become closer to each other than ever before. 'We knew something was going on on the train,' said Bruce.

In Cliff, Carol was finding the tender affection, support and care she had lacked in her marriage to Jet and, because of Jet's infidelity, she was prepared for the marriage to end.

She said: 'He'd been having an affair while I was in hospital giving birth to Ricky. The hurt I had was so bad, really bad, so I decided: I'm not going to forgive this any longer. I've done this once, I'm not going to do it again.'

Despite their growing affection for each other, Carol and Cliff had not yet become lovers, which puzzled Carol. She said: 'When you're together and you love one another it's very difficult not to make love. Also, I'd also been married, and I used to think: there's something wrong.

'When we'd been together a little while, he told me one night he was a virgin – and then I understood everything. Because of who he was, very sexy – and they'd marked him out to be a sexy pop star – you can understand, really, him not wanting anyone to know.'

Not long afterwards the romance moved to another level when they consummated their love in the attic room of a house in Ealing belonging to a dancer who had appeared in two of Cliff's movies.

Carol said, 'Then we made love. It wasn't planned. The definition of making love . . . some people say sex is the be-all and end-all of making love. I don't believe that. I believe we were making love before that. But to actually consummate it took time. In the end we did, and very beautiful it was, too.'

The affair might have blossomed had not an intimate letter from Carol to Cliff been intercepted by Cliff's mother, believing it to be just another fan letter. Dorothy was shocked and made it clear to her son that the affair was morally wrong and must end. Now the secret was out within the family, Cliff was fearful that any press scandal might be fatal for his father, who had been taken seriously ill with thrombosis.

Tony Meehan recalled that Cliff realised his best course of action was to let Carol go: 'Eventually it became very difficult because Jet was still part of the band,' Tony explained. 'I was quite close to Cliff, having just been on holiday with him. We sat down and spoke about it and he said: "Yes, I agree with you, what am I supposed to do?" I said: "You've got to ring her, you've got to speak to her and call it off if you're not serious and you don't want to go through with it," because just at that time Marty Wilde's career had broken up pretty badly because he'd just got married – that was the silliness that was going on at that time. But he couldn't bring himself to do it. He just said: "Would you do it? Would you ring her and say it's over and that's it?" And I did.'

Carol was dumbfounded at Cliff's sudden U-turn: 'I couldn't understand it. I thought: he left me last night and it was wonderful, and today I get a phone call to say it's over. I must speak to Cliff. You can't tell me this. It must come from Cliff.

Then Cliff came on the phone and he was crying and I was crying, and I said: "What's happened?" He said: "It's got to end." That was it, really, and I just left, absolutely heart-broken.'

Cliff later commented on his brief liaison with Carol: 'What should have been really rather a fantastic thing turned out to be nothing much at all, and she was probably resenting it and regretting it to a great extent too. Some people might say: "Oh great! He's just one of the guys after all." No, I'm not. I just made a big mistake.'

Cliff's very brief affair with Carol hit Jet Harris hard. 'Jet started on the drink – as most of us would at that moment in time,' said Bruce Welch. 'That was the start of Jet's downward spiral. And the more money we made, the more he drank.'

Jet says: 'The first thing I knew was when Bruce and Hank said: "Hey, I should watch your wife if I were you." Nothing more was said. I didn't want to know about it. It was another thing to run away from, I suppose.'

Always nervous before he went on stage, Jet was insecure about where he was going in life. 'I was an absolute wreck before I went on stage, but as soon as I stepped up there and started to play, I felt good. When I stepped off, I came down and was back in a life I wasn't happy with. It took its toll.'

In Mike Read's book *The Story of the Shadows*, Jet is quoted thus: 'Cliff and my wife had been going together quite a bit and it was getting me down, so I started hitting the bottle, although I think Carol really encouraged him, so I never blamed our little bachelor boy, really. It was another excuse for me to have a drink. It was bloody hard, standing up on stage every night behind Cliff thinking that he was having it off with your wife. I couldn't really stand the pressure, so I started drinking fairly heavily, until it became a state of mind. Bruce was always having a go at me about drinking! He was like a bloody sergeant major.'

Jet has said, 'Much later I realised that he [Bruce] was really watching out for me because he was worried and concerned. But when you're drunk, you don't see things like that, so it led to a lot of rows and tensions between the two of us.'

The other members of The Shadows, especially Bruce, increasingly came to regard Jet as a liability. At gigs they found themselves too often having to apologise and cover up for Jet. During a performance at the Cavern Club in Liverpool, the group were strutting through their famous routine, known as 'The Shadows walk', when Jet fell into the audience. Bruce explained to the tightly packed crowd that Jet was unwell. But the Scousers weren't fooled and shouted back: 'He's pissed!'

Hank Marvin once recalled: 'We'd have terrible fights before going on stage, with blood flowing. We'd be arguing all the time about how to present ourselves on stage. We'd have flaming rows about drink, really ugly shouting matches.'

As a pop group who prided themselves on being musically tight when they played live, The Shadows could not afford to carry a passenger, and an inebriated one at that. Bruce, so meticulous and precise that he even made chalk marks on the stage where each member of the band should stand, knew that Jet's days in The Shadows could not last much longer.

The end came at the 1962 *NME* Poll Winners' Concert at Wembley, when Jet took full advantage of the all-day open bar for artistes before meeting up with the other members of the group. According to Jet, Bruce turned on him and simply said: 'We don't really need you, Jet,' and the bass guitarist walked out, never to return.

Jet's departure occurred while 'Wonderful Land', the group's third chart-topper, was still high in the hit parade, and he soon went into the recording studios to pursue a solo career. He achieved limited success as a solo artist before teaming up to make records with Tony Meehan, and they went on to have three Top Ten hits together, including reaching number one with 'Diamonds' in the summer of 1963.

They were a natural duo because eight months earlier, in autumn 1961, Tony had himself left The Shadows after his timekeeping and his general haphazard and lackadaisical approach to his role within the band had become unacceptable to Hank, and to Bruce in particular. The final straw for the other members of The Shadows came during a performance at the Blackpool Opera House when, with no sign of Tony, there was no option but for Hank, Bruce and Jet to take to the stage without him. They had already finished playing their first number, 'FBI', with no drum accompaniment, when Tony ambled onstage still casually dressed in his street clothes.

Brian Bennett and Brian Locking, old friends of both Hank and Bruce from the 2 I's days, were thoroughly competent and ready-made replacements for Tony and Jet. The two Brians had both played with Marty Wilde's Wildcats, and Brian Locking, known to everyone as 'Licorice', had also toured with American rockers Eddie Cochran and Gene Vincent. Brian Locking had earned his 'Licorice' moniker due to his ability to play several other musical instruments apart from bass guitar, including 'the licorice stick' – the clarinet.

Licorice joined The Shadows to replace Jet in April 1962. And by the time he quit the group eighteen months later, he left having had a greater influence over Cliff Richard's future than anyone could possibly have imagined.

'It turned out he was a Jehovah's Witness,' said Bruce. 'We had an inkling he might be, but when a new bass guitarist is joining the band, you don't ask what religion he is, do you? It was Licorice who kicked off the whole religion bit with Hank and with Cliff.'

11. FILMS

It's a film very much of its time, but decades later it is still highly enjoyable and very entertaining.

Sidney Furie, director of *The Young Ones*

After Cliff's two brief forays into films in *Serious Charge* and *Expresso Bongo*, the search was on for a movie that could be built around him as the major star. The formula had worked for Elvis Presley, and movie stardom was considered by Cliff's management to be the natural progression for him, too.

Cliff Richard's first starring film role came in the 1961 movie *The Young Ones*. His performance as unknown singer Nicky Black, whose voice helps save a run-down youth club from demolition, brought a box-office bonanza, a string of hit records and joy to Cliff's fast-growing fan base.

The Young Ones became one of the most popular British films made since the war, but from the first moment he saw it, Cliff simply hated the sight of himself in the leading role on the big screen. 'I look like a fat slob,' he said afterwards and promptly put himself on a strict diet.

Fortunately for ruthlessly self-critical Cliff, the fans either didn't notice the extra pound or two that had been added to the famous frame or they didn't care. The long search for a movie vehicle for the rising star had been an undeniable success. Freelance film producer Kenneth Harper was the driving force behind the movie and had joined top agent Leslie Grade to start a film division of the Grade Organisation. He had witnessed Cliff Richard filling cinema seats on Sunday nights with his gruelling tours of one-nighters at a time when films were struggling to attract large enough audiences.

Harper had an excellent script written by sophisticated revue writers Ronnie Cass and Peter Myers which carefully kept wholesome Nicky Black close, but not too close, to the character of Cliff Richard.

Writer Ronnie Cass said: 'The first thing we decided was that we would try to make a film that would cater for all age groups, not just Cliff's young rock 'n' roll fans. And we succeeded. I think the reason was that the film shows kids enjoying themselves and doing something worthwhile. They're not beatniks and they're not bored or looking for trouble.'

But at a time when London was famously starting to swing, with Carnaby Street establishing itself as the fashion favourite of the young and the hemlines rising so fast down the King's Road that even *Time* magazine noticed, it was across to the other side of the Atlantic that Harper reached for the creative talent that would help launch Cliff Richard as a movie star.

He hired elegant dance deviser Herbert Ross as choreographer, in a move that impressed Cliff. 'I was flattered,' said the star. 'Herb Ross had been responsible for the choreography in many big stage, TV and film musicals not least *Carmen Jones* with Sammy Davis and Dorothy Dandridge. It was great to hear he was part of the team.'

'We needed the American polish for the dancing,' said Kenneth Harper. And to direct *The Young Ones*, Harper called in the brilliant Canadian film-maker Sidney Furie, who went on to have a long and highly successful career and to direct the iconic Len Deighton thriller *The Ipcress File*. But, in 1961, Furie was just 27 years old, full of youthful enthusiasm and easily young enough to relate to the star and the story.

Filming began on *The Young Ones* in May 1961 and Cliff confessed to journalist Mike Hellicar that behind the confident smile he was uncharacteristically anxious about the job in hand. 'It's not often that I get nervous,' said Cliff. 'But, boy, those butterflies really got at me for the whole of the first day's shooting and stayed for almost the rest of the week. I've been hoping and longing to get back on to the film set. It must be nearly two years since we made *Expresso Bongo* and I made up my mind then that film-making is something I really love. I have definitely missed the excitement of movie-making.'

The master plan devised by producer Harper and director Furie was to capitalise on Cliff's wide appeal and come up with a strong MGM-type movie. There are certainly great similarities between the story of *The Young Ones* and the plot of the classic 1939 Rodgers and Hart musical *Babes in Arms*, which starred Mickey Rooney and Judy Garland as the teenage children of retired vaudeville performers who put on a show to raise money. Then again, *The Blues Brothers* movie followed pretty much the same lines in 1980.

Furie was delighted to discover that the writers Myers and Cass were great enthusiasts of both screen and stage musical and had put together a highly competent script and that Cliff Richard was a genuine talent and a pleasure to work with. 'Cliff was a huge star in Britain by then,' the director recalled in the commentary to a DVD version of the film. 'Whenever he was seen in public there would be screaming fans. But he didn't let any of that get in the way.

'We didn't have many locations; mainly we worked on the lot. Cliff is a very natural performer and a terrific person. I really enjoyed working with him. He was always very down-to-earth and very professional, a genuine nice guy.'

The story of *The Young Ones* begins with young workers merrily clocking off for the weekend and joyfully singing 'It's Friday Night' as they head for a night out in their ramshackle wooden youth club, which makes up in atmosphere for what it lacks in luxury. But the teenagers' precious base is threatened by ruthless property developer Hamilton Black, who wants to demolish the club and build a twenty-storey office block on the site.

Nicky/Cliff is on stage when breathless young Ernest, played by Richard O'Sullivan, rushes in with the bad news. The club members are outraged and wilder members suggest barricading themselves in and fighting any attempts to evict them. Nicky counsels reason and, in a late-night meeting with pretty Toni, played by West End star Carole Gray, he sings 'Nothing's Impossible', swinging energetically around Belisha beacons in a lively fantasy sequence.

But Nicky has not exactly told his pals everything. He is the son of the dreaded Hamilton Black and he angrily has a go at his father. The grasping tycoon is wonderfully played by Robert Morley as he sneers about 'young thugs polishing their coshes'. Toni is a bit startled when Cliff confesses to his father's identity, but she soon comes round after the action switches to a sun-drenched lake and Nicky sings 'The Young Ones' to her.

The kids need to raise the then massive sum of £1,500 to buy the lease to allow their club to continue. It seems a hopeless task until Nicky suggests putting on a concert to generate funds. 'Let's put a show on to raise the money and we'll show Hamilton Black he's not just dealing with a few of us, but with every kid in town!'

The kids, of course, find a theatre, along with props and costumes, and prepare for the big show. They even stage a subversive advertising campaign with Nicky as the 'mystery singer' who keeps bursting into television programmes to promote the event. The classic 'You're never alone with a Strand' cigarette commercial and newsreader Richard Baker are among those interrupted by the kids, who suddenly turn into technical wizards. In the end, evil Hamilton becomes so inspired by all that youthful idealism he finishes up dancing rather well on stage in a traditionally happy ending.

'The difficult part was fitting the production numbers into the story,' said Sidney Furie. 'But it worked well, even if everything in England took forever when it came to movie-making in those days. We had tea breaks in the morning, tea breaks in the afternoon and there was no such thing as overtime!'

In those days, drinking alcohol at lunchtime was the norm. Furie remembers the crew heading for pints all round at the pub, while he and other senior staff enjoyed wine and whisky in the executive dining room. Times have certainly changed, but even then clean-living Cliff was never part of the drinking culture.

The initial budget for the film was just £100,000, but it ended up costing around £230,000 to make at Elstree Studios, which, much later, was to become home to *Raiders of the Lost Ark* and many other memorable hits. 'Expectations were high because Cliff was so hot,' said Furie. 'But I was still surprised how well it did. I loved Robert Morley. He is exactly as he seems, an erudite, fabulous person who loved the movie because his kids were thrilled he was acting with Cliff Richard.'

Even when it was in production, it was clear that *The Young Ones* could be something special. Cliff said at the start: 'There is something about this film. It is different from anything I have ever done before. I have put in more work into the rehearsals for *The Young Ones* than I did for the entire shooting schedule of *Expresso Bongo*. Sidney Furie is a man I admire. He is like everyone else here – so patient with me. If anything goes wrong, there is a smile and a discussion to put it right.'

The relationship between Nicky and his avaricious father is key to the credibility of the film, and Cliff was anxious that he might not hit it off with the celebrated, but not always easy-going, Mr Morley. It turned out happily enough, but Cliff was especially concerned because he had been warned that playing alongside Robert Morley would be difficult. He had a reputation for not suffering fools gladly and a bunch of raw beginners was always likely to try his patience to its limits. In the event, Cliff was so nervous that he blew a couple of his very first lines with his booming-voiced co-star, which meant a major retake.

Cliff recalled the incident years later: 'Before I could get a word in, Robert said: "I'm awfully sorry, Cliff, you'll have to excuse an old dodderer like me, but I've made a mistake." I knew full well it was my fault, but I felt it was tremendously kind and generous of him to take the blame. I'm sure he didn't have any respect for me as an actor because I wasn't one, but his thoughtfulness for me as a person was quite a lesson. And the less nervous I became, the fewer mistakes I made.'

Cliff formed a friendship with Robert Morley that lasted way beyond the end of filming and he was always full of respect for the older actor. As production on the movie drew towards a close, Cliff said: 'Mr Morley is the sort of artiste who brings out the best in people with whom he is working. His acting radiates so strongly that sometimes you just have to act back at him. As this is easily my most important film role to date, I'm very thrilled to have someone around who is so experienced in the art of acting.'

The process of film-making requires endless patience, because there is inevitably a great deal of hanging around while shots are set up. 'That's the one trouble with filming,' said Cliff. 'It's grand and I love it, but there is always a lot of waiting while they get everything just right. To occupy my time more usefully I installed my record player in my dressing room to fight off any boredom and I play my guitar as well.'

The Finsbury Park Empire was the location for the kids' big show in *The Young Ones*. The poor old place was well qualified to play a dilapidated, disused old theatre, because that was exactly what it had become. It had been closed down in 1960 and was being used only to store props for Moss Empires. Cliff was deeply saddened when the theatre had been closed to the public, because he had delivered some great performances with The Shadows in a three-week run to packed houses only months earlier.

'It seemed a great pity for a house with such a long-standing tradition to be shut,' said Cliff in an article he wrote for the *New Musical Express*. 'But I never dreamed that within a matter of months I would once again find myself working at the dear old Finsbury Park Empire.'

The designers festooned the old theatre with artificial cobwebs, imported plenty of dust and made sure the paint was peeling in what looked like terminal decay. The theatre looked derelict and Cliff's reaction was one of genuine shock when he saw it. 'I was astonished,' said Cliff. 'It looked in a really bad way.' But *The Young Ones* breathed real life back into the Finsbury Park Empire as all the equipment and staff arrived to shoot the film's crucial final sequences.

Enough seats were restored for four hundred fans to provide the essential reaction to the unmasking of Nicky as the mystery singer and see ruthless Hamilton Black reduced to a soft-hearted supporter who gives the kids a brand new youth club instead of turfing them out into the cold. Cliff's dressing room was a hastily converted corner of the stalls' bar. He had to work hard on his dancing for the many colourful sequences and got a great deal of help from gifted young dancer Teddy Green. 'Teddy was great,' said Cliff. 'He devoted a lot of time and patience to teaching me the right steps. He taught me a soft-shoe routine, a top hat and cane dance, and how to link in with the chorus line. I was very grateful.'

Finding the fans for the big finale scenes was no trouble at all. Sidney Furie later recalled: 'We could have filled the place hundreds of times over because Cliff was so popular. And getting them to scream was no trouble. Persuading them to react to the story was harder, but they came through really well in the end. And we got a complex sequence of scenes in the can all in one day.'

The film was distinctive in many ways. Furie used a highly innovative split-screen technique to great effect early on in the movie as the kids were preparing for a big night out. And he many times marvelled at the professionalism of the highly experienced British character actors and technicians. Melvyn Hayes played a role that was to have been taken by Jet Harris, which explains why the actor's hair went blonde for the film. The idea of giving the members of The Shadows speaking parts in the movie was dropped at quite a late stage and Melvyn certainly made the most of the comic potential of his role.

The Young Ones was a huge success. The simple plot and its high-energy execution struck a chord with filmgoers, who caught on to Furie's dream of recreating the old MGM-musical style in a British setting. The reviews were mostly upbeat and positive, and the soundtrack album was the first pop album to enter the charts at number one.

'Cliff brought enormous energy to the screen,' said Furie. 'And there was a great innocence about all of the action. There was absolutely no sex, in fact I think there was scarcely a kiss.

But there was still a truth about the writing and acting that we were all impressed by. It's a film very much of its time, but decades later it is still highly enjoyable and very entertaining. I'm proud of the movie. It was just a dream I had to bring some colour, because everything seemed very grey in London. This was Cliff's big breakthrough and it was mine as well. All of a sudden I was a known commodity and everything changed for me.'

Shortly after completing filming of *The Young Ones*, Cliff said in an interview with *Top Pop Star*: 'Goodness knows what my fans will think. I'm even seen wearing a bowler hat. I didn't think I'd maintain anything. There were so many one-hit wonders and everyone was calling us here-today-gone-tomorrow and they weren't really concerned with us. I thought it would be all over by the time I was twenty-one. But now I think I can go on until I'm at least twenty-five.'

Cliff later reflected: 'It requires dedication, commitment and a heck of a lot of work. You really have to work at it. You have to be in contact with those who buy your records. They need to see you, touch you, feel you and enjoy you as a person as well as a musician. The movies brought me a massive audience that were accepting me in other ways.'

When the title track from the movie was released as a single in January 1962, it established a number of records. 'The Young Ones', written by Americans Sid Tepper and Roy Bennett, who had also written 'Travellin' Light', was Cliff's second million-selling single, and only the fourth single in the history of the charts to go straight in at number one.

It was also the first single by a British artiste to enter the charts at number one, having amassed advance orders of 524,000, which was also an all-time record.

Sadly for Cliff's American ambitions, the impact of *The Young Ones* was a great deal more subdued on the other side of the Atlantic, where the movie was retitled *It's Wonderful To Be Young*. The change of name inevitably lessened the impact of the single 'The Young Ones' – it was no longer the title tune.

And, much to the horror of director Furie, the opening of the movie was drastically changed. The 'It's Friday Night' number was replaced by the new title song, which was specially written by Burt Bacharach, but it was not a success. Cliff was his usual diplomatic self regarding the American version of *The Young Ones*, but director Furie was much more outspoken. Years later he was still fuming and said that the alterations to the hit British film to cater for the American market were 'moronic'.

But the news from the British box office was all good. By the end of 1962 cinema favourites like Peter Sellers, Kenneth More, Frank Sinatra and Sophia Loren had all been eclipsed by the boy from a council house in Waltham Cross. According to a survey by the *Motion Picture Herald*, the 22-year-old Cliff was the most popular film star and his film was beaten at the box office in Britain only by spectacular war movie *The Guns of Navarone*, with its stellar cast led by Gregory Peck and David Niven. And as the epic tale from the Second World War had taken more than two years to make at ten times the cost of *The Young Ones*, it was quite an achievement.

For the record, the ten most popular film stars of 1962, in order, were: Cliff Richard, Elvis Presley, Peter Sellers, Kenneth More, Hayley Mills, Doris Day, Sophia Loren, John Wayne, Frank Sinatra and Sean Connery.

Cliff was surprised and typically modest when the survey's figures were relayed to him. 'It really is fantastic,' he said, especially relishing the fact that he had pipped his idol, Elvis. 'I'm terribly proud, but if I was making the choice of my favourite film star I wouldn't choose me – at least not until I had made a couple more films and showed how consistent I could be. I knew I was being used as a guinea pig to see if a British musical could be a success. I think it happened because *The Young Ones* is a simple film with a kind of amateur charm. The public like something simple. We've found the same thing with records – give them something catchy and very simple that's made in five minutes and it can sell a million.'

Not surprisingly both Cliff's public and his producers wanted a follow-up and work swiftly started on a brand new movie called *Summer Holiday*. Again, it was written by the prolific Myers and Cass partnership, produced by Kenneth Harper, and Herbert Ross was in charge of the colourful and ambitious dance routines. But Sidney Furie was unavailable, so another young director was found in the shape of Peter Yates. In 1962 he was unknown, but producer Harper showed his talent-spotting ability again, as Yates was to go on to enjoy a glittering career, which included directing the memorable Steve McQueen car-chase movie, *Bullitt*.

'*Summer Holiday* was the first film I ever directed,' said Peter Yates on the director's commentary on the DVD release of *Summer Holiday*. '*The Young Ones* had been a great success and they wanted to repeat it . . . They were searching for a young director who would get on with Cliff and share his energetic attitude. I went down for some tests to be shot and met Cliff. I found his voice was extraordinary and his enthusiasm very refreshing. He was a marvellous guy to work with.'

The story is appealingly simple. Four young guys persuade London Transport to loan them a big red London bus to convert into a mobile hotel and tour Europe. Along the way they meet three pretty young singers, led by Una Stubbs, and acquire a young girl stowaway, who was rather improbably disguised as a boy and played by American singer Lauri Peters.

The film opens with bold black-and-white footage of relentless rain ruining yet another English summer and Cliff as bus driver Don bringing colour into everyone's lives, as well as the screen, as he rolls up on the gleaming bus. 'It was very important to get lots of pace into the movie from start to finish, because this is a film based almost entirely on energy,' said Yates.

And that was something the new slimline Cliff seemed simply brimming with at the time. Years later Cliff said: 'I think *Summer Holiday* is a much better film than *The Young Ones*. Watching myself in *The Young Ones*, as I have done a few times, I look like a fat slob.'

Cliff's concern about his weight grew in 1963, when he was sitting at home watching *Coronation Street* and to his horror he heard Minnie Caldwell remark in the snug of the Rovers how much she liked: 'That chubby Cliff Richard.'

Cliff was already much slimmer, but the description made him shudder. To most fans, of course, Cliff has always looked good. But he did put on a few pounds and, as he explained, it was partly his own success that was to blame. 'When I went to America, for the first time in my life I had money and there was all this fantastic food laid out in front of me. I just went mad,' said Cliff. 'I would eat piece after piece of cheesecake covered in cream. I couldn't believe that there was all this fine food and I could pay for it.

'Of course I just piled on the pounds. I didn't realise what was happening until I saw myself on screen. I'd turned into this chubby boy, and I hated the way I looked. My weight at that time ballooned up from eleven stone to twelve stone seven pounds. I realised very quickly that if I didn't do something about it, I was just going to get bigger. I knew that if I let that happen, it certainly wasn't going to do much for my career. I couldn't see my audiences screaming and cheering a blob, unless it was in horror.

'There was a very simple solution. I just stopped eating so much. I cut myself down to one meal a day. It's a regime that I've stuck to ever since. I have a very light breakfast, no lunch, and for dinner I eat whatever I want. I've found it very easy to keep up and it's not too strict because I can enjoy all my favourite food.

'By the time I made *Summer Holiday* I had started a diet . . . so I look more the part. But there again, I think it was a better film in lots of other ways too. It had that brightness that you can't fail to get when you take the bus across Greece. Almost all of the movie was shot outside. And we had a great team by then. I can't ever remember enjoying working quite as much as that.

'I remember standing with the Acropolis behind me and thinking: why can't life go on like this for ever?'

Once the gloomy English weather disappears from the screen, the action switches to a giant London Transport bus garage not far from Elstree Studios. Don/Cliff brings great news to his three pals – Cyril played by Melvyn Hayes, Steve played by Teddy Green, and Edwin by Jeremy Bulloch – that they have got the bus they need to make their dream of starting a holiday business come true.

The dialogue might not always have been exactly sparkling, with lines like, 'Don's got something up his sleeve. His arm.' But the youthful enthusiasm was irresistible. The film company had to buy two buses out of its far-from-generous £300,000 budget. 'You always need a standby with vehicles in case one breaks down,' said Yates. London Transport offered lots of help and advice, and they got some massive positive publicity in return.

'I thought innocence was the secret of Cliff's success,' said director Yates. 'You really believe what you see on the screen and you trust him as a performer. He is very untheatrical when you consider he is singing songs and dancing. He captures an air of reality, which is a very difficult thing to do.'

The director regarded *Summer Holiday* as a knee-jerk reaction to the wave of frequently grim kitchen-sink dramas that were so popular at the time. '*Summer Holiday* was an entertainment, pure and simple,' said Peter Yates. 'And I've always thought that, basically, we are here to entertain.'

Yates happily acknowledged that he had a very good team. 'Melvyn Hayes is a fine comic actor, and Una Stubbs was very funny as well as being able to dance brilliantly,' he said. 'Jeremy Bulloch had several scenes with a large St Bernard dog and he had such charm and a lot of presence that's what he always reminds me of!'

Jeremy Bulloch and Melvyn Hayes were not the greatest dancers in the world, so Herb Ross often had to work hard to feature others more prominently. 'It's very important to integrate the musical numbers into the story,' said Yates. 'Herb had a lot of experience and he was expert at doing this.'

As the bus sets off into France with Cliff at the wheel, they pass The Shadows, all looking very French in their berets! But one ingredient is still missing for the boys in the bus – girls. That is quickly put right after the big red bus tangles with a small purple sports car containing Una Stubbs and two other equally attractive young girls who made up a singing trio. If that seemed a shade uneven, young American singer Lauri Peters, who had just enjoyed a huge success on Broadway, played runaway Barbara, the fourth girl.

That gives rise to some fairly tame embarrassing moments as the newcomer is recruited to hand naked Cliff a towel as he emerges from the shower, but it was all done in the best possible taste. Director Yates handled the scenes with such gentle humour no one could have been offended, and he later pointed out that the device of a young girl disguised as a boy had been used by Shakespeare, so it couldn't have been such a bad idea.

In fact, Cliff pointed out later that he might have had Barbra Streisand playing alongside him. 'But in our wisdom we turned her down,' said Cliff. 'Choreographer Herb Ross had staged Barbra's first Broadway show and was overboard about her. Every night, apparently, there was fantastic audience reaction. But would you believe that when the producer flew over to see her, he thought she wasn't right for the part! Maybe for my sake it was just as well. She would probably have stolen every review going, but imagine the billing: Cliff Richard and co-star Barbra Streisand! As they say, you can't win them all!'

But there were some up-to-date ideas as well, as Don/Cliff dances in an elaborate dream sequence with a series of everyday French characters who become transformed into sexy, bikini-clad women. When the dance is over they revert to outraged locals who chase our hero until he falls into a lake in a park. The captivating switches were achieved by simply freezing the camera, putting the dancers into exactly the same positions, and then linking the two with a jump cut.

'Nowadays it would cost a fortune in computer time,' said director Yates. 'Cliff got on very well with everyone and could not have been more helpful. He's a lovely person and was only too happy to fall in the water. It helped give the musical a very happy feeling. A lot of us were making our first feature movie and the friendly, relaxed atmosphere was essential to bring out the right feelings. *Summer Holiday* was to cheer you up and make you feel better.'

As the kids cross Europe in the bus, Barbara's manipulative mother, played by Madge Ryan, and her agent, brought to life by Lionel Murton, scheme to have them all arrested. No one could call it a thriller exactly, but there are dramatic moments. In fact the scenes showing Cliff and the team arriving in the former Yugoslavia were later seen as shocking enough to have him banned from the country!

'We never actually went to Yugoslavia, but we still got banned from ever visiting the country,' said Peter Yates.

The Yugoslavs evidently did not like the scenes showing their countrymen as arrogant, swaggering border guards or wild and primitive villagers who take a violent dislike to their young British visitors. Considering the content of the film, it is very hard to see how anyone could have objected. Cliff and the gang get through a heavy-handed search at the frontier and then try to persuade a frightened young girl to tell them where they can buy some bread. Only they get the wrong word for bread and instead suggest Cliff is searching for a bride.

'I think the Yugoslavs thought we represented them as being wild and ignorant,' said Yates. 'But it was never supposed to be taken that seriously. It was never a political statement about Yugoslavia. It was just a wonderful dance routine that Herb choreographed brilliantly. We weren't saying the whole country was like that!'

It was in the 'Yugoslav' sequences, which were filmed in Greece, that Cliff started wearing a curious string vest-type T-shirt, which he used in many scenes after that. Sales of that particular garment went through the roof after the movie was screened.

Don's romance with American singer Barbara was one of the main themes of the film, and Cliff and Lauri Peters shared many tender scenes together. But off screen, Cliff and Una Stubbs were becoming very close and a real-life attraction between the two stars was one of *Summer Holiday*'s most surprising by-products, although it didn't develop into a romance until they were working on their next movie together, *Wonderful Life*.

One of the film's big hits, 'Bachelor Boy' was only shoe-horned into the action two months after filming had ended.

'"Bachelor Boy" is the one song that, no matter where in the world I am, people know it,' said Cliff. 'They've heard that chorus before and if they don't know all the words they hum along. It's one of the first songs that I had a part in writing with Bruce. The Shadows are amazing, because when we did the film it was not in the original score but suddenly they said: "We need a bright number here." And it was Bruce, really. Bruce has to take credit for writing most of that song. I think I contributed some lyrics.

' "Bachelor Boy" was a song that was in fact edited in so late that if you watch the film very closely you will see it suddenly go from exterior to interior. There's cork on the floor to look like mud and a big red bus and a load of fake trees. Next time it's on telly watch it and see.

'Having sung it so often, I've often been asked if I ever considered the lyrics. Is that why I'm not married? The answer is no. I've had to do with the press asking me about marriage, but no. "Bachelor Boy", to me, is just a nice old knees-up song. The fact I'm not married is because I am not in love. Not enough to get married.'

The other huge hit that came out of the movie was, of course, the title song, 'Summer Holiday'. Cliff recalled years later: 'I think Brian Bennett started that one. We thought it was nice, but we didn't think it was a number one. But it was obviously a perfect title for the film.'

'Summer Holiday' saw Cliff's popularity reach a new high. The movie struck a real chord with the public. 'The premiere was like a bear garden,' said director Yates. 'There were lots of girls banging on Cliff's car and the crowds were enormous because he was so incredibly popular.'

In fact, the fan mania that night was so extreme that, much to his own disappointment, Cliff failed to attend his own premiere. He had delayed the start of his tour of South Africa to go along, but when he drew up outside the Warner cinema in a chauffeur-driven Cadillac, the crowd broke through the police barriers and surrounded the car from all angles. Cliff tried twice to get out, but both times he was forced back by pressure from the crowd until he was advised by the police to drive on.

'The premiere was in Leicester Square in the days when you could drive around the square,' Cliff recalled, 'and as I approached the square I was amazed at how many people had turned out. The car inched forward with fans banging on the windows and when we got to the edge a policeman stopped us. The window went down and the policeman said: "Move on." I said: "But it's my premiere." He said: "I don't care whose premiere it is, move on." So we moved on to my manager's house in Abbey Road and I watched it on television with the announcer saying on the news: "Cliff Richard couldn't make it to his premiere."'

Cliff was thoroughly depressed and disappointed at having to watch the proceedings on TV just a couple of miles away. But even without the presence of the star at the launch, the film was a huge hit. *Summer Holiday* earned more money than any other British musical, playing to packed houses all over Britain and Europe. Impresario Leslie Grade said: 'What you must not forget is that Cliff has developed tremendously as an actor. He is a talented, contented boy who loves his work. I remember there were people who said he wouldn't last five minutes, but he has been a big star for six years. Groups come and groups go, because it is not the hardest thing in showbusiness to make a star. The hardest thing is to make a star stay a star, and Cliff's films have helped to do this.'

But in the film world, as in every other facet of showbusiness, once you have reached the top, there is only one way to go. The talented team carefully guiding Cliff Richard's screen career were about to make their one great mistake – *Wonderful Life*.

Towards the end of 1963 and shortly before Cliff embarked on filming *Wonderful Life*, he moved into Rookswood, a sumptuous new £30,000 house in Upper Nazeing, Essex. Set in eleven acres with sweeping manicured lawns, the Tudor-style house stood at the end of a three-hundred-yard drive and boasted seven bedrooms, four bathrooms, a snooker room, two reception rooms, a Louis XIV lounge, a large kitchen and a five-car garage, stables, several greenhouses and a tennis court. Especially prized was a section of panelling that originated from Hampton Court, and a water garden with a forty-foot waterfall and deep pools.

It was a home fit for Britain's foremost entertainer, and Cliff set about organising major improvements, including new tennis courts. But right from the start security proved to be a major headache once the fans discovered the location. Cliff had only been in residence for three weeks when his mother felt compelled to call the police after inquisitive fans determinedly crowbarred their way through the four-foot-high gate and drove their cars up to the house, carelessly churning up lawns and damaging flower beds in the process.

As cops ordered the cars out of the grounds, Cliff was furious to discover that some of the fans had reacted unpleasantly when his mother had asked them to move their motors, 'It's the limit when they are rude to Mum, as a few have been,' he said. 'Lots of people have been descending on us. Some hang about and we find them all over the place. I found two girls in the pantry.'

At least Cliff's very public departure for the Canary Islands to film *Wonderful Life* provided Dorothy with some temporary respite. *Wonderful Life* saw Cliff with old friends Melvyn Hayes and Richard O'Sullivan as stewards on a cruise ship, with The Shadows given a much more prominent role as the resident band.

The happy life afloat ends early after the gang is cast adrift in the Atlantic in a life raft after causing an explosion on board. It is soon very clear that realism is not a strong point for the movie as Cliff and his gang step out of the life raft in the Canaries still looking immaculate.

The film, with its complex story and confusing dream sequences, sees Cliff and Co. accidentally become involved in the making of a movie. The story starts to become seriously complicated and badly bogged down in heavy-handed cinematic jokes and bewildering costume changes. Hollywood veteran Walter Slezak is good value as the outraged director, storming around shouting lines like: 'When I stage an orgy, I stage an orgy. I want two hundred more slave girls flown in tomorrow. When I make a picture I make a picture, not a snapshot.'

The wind in the Canaries played havoc with Cliff's quiff and the story became lost, particularly in a bizarre history-of-the-movies section, which features such unlikely moments as Cliff impersonating Groucho Marx and Sherlock Holmes, and Hank Marvin playing Tarzan. Cliff managed sixty costume changes.

In one scene Cliff and Richard O'Sullivan were dressed as cowboys for a Western shootout, which the villagers of a small place called Castelroma turned out to watch with their families. They were fascinated by the rehearsals, but when Furie went for a take and the two cowboys started blasting away with blanks, everyone panicked and ran for cover.

But there were bright moments, particularly when Susan Hampshire reprised Ursula Andress's famous bikini-clad walk out of the sea from the first James Bond 007 movie, *Dr No*. Susan looked stunning as she emerged from a tropical lagoon and went into a clinch with Cliff as Bond. 'After the kisses I was going around bumping into furniture for hours,' she told the press.

But, sadly, in the main *Wonderful Life* did not work.

One of the main problems in the Canary Islands was the weather. It rained almost every day. 'We had chosen to film in the Canary Islands because of the exceptional sunlight and golden sands,' said Cliff. 'We should have been there for three weeks but everything took so long we were there for almost three months.

'So for the first couple of days everything was fine when we filmed in beautiful sunshine in a place called Maspalomas. And then when we came to do the close-ups the next day, it had rained and everything was black. It looked more like a Welsh mining village than a tropical island. So we waited and waited, and when the rain eventually stopped the sand took four days to dry out and regain its colour. Our stint there was terrible. The budget went up and up and in the end the film cost about three-quarters of a million pounds – in those days. It took seven years for the film to make its money back. Now it's in the black.'

Even director Sidney Furie, who returned to take charge, admitted in his revealing director's commentary: '*The Young Ones* had heart but *Wonderful Life* hasn't got heart. There's a magic that only comes into certain things. You can have all the production in the world, but the simplest little story can work better. *Wonderful Life* did not do what *The Young Ones* did even though the budget was much bigger.'

While Cliff was in the Canary Islands filming *Wonderful Life*, it became apparent that his short-lived romance with a stunningly beautiful dancer called Jacqueline Irving had come to an end. 'I don't see Cliff any more,' Jackie revealed in a newspaper interview on 4 February 1964. 'I haven't heard from Cliff since he went away filming. Not a letter, a postcard, nothing.

'We never had any rows or anything,' she stressed. 'Although we don't see each other now, I imagine we're still friends.' It was the end of a romance that could conceivably have led to marriage for Cliff.

From a humble background in Manchester, Jackie had, without any formal training, become one of the most sought-after dancers in variety television. She also had head-turning good looks. 'She was absolutely beautiful,' said Bruce Welch. 'A lovely girl. Different class.'

Jackie had first caught Cliff's eye when she appeared with him at the London Palladium. Then, early in 1963, they became better acquainted when they were both in the same touring show in South Africa. At first they went out together with a group of other people from the show, but back in England Jackie received a call from Cliff's manager Peter Gormley asking if she would like to accompany Cliff to a film premiere. 'It seemed I was the only girl Cliff knew well,' said Jackie. 'He's a very shy boy, and as I'd never been to a premiere, I accepted.'

Jackie was one of eight dancers subsequently signed up for Cliff's summer season at Blackpool ABC, which opened on 1 June, followed by an after-show supper party attended by four hundred people. Cliff had invited Jackie to the cinema with him one night after rehearsals and soon they were dating regularly, sometimes going out together as often as three times a week.

During the run, Cliff stayed at a house in Lytham St Anne's, some five miles south of Blackpool, but he had to move for the sake of his neighbours after he woke up one morning and found 150 fans milling around outside. When Dorothy and two of his sisters joined him in Blackpool, Cliff was able to introduce Jackie to his mother and she in turn introduced Cliff to her own mum, Minnie, who ran a boarding house in Blackpool.

At first they dated quietly to avoid the press finding out, but after a while they made no secret of it. The beautiful girl who sat beside Cliff in the 160 mph Corvette he now drove after trading in his red Thunderbird was bound to turn heads, and inevitably their romance was seized upon by the newspapers. It prompted feverish speculation that the couple were about to get married, although Jackie and Cliff both denied it. 'There is one girl I'm very friendly with – dancer Jackie Irving,' he said in July 1963. 'But she and I know that marriage is out of the question.'

'Obviously I like him a lot,' said Jackie. 'So does my mother. She has met him on odd occasions and has shaken hands with him. She thinks he's a nice boy. Neither of us is planning to get married. There's nothing like that.'

Tellingly, Jackie said of their dates: 'Afterwards he takes me home and says goodnight on the doorstep. It's usually pretty late and he has to get back to his hotel.'

Ironically, while the press speculation of impending marriage was at its height, Jackie was introduced for the first time to the man she would eventually wed – Adam Faith. Jackie and Cliff were at a Blackpool restaurant when Adam walked in with some aides after giving a concert at the Queen's Theatre, Blackpool. Adam remembers being instantly struck by Jackie's extraordinary, radiant beauty. 'She was the most stunning girl I'd ever clapped eyes on,' he later recounted. 'It was love at first sight.'

After chatting to Cliff for a while, Adam gazed admiringly at Jackie from a distance all evening. And when she got up from the table to go to the ladies' room, Adam briefly thought about sending over one of his friends to ask Jackie for her telephone number on the sly. But Cliff was an old friend, and he thought better of such subterfuge. 'Up to then I'd only envied Cliff for making a record as great as "Move It",' Adam said. 'But tonight, as far as I was concerned, he had it all.'

Perhaps Cliff was aware Adam had his eye on Jackie when he subsequently came up with some lyrics for a new Bruce Welch song while he was in Blackpool that summer. Cliff co-wrote 'Don't Talk to Him' with Bruce and it went on to reach number two in the charts in November 1963. The lyrics involve imploring a girlfriend not to listen to the words of a love rival while reassuring her his own love for her was not 'plain'.

Adam would not meet up with Jackie again until her romance with Cliff had long fizzled out. The next time Adam saw her, it was at a party and she was on the arm of Beatle George Harrison. But Adam never forgot her and Jackie eventually became his wife in 1967.

Back in the winter of 1964, after her romance with Cliff had run its course, Jackie was able to look back philosophically at its conclusion. 'Cliff and I only seem to have gone out together while we were working together,' she reflected. 'Since the Blackpool show ended, we've only met at parties to which we've gone separately.'

Jackie would not be the first girl to conclude that she would never become Cliff's wife. 'I have plenty of other boyfriends,' she said, 'and I realise it wouldn't do Cliff's career any good at all if he got married. It would only annoy his fans.'

In her frustration at the way their romance was failing to progress any further, Jackie had at one point sought out Cliff's mum for a woman-to-woman chat. Jackie believed Dorothy was partly responsible for holding Cliff back from marriage, but she was told in no uncertain terms by his mother that Cliff was his own man and that if he did not want to get married, then he would not do so.

Cliff eventually broke the news to Jackie that their romance was over when she visited him in the Canary Islands. There would be no wedding, he told her, and Jackie disconsolately flew home.

Cliff was then only 23, but there is no doubt that he had seriously considered marrying Jackie. 'The Shadows had all married,' he said later, 'and I'd been going around with Jackie Irving for three years and we'd got along very well. So when The Shadows got married one after the other, I really began to worry. I kept thinking: why not me? I did think about marriage then, but I decided I couldn't love her or we'd have been married earlier.'

In 1975, more than a decade after they had split up, Cliff looked back and, upon further reflection, said: 'I was madly in love, but I had doubts at the last moment. Jackie is the only girl I have contemplated marrying. I thought I was in love with her, but time showed I wasn't.'

A major factor in Cliff choosing to stay single was the damaging effect getting married would have on his fans. He had seen Marty Wilde's career nosedive after the singer tied the knot. The teenage girls who formed the core of his fan base transferred their devotion elsewhere.

Cliff also knew from personal experience that his female fans found it hard to see him getting close to any one girl. And one incident, in particular, shaped his attitude towards girlfriends for many years to come.

'Early on I didn't get married because my career was everything to me,' he has admitted. 'You just didn't get married if you were a pop singer, your fans would slay you.

'You had to be very careful in those days because the fans really cared. I remember one girlfriend, Jean. She was a very attractive girl, but I only knew her for a short time. She was a fan at first, probably the only fan I've ever taken out. I remember one night we were coming out of the Finsbury Park Empire and she got into the car and sat on my lap. Then I looked behind me, and I was shattered. I felt I wanted to die inside. I remember sitting in the back of the car with my girlfriend on my knee and I turned round and saw these young girls looking at the car and trampling my photographs in the gutter.'

This image of jilted fans, distraught at their idol apparently intimately involved with a female, may have contributed to Cliff finally dismissing any idea of asking Jackie Irving to marry him. But the end of his romance with the dancer had also happened to coincide with Cliff becoming increasingly en-amoured of his *Wonderful Life* co-star Una Stubbs, who played Walter Slezak's script girl.

They are both much too discreet ever to talk in detail about the relationship, but a source who worked on the film told the authors of this book: 'They were very young and for a while they were very much in love.

'There's always a sort of heightened emotion about filming on location. You're all thrown together and people do become close. But it was more than that between Cliff and Una. You only had to look at them to see they were head over heels in love with each other, and everyone did what they could to make sure they got plenty of privacy.'

Una said years later in a television interview for ITV's *South Bank Show* that she became romantically involved with Cliff. She said: 'I was very unhappily married [to actor Peter Gilmore] at the time.' She was asked if she thought she was in love with Cliff and replied: 'Oh, I think so, as indeed most women are that meet him. I suppose for a period I was in love with him. I was very young.'

It seems it was a very innocent affair. Cliff has said that while he has very fond memories of the relationship, it involved kissing and holding hands rather than spending nights of torrid passion together. 'We didn't go to bed together,' said Cliff in the *Daily Mail* in September 1993.

The closeness of the relationship was interrupted by the end of the film, but the couple remained very good friends and are still fond of each other to this day. Years later Una was offered a large sum of money by a newspaper to tell exactly what happened between them. Cliff cheerfully advised Una to take it. 'What can you tell them?' he laughed. 'They'll only be disappointed.'

The public reaction to *Wonderful Life* was very disappointing, but Cliff was determined to take the impact of the letdown on the chin. '*Wonderful Life* was a flop,' admitted the star with refreshing frankness. 'It was a disaster from the word go.'

To a star used to success after two hit films, *Wonderful Life* was a blow. Cliff's budding film career was stopped in its tracks. Cliff remembers with sadness: 'We started getting scripts that were full of red buses and we decided to pass for a while. Everything else was going very well and I was busy and I think: this is where the good management comes in. We thought it was just wrong to keep doing the same sort of thing. And with hindsight, I think we were right.'

By the time Cliff returned to movie-making with *Finders Keepers* in 1966, Liverpool's Fab Four had taken film musicals in a different direction with *A Hard Day's Night* and *Help!* and Cliff found himself having to play catch-up. 'The Beatles were doing films that were really avant garde movies of the time,' he says. 'We were trying to do films that were one step on from *The Young Ones* and *Summer Holiday*, but they were not different enough.'

Finders Keepers was a light-hearted, spy spoof musical loosely based on an incident in 1965 when the Americans contrived to lose an H-bomb in the sea off the coast of Spain. The upshot was a movie featuring Cliff and The Shadows turning up at a Spanish town to find the area deserted after a small unexploded bomb had accidentally landed on the town, causing the villagers to flee in panic fearing it will go off. Disguised as a roving guitar troupe, Cliff and The Shadows set out to find the bomb and restore peace to the town.

The movie, which also starred Robert Morley, and Vivienne Ventura as Cliff's glamorous new leading lady, encompassed nine weeks of studio filming and some exterior filming on the south coast.

'Although it was set in Spain, we never left Pinewood,' Cliff recalls. 'We used the Walt Disney set of a Gothic village that they had put a few daubs of white paint on and a couple of Spanish tiles and a few geraniums.'

Despite a promotional tagline that proclaimed: 'The beat is the wildest! The blast is the craziest! . . . and the fun is where you find it!', *Finders Keepers* failed to set the screen alight.

'It was one of those films that never really quite made it,' was Cliff's verdict. 'It never got off the ground, but it was the best music we'd had in any film up to then and it went in a different direction in that it mixed up rock 'n' roll with show numbers.

'The film did all right, but in terms of films we were going through a kind of lull,' Cliff said on reflection. '*Wonderful Life* had kind of cooled people off because it wasn't as good as the others.'

Cliff's interest in acting continued, however, and he made his straight acting stage debut at the New Theatre, Bromley, in Kent, in Peter Shaffer's play *Five Finger Exercise* in 1970. He was due to return to Bromley the following year in Graham

Greene's *The Potting Shed*, but the theatre burned down two days before opening night and the production was forced to transfer to the Sadler's Wells Theatre in north London.

Cliff also made occasional forays into TV drama before being asked in 1973 to star in a new film, *Take Me High*, with Anthony Andrews as his co-star. The plot centred on a young merchant banker called Tim Matthews, played by Cliff, who goes to Birmingham and ends up running a restaurant with his girlfriend, Sarah (Deborah Watling). Together they transform the eaterie's fortunes by inventing the Brumburger.

Premiered in London, *Take Me High* failed to draw big audiences and the title track issued as a single fared little better. The highest position it reached in the charts was a disappointing 27, although 'Time Drags By', one of the best songs from the film, provided Cliff with a Top Ten hit.

12. HITS

Don't get too fond of Cliff, he's got his career ahead of him.
Dorothy Webb to Cliff's girlfriend, Delia Wicks

S ome pop stars are so intoxicated by their first taste of big money that it instantly goes to their heads in a flurry of drink, drugs and flash living, with hot and cold running women in every room. Cliff Richard bought his mum and dad a semi.

In April 1960, months after returning from his first tour of the US, Cliff was ready to move himself and his family out of their Cheshunt council house and into a new home. By now he was earning very highly – in one interview in November 1959, just twelve weeks after the release of 'Living Doll', ever-honest Cliff revealed: 'I get the royalties for myself, and that number-one hit has so far brought in about six thousand pounds.' Cliff was then estimated to be earning £30,000 a year – at a time when the average teenage male took home £8 a week and the average female £6 a week.

The big pay cheques enabled him to buy a semi-detatched corner house at 2 Colne Road, Winchmore Hill, in a middle-class area of north London. He was able to pay £7,000 for this five-bedroomed property – which of course had to be large enough to accommodate his entire family – and to spend a similar amount on alterations and redecoration.

'When I was nineteen or twenty and used to get asked whether money and fame had changed me, I used to say: "No, not at all,"' Cliff reflected years later in a TV interview with Gloria Hunniford for the *Biography Channel*. 'What I meant was, I don't think it spoiled me or corrupted me in any way. But now, when I look back, it's changed absolutely everything. Not just for me but my whole family. When you're a child and sitting on your mum's knee, you say: "One day I'm going to buy you a house." Well, I did!'

In the first flush of success Cliff had asked his dad whether he should splash out on a car first or a house. 'I told him to get a car,' Rodger revealed, 'but he came back a bit later and said no, he'd get the house first.'

The car followed soon afterwards, when Cliff passed his driving test first time in June 1960. He paid £1,300 for a pale silver-grey Sunbeam Alpine two-seater sports car with red leather seats to replace the nasturtium and black motor scooter he had owned as his means of getting around Cheshunt. His mother also started taking driving lessons and, as an incentive for her to pass her driving test, he bought her a car of her own. It came as a complete surprise to Dorothy when she returned home one day to find a gleaming white Renault Floride waiting for her.

While house-hunting the previous summer, Cliff and his parents had viewed several much larger properties than the one he eventually bought, but they had all agreed that they didn't want to rattle around in a sprawling mansion. They felt it was inappropriate for such a close-knit family.

Cliff's new home did not look especially imposing from the outside, but it proved to be deceptively roomy inside – especially for a family who had endured the claustrophobic one-room existence of their first few years in England.

The solid oak front door opened on to a wide hall, which led into a spacious sitting room-cum-dining room, and the first floor contained four bedrooms. Cliff chose the top-floor attic bedroom with dormer window for himself.

Visitors expecting Cliff's home to boast the garish, over-the-top, self-indulgent opulence and excess of Presley's Graceland were disappointed. Just about the only concessions to luxury were a white leather-covered bar, a 21-inch TV set, and a top-of-the-range radiogram.

Cliff's mum took charge of the décor and plumped for a tasteful semi-Regency style. After the bare essentials of their previous dwellings, now every room had wall-to-wall carpeting, including the bathroom. Plush, red-velvet curtains hung in the sitting room, where the focal point of the room was a large sideboard with all Cliff's showbusiness awards on display, as well as the athletics silverware he had won at school.

It was only Cliff's bedroom that reflected a hint a showbiz glitz. The wallpaper was a brash red, the carpet was black and Cliff slept on a divan that boasted a leopardskin bedspread. Two big fitted wardrobes were crammed with his ever-growing collection of suits and shoes.

It did not take long for Cliff's fans to discover the location of his new home, and they started turning up from all over the country, much to the family's irritation. The Webbs accepted that their son's success would bring fame, but they were not prepared for the onslaught of uninvited visitors and their patience was tried to the limit. And the neighbours were definitely not amused. The days when Dorothy Webb would happily invite fans in for a cup of tea and cakes at Cheshunt had long gone. Now there were simply too many of them and they were more obsessively intrusive. The gate outside the house would be locked at all times but the fans simply clambered over it or climbed the fence.

Later on, Cliff splashed out to buy five hundred acres in Wales to plant trees after learning that forests were dwindling. He set about organising the planting of firs and hardwood and enjoyed going off for weekends for a bit of peace and quiet to the cottage with thick stone walls and huge hearth that came with the land.

The Winchmore Hill house was a timely purchase. Cliff was soon to embark on a highly lucrative six-month engagement at the London Palladium in a variety show called *Stars in Your Eyes*, and the Palladium was a relatively easy commute from Winchmore Hill.

* * *

By the time Cliff was filling the Palladium in *Stars in Your Eyes*, he was top of the charts once again, partly thanks to a clever marketing ploy by EMI's Columbia Records, which threw a party for eighty teenagers to help them decide which of 21 recently cut tracks should be Cliff's next single. Over tea and biscuits the youngsters listened to all the tracks and then voted 'Please Don't Tease' the clear winner.

Their choice put Cliff back on top of the singles charts for the third time. He was especially pleased to hit number one again after his last two records, 'Voice in the Wilderness' and 'Fall in Love With You', had both peaked at number two.

'Please Don't Tease' was a song co-written by Bruce Welch and his friend Pete Chester, son of a popular comedian of the day, Charlie Chester. 'We got into writing songs really early when we were [very] young,' said Bruce. 'An influence for me was Buddy Holly, who wrote his own stuff, unlike Elvis. That's why Hank and I wanted to be like Buddy, who'd churn out these little two-minute songs with three chords, which were perfect for me. From 1959 we were writing album tracks and B-sides for Cliff.

'As The Shadows, we were blessed – we were the backing group to the biggest star in Britain and he recorded almost everything we wrote. We were in the right place with the right man at the right time, and we've always been grateful for that.'

Cliff was grateful for this constant supply: 'Hank and Bruce wrote some wonderful stuff. The writing of the songs used to go on in the coaches and in the hotels and I used to write with The Shadows, too. With Bruce I co-wrote "Bachelor Boy", "On the Beach", "Don't Talk to Him". But The Shadows would say to me: "You're the star, you go and do the press conference." I quite liked it when they called me the star – I liked being the frontman. But when I got back two hours later, they'd written three great songs – but without me, of course.'

Ironically, it was The Shadows who knocked Cliff's 'Please Don't Tease' off the top spot after just three weeks with a wonderful instrumental, 'Apache'. The group had first heard the rudiments of 'Apache' while they were on a tour bus with singer-songwriter Jerry Lordan. Hank and Bruce were chatting to Jerry at the front of the bus when he got up to fetch his ukulele from the back of the bus and returned to play them a number he had penned. The two Shadows guitarists knew at once they wanted to record it. But there was a snag. Lordan informed them that guitarist Bert Weedon had already beaten them to it.

Lordan suspected, however, that Weedon, whose guitar instruction book *Play in a Day* was helping to generate unprecedented sales of guitars in the UK, was seemingly not planning for his version of 'Apache' to be released as a single. So Lordan gave The Shadows his blessing to record their own single.

The group made a little demo of 'Apache' for Norrie Paramor to listen to and Norrie subsequently recorded 'Apache' and another number called 'Quartermaster's Stores'. Just as he had done with Cliff's first two recordings, Norrie took both numbers home to play, this time to his two daughters, to see which they liked best. They picked 'Apache' as the A-side.

'Apache' came along at an ideal time for The Shadows. Just then guitar-based instrumentals were prominent in the hit parade in their own right as never before, and 'Apache' had 'hit' written all over it as soon as it was released. It was perfect timing. Also in the charts around this time were American guitarist Duane Eddy with his twangy instrumental 'Because They're Young', and the American group The Ventures were vying with the UK's John Barry Seven for chart supremacy with the heavily guitar-influenced instrumental 'Walk Don't Run'.

Lordan's distinctive composition was instantly a smash hit for The Shadows, and the record shot to number one although, as Bruce Welch has pointed out, the group were disappointed not to repeat the UK success in America. In the UK, 'Apache' stayed on top of the singles charts for five weeks and elevated The Shadows from being just Cliff's backing group into stars in their own right. By the end of 1960 they had won a clutch of awards, including Top Instrumental Group of the Year. 'Apache' was also voted Top Record of 1960 by readers of the *New Musical Express*.

'Once The Shadows had made it by themselves in the mid-1960s, you then had two big acts on one show,' explained

Bruce. 'We would close the first half, and then we'd change our suits and do the whole of the second half with Cliff.'

Still not daring to believe that rock 'n' roll really was here to stay, EMI released Cliff's tenth single, 'Nine Times out of Ten' to cash in on his popularity as quickly as possible, while 'Please Don't Tease' was still showing healthy sales in the Top Twenty.

'Nine Times out of Ten' went straight into the Top Ten after setting a new record for advance sales for a single in Britain – a then staggering total of 180,000. It was quickly followed by an EP and, in October, an album, *Me and my Shadows*, which some of Cliff's fans believe to be their best LP together. That same month EMI's managing director, Len Wood, was able to endorse Cliff's extraordinary popularity by revealing that, in his two-year career, his sales of singles now totalled 5.5 million.

On the recording front, a pattern evolved of releasing three to four singles a year. Television was a natural progression for Cliff, and it was no surprise when, during October 1960, that month of unparalleled success, ATV announced it had signed up Cliff for a series of six half-hour shows to be screened the following year, 1961.

By the end of a golden 1960 for Cliff, EMI chairman Sir Joseph Lockwood was able to claim that the singer was a major factor in the company achieving 25 per cent of the world's total record sales during the year, with Cliff way out in front as their best-selling artist. He had topped the charts in South Africa, New Zealand, Australia, Singapore, Sweden and Holland, as well as the UK.

Of particular satisfaction for Cliff was ending the year by displacing his great idol, Elvis Presley, at number one. His eleventh single, 'I Love You', another composition by Bruce Welch, knocked Presley's 'It's Now or Never' off the top.

After such unprecedented success, it should have been a perfect Christmas for Cliff and his family. But, on 27 December, the Webbs' seasonal festivities were worryingly interrupted when Cliff's father was suddenly taken ill. Heavy smoker Rodger was taken to hospital and treated for heart trouble. He had to stay in hospital for four weeks and, although none of the family knew it at the time, Rodger was becoming seriously ill and had just four and a half months left to live.

One of Rodger's last acts for his famous son was to pave the way for a new personal manager to take control of Cliff's career. Cliff was grateful that Tito Burns had enabled him to get into movies, but father and son both felt Tito was overly concerned with going for instant money-spinning returns on his client's talents rather than planning for a long-term, lasting, showbusiness future for Cliff.

Tito had never enjoyed the easiest of relationships with Cliff's dad. He resented Rodger Webb constantly looking over his shoulder when it came to handling Cliff's bookings and business affairs.

'He didn't want to be Cliff's manager,' Tito said of Rodger, 'and yet he wanted to be his manager, if you know what I'm trying to say. It may have just been paternal protectiveness, but he began to delve into things and came up with weird situations. He wanted to put his spoke in.'

Cliff's contract with Tito was due to expire when the singer turned 21 anyway, but when Rodger's differences of opinion with Tito became ever more prickly, Rodger decided it would be best for everyone if their agreement was terminated early. Tito was duly dismissed and, on 1 March 1961, it was announced that Peter Gormley, an Australian who had arrived in England in 1959 to launch Aussie singer Frank Ifield – who later became a major star after topping the charts with 'I Remember You' – would now be Cliff's new personal manager.

With the musical assistance of Norrie Paramor, Gormley had quickly achieved a breakthrough for Ifield in the UK with a minor hit, 'Lucky Devil', on Columbia, the same label as Cliff's recordings. Soon afterwards Gormley also became manager of The Shadows after impressing the group with his plans to expand their talents. With these links, Gormley was therefore the obvious choice to succeed Tito Burns as Cliff's manager

Rodger, ever wary of Cliff being greedily exploited, was particularly impressed by Gormley's insistence that he would not take a percentage of Cliff's earnings for the first year, as he had played no part in helping to generate them. It was a rare gesture of generosity in the hard-nosed, grasping world of showbusiness. And, unlike showman Tito, who was comfortable in the limelight, Gormley preferred largely to be an unseen presence when it came to taking control of Cliff. But he was, nonetheless, astute and shrewd, as well as effective for going about his business quietly.

Gormley had been installed for only a few weeks when the Rodger's health took a turn for the worse, meaning he had to rely on other people around him. He bitterly resented being so helpless and dependent, but it allowed Cliff to show his father he was quite capable of changing an electric plug or mowing the grass.

Despite his failing health, Rodger remained stubborn to the end. Always a very heavy smoker, he was under orders to cut out the habit. But Cliff remembers that even when his father was in an oxygen tent in hospital, a nurse caught him trying to light up a cigarette. He had somehow managed to unzip the tent from the inside.

Cliff's father died on 15 May 1961, on the very first day rehearsals started for *The Young Ones*. By then, Rodger's death was not unexpected and, in the weeks leading up to it, Cliff was able finally to forge a closer relationship with his father than he had enjoyed hitherto.

'When he got ill with thrombosis problems I did get closer to him,' he has asserted. 'It wasn't until he was ill and I had to do everything that we got on really well. We never had any closeness till he was too desperately ill to be stubborn. Even so, I don't think we said much to each other at the end. But looking back now, I'd have liked him to have seen the best part of my career.'

Mingled with the collective family grief at Rodger's passing was the realisation among Dorothy and her three daughters that Cliff was now head of the family at the tender age of twenty. It was a responsibility that immediately registered with Cliff himself and it weighed more heavily upon him than he could have possibly imagined. 'I was already the breadwinner, but then I also became the man of the house overnight and everything changed,' Cliff said. 'Not only was I the breadwinner, I was the only one who could do anything. My mother was almost helpless with worry and my sisters were young. We'd actually had a much better time when he wasn't well, which was a shame, really.

'Nevertheless I'm grateful that we had that time and that we finally understood each other better, otherwise my memory would have just been of a man who was bordering on tyrannical. In fact, he was just very firm and I now recognise that I actually needed that discipline.'

Rodger's death had far-reaching repercussions upon Cliff, and the singer believes it was the catalyst for his eventually turning to God. 'I was really far more upset than I ever thought I'd be by my father's death. I felt cheated, because it was 1961, and it was just beginning for me. I was twenty and *The Young Ones* was about to happen and I'm there thinking: what will I do without my dad?'

One who was soon to notice a marked change in Cliff was Delia Wicks. She was a pretty, blonde dancer the singer had initially taken a fancy to during his Palladium show *Stars in Your Eyes*, in which Delia was chosen to step out of the chorus line to perform a little routine with Cliff, which ended in a kiss. 'I was the first girl ever to dance with him on the stage,' Delia recounted many years later. 'The screams from the girls in the audience were tremendous. At the end of the dance, Cliff kissed me. It started on the cheek but as the weeks went by, it moved round to my lips. And that was the start of it all.'

When the Palladium run came to an end, they dated intermittently, when Cliff's hectic schedule allowed, and Delia had soon fallen head-over-heels in love with the famous singer.

'When the show closed, he rang me up all of a sudden out of the blue,' Delia has revealed, 'and he said: "Delia, I've got to come over and see you." My heart was beating so fast. He came over early in the morning because nobody would see him, about six o'clock, and parked the car outside. As soon as he arrived he had to phone his mother to let her know where he was.'

As the romance progressed, Cliff's mother was to play gooseberry far more often than Delia might have liked.

In a frank TV interview, Delia explained: 'His mother used to come to the cinema with us and everything. She always used to come with his sisters. He'd say: "Oh, Mummy's coming," and she'd be sat in the front row of the circle.'

Dorothy Webb later went on to make it plain to Delia that any hopes the latter might harbour of the relationship leading to any permanency or, ultimately, even marriage, should be forgotten. Cliff's mother chose to make her point forcefully one night when Delia and Cliff were about to step out together to see the legendary American singer Peggy Lee in concert. Delia was dolling herself up in one of the bedrooms at Cliff's Winchmore Hill home when Dorothy walked into the room and had something to say.

'His mother said: "Don't get too fond of Cliff, he's got his career ahead of him," Delia remembered. 'And I said: "Well that's up to Cliff, isn't it? He can make his own mind up." And she said: "Well, I'm just warning you." '

Those were not the words Delia wanted to hear. 'I would have married him like a shot. I was deeply in love with him.'

The romance with Delia continued off and on, but in great secrecy. Cliff was at pains to distance himself from Delia if they attended the same public function, so that they were never photographed together. Loyally, Delia went along with a clandestine relationship and never even held Cliff's hand in public when there might be a risk of their being photographed together. The press were given no inkling that they might be an item. Time spent together as a couple became a rarity. If Cliff's mother wasn't around, his manager was never far away. 'It was like being with royalty,' Delia said. 'We never had a moment alone.'

Rodger Webb's death also hastened the demise of Cliff's romance with Delia. 'When his father died, I didn't hear anything from him for a long time,' she said. 'And then, of course, the pressure was on him because he'd got to leave for Australia with his mother and sisters. I think that's when the pressure started, and that's when I got the letter.'

In the autumn of 1961 Delia, who was living in Earls Court, London, received an airmail letter postmarked Melbourne, 26 October. It was from Cliff, who was enjoying a hugely successful tour of Australia.

His letter read: 'Dear Dellia [sic], I want you to understand the position I am in as a pop singer. I'm going to have to give up many things in my life, but being a pop singer I have to give up the most priceless things in my life that is a long-lasting relationship with a special girl. I couldn't give up my career and besides the fact that my mother and sisters since my father's death rely on me completely. I have showbusiness in my blood now and I would be lost without it. D all I can say now is goodbye and don't think too badly of me. Love Cliff.'

Delia was shaken to the core, and deeply upset. The bad news had come out of the blue, and once again Cliff had shown a reluctance to deliver it face to face. He had essentially ducked the issue. 'He made a decision: my career is more important that anything else,' said Bruce Welch. 'I'm not going to go out with women – it's my career. But he didn't have the courage to face her and tell her, so he wrote her a letter.'

In truth, Cliff's relationship with Delia was never a grand passion. It was 1960, when the permissive age had barely begun, so they kissed and cuddled, but they never slept together. 'Don't forget we didn't have the Pill in those days,' Delia said. 'We would cuddle up and go to sleep together but we never took our clothes off. It would have happened eventually.'

Times were different then, but even allowing for the stricter moral code of the day, Delia acknowledges their relationship was incomplete. 'Everybody needs company and companionship,' she said, 'but somehow with Cliff I always felt there was something missing or lacking, I don't know what it was.'

But asked if the thought ever crossed her mind that Cliff was gay, Delia told the *Daily Mail*: 'Without going into details, I can categorically say he was not homosexual when we were dating.'

Weeks after Delia had been dumped by airmail letter from the other side of the world, Cliff flew to South Africa to attend the premiere of *The Young Ones*, opening in Johannesburg, Cape Town and Durban. With him went not Delia, but his mother.

This strong maternal bond prompted Shadows drummer Tony Meehan to observe: 'Cliff had such a very close relationship with his mother that I think it precluded any chance *ever* of there being a girlfriend.'

And in an interview for ITV's *The South Bank Show*, Meehan added: 'For the bulk of his adult life he has avoided any kind of physical contact to my knowledge, so he arrived at that decision. There is suppression, but whether it's suppressed homosexuality or repressed heterosexuality, I couldn't answer.'

While he had been on tour in Australia, Cliff had clearly done a great deal of soul-searching. The reception he was being given by Aussie fans wherever he performed could hardly have been warmer, and yet he felt increasingly empty inside, accentuated by the fact that times were changing close to home. He had to face the fact that the Webb family, so solid for so long, was beginning to break up. Within a few months of his father's death, Cliff's sister Donella had got married and left the family home.

Cliff was desperate for Donna's wedding on 5 August 1961 to be the most perfect day of his eldest sister's life but, much to his anger, it was anything but. Thousands of Cliff's fans besieged Waltham Abbey parish church in Essex and when Cliff, who was giving Donella away, arrived with her for the wedding ceremony, they were mobbed by a frenzied crowd the minute they emerged from their car.

Despite the best efforts of Cliff and a police cordon to protect her, Donella's bridal veil was half snatched from her head in the ensuing scrum and she fainted in the crush.

Helping hands finally enabled her to reach the church, her wedding dress crumpled and tears filling her eyes. Cliff was appalled and had a face like thunder.

To avoid similar chaotic scenes after the ceremony, Cliff made good his escape through the vestry door, taking the bride and groom with him. This furtive exit meant the official wedding photographer was unable to take the traditional post-ceremony photographs outside the church. Cliff was upset at the way Donna's big day had turned out, and, although he had been powerless to intervene and could hardly be called to account for the intrusive behaviour of his fans, of course he blamed himself.

It was just a few weeks after Donna's wedding that Cliff headed off to Australia and started to miss his father so much more than he had possibly imagined. Cliff appeared to have it all, but, with his father now gone, he began to feel the first signs of a creeping sense of emptiness inside.

Partly out of curiosity, Cliff decided that he would seek out a spirit medium in a bid to try and contact his father in the after-life. A séance, he felt, might give him a clue as to whether there really was life after death, and if he could get through to his father, then Rodger might be able to tell him why he was feeling so empty.

The séance might well have gone ahead had Cliff not mentioned his plan to Licorice Locking. Cliff was totally unprepared for the bass player's reaction – Licorice simply erupted in anger and horror and forcefully gave Cliff a piece of his mind. He told him that attending a séance was not only wrong, it was dangerous, too, and to ram home his point, Licorice suddenly produced a Bible from his pocket and started reading out passages that expressly forbade any dealings with spirits or mediums.

Cliff was taken aback, not just that the Bible had provided some sort of an answer as to whether he should try and contact his father beyond the grave, but by the force of Licorice's argument. Cliff was aware that Licorice was a religious man, but now it emerged that he was a devoted Jehovah's Witness. Cliff was impressed, too, that Licorice thought enough of him to warn him away from dabbling in séances and suchlike.

That might have been the end of the matter, but Licorice's impromptu lecture led Cliff to seek out his own Bible. The upshot was that he began attending Jehovah's Witness meetings alongside Licorice, as well as Hank Marvin and Brian Bennett, who were both showing interest.

Over the next two years Cliff continued to explore various aspects of the Jehovah's Witness movement, which dates back to the nineteenth century. He even underwent a formal course of Bible studies during a summer season in Blackpool, which involved attending a meeting every Sunday afternoon. He subsequently invited a local Jehovah's Witness into the family home after he fired up similar enthusiasm for the movement among his mother and his sisters.

Despite his growing interest, Cliff somehow could never quite bring himself to volunteer for a public baptism as a Jehovah's Witness. He always had doubts and baulked at this final declaration, despite constant entreaties by eminent Jehovah's Witness converts that he stand up and be counted.

Cliff's doubts led him briefly to explore Judaism, but his search for spiritual enlightenment took a different turn when Jay Norris, Cliff's former English teacher, invited him to a car rally in 1965. Jay had kept in regular contact with Cliff ever since he had left school, and when they had met up the previous year on one of his occasional visits, Cliff had told Jay of his interest in the Jehovah's Witnesses and she was worried that her former pupil was being led astray. Artfully, she now paired Cliff off in the car rally with Bill Latham, head of religious education at his old school.

'I only knew Cliff as the most notable old boy from our school,' Bill said in a rare interview. 'Jay knew he was involved in Jehovah's Witnesses and, as she had a Catholic background, did not want him to get involved. So she put me in a car with him on a rally and told me: "Try to talk him out of it." Of course, it was an entirely superficial situation and we did not have time to talk properly.'

Cliff and Bill came second in the car rally, and although Bill had made little headway on Jay's behalf, a date was arranged for her to bring Bill to Rookswood, Cliff's new family home in Upper Nazeing, for a meeting where the topic of religion would be on the agenda.

'I had been invited to the house for a specific reason,' said Bill. 'To talk about religion. I remember being impressed by what a strong-willed person he was. He certainly had fame and money, but was looking for something else in life and had not found it.'

The young Christian teacher gently tried to turn Cliff away from his Jehovah's Witness stance, but at first Cliff showed a stubborn streak worthy of his father. By the end of the evening Bill had certainly made a point. 'I think our talk had enough impact on him to pursue religion, and he was open in wanting to talk some more.'

Bill followed up by inviting Cliff to his home in Finchley, north London. 'I introduced him to various church friends and he seemed to enjoy the non-showbusiness orbit of it all,' Bill noted.

'They talked about Jesus as though they knew Him,' Cliff once explained. 'Gently, and at first imperceptibly, my JW platform began to rock.'

For fully a year Cliff wrestled with his thoughts during many a conversation with Bill Latham, and gradually his interest in becoming a Jehovah's Witness diminished. Fittingly, the moment of truth for Cliff came while he was staying with Bill in Finchley while making the movie *Finders Keepers*. Bill offered him the use of his spare front bedroom in his home so that Cliff did not have to make the long trek from Upper Nazeing to Pinewood Studios and back each day.

Recounting his own personal path to becoming a Christian, Cliff told Tim Rice in a Radio 1 interview: 'It was a gradual thing, but I can whittle it down to one of the last items that hit me. Like most people, I didn't go into Christianity to prove it – I tried to disprove it. I asked a lot of questions, but the more questions I asked, the answers I got were phenomenal and beyond my expectation.

'I didn't know that Christians could be so rational, and one of the final things was when I came to a point to think: yes, I do believe Jesus did exist. Yes, I believe he is the Son of God. Yes, I believe he died. Yes, I believe he is alive. And then I thought: well, so what? That's just a lot of beliefs. I could go on believing that for ever but it wouldn't make me feel any different. Someone said to me: "Read the book of Revelation, Chapter 3, Verse 20." It is ever so simple and it is the last little thing that clicked into place for me. It's Jesus' words and he says: "Behold I stand at the door and I knock and whoever opens the door I will come in."'

Cliff then proceeded to lie down on the bed in Bill Latham's front bedroom in Finchley and mouth a very hesitant prayer. 'I thought then: "If you're knocking on my door then I want you in my lifestyle."

'I can't say it was a dramatic conversion. There was no thunder and lightning, but that is the moment that I can trace my Christian life back to. That is the moment I became a Christian.'

Cliff added that without the faintest shadow of a doubt, 'that sober and almost anticlimactic evening in suburban London marked the turning point of my life'.

It was also the start of an unlikely, but long-lasting, friendship between a pop idol and a comprehensive schoolmaster. From this point onwards, Bill Latham took charge of Cliff's Christian diary while Peter Gormley, sympathetic to Cliff's religious feelings and supportive in every way, continued to look after his secular career.

A source of worry for Cliff at the time, however, was that his mother and two sisters became Jehovah's Witnesses, and his eldest sister Donna was on the point of commitment, too, when a crisis in her health caused a change of direction. In 1973 Donna became desperately ill and required a blood transfusion, something which went entirely against the teaching of Jehovah's Witnesses.

Cliff is on record as saying that Donna steadfastly refused to have a transfusion, and it was Cliff's mother who took it upon herself to take the decision to tell the doctors to do whatever was necessary to keep her daughter alive. This action resulted in Dorothy, who was a baptised Jehovah's Witness, being hauled before a JW tribunal.

13. CHRISTIANITY

To declare yourself a Christian in 1966 was the most unfashionable, the most daring, courageous, brave act you could imagine. You could have said that the world was flat and people would have had more time for you.

Bruce Welch

As a boy, Cliff Richard often attended church with his mother and, although his father insisted, 'Church is not for people like me,' Rodger Webb regularly held family Bible readings at home.

At the age of fourteen, however, young Cliff abandoned confirmation classes when he fell in love with rock 'n' roll. But as an adult, following the discovery that he needed Jesus in his life, Cliff decided he had to tell the world. And on the evening of Thursday 16 June 1966, at London's Earls Court, in front of a crowd of 25,000 drawn to a crusade by American evangelist Billy Graham, Cliff purposefully made his way to the stage to make his dramatic announcement.

Soberly dressed in a brown corduroy jacket, striped tie and flannels as befitted the occasion, and with heavy-rimmed spectacles on his nose, the singer once deemed too sexy for TV proceeded to make the very special announcement that he was a Christian.

Cliff told the congregation he felt fortunate that during his childhood his mother and father had always had the Bible at home. He then went on: 'I can only say to people who are not Christians that until you have taken the step of asking Christ into your life, your life is not worthwhile. It works – it works for me.'

Cliff followed up by singing, accompanied by just a piano and an organ, 'It is no Secret (what God can do)', a gospel song composed by a Billy Graham convert twenty years previously, and one that Cliff knew from Elvis Presley's version on the Presley LP *Peace in the Valley*. The massed congregation listened intently and at the end broke into restrained applause.

Cliff's public avowal that he had found God was not totally unexpected, but it still came as something of a surprise to the crowd crammed into the huge stadium, many of them teenage pop fans, and to the 5,000 locked out after the overflow halls were filled.

Billy Graham was full of admiration for Cliff. 'I think this has tremendous impact on young people who have listened to Cliff or seen his films,' he said. 'For him to stand up and say: "I am a Christian" gets thousands of young people thinking.'

For many months before Cliff chose Billy Graham's platform to profess his faith, rumours had been circulating that he was contemplating giving up his showbusiness career. It was by now well known that he went to church regularly and that he was involved with the Crusaders, a Christian youth movement.

But within Cliff's showbusiness circles, his Earls Court announcement was still greeted with incredulity by some. Former girlfriend Delia Wicks said, 'I thought it was strange. I thought: gosh, what's happened to Cliff? He didn't seem to be the Cliff that I knew.'

Pictures of a bespectacled, smartly attired Cliff standing up to be counted as a Christian at the Billy Graham rally inevitably made headlines in the newspapers next day. 'He looked like a bank manager,' said Bruce Welch. 'He had the horn-rimmed glasses, the suit and tie. He was professing to be a rock 'n' roll star but he didn't look like a rock 'n' roll star.

'To declare yourself a Christian in 1966 was the most unfashionable, the most daring, courageous, brave act you could imagine. You could have said that the world was flat and people would have had more time for you. We thought: that's his career down the pan. But it made him bigger and bigger.'

Bruce's fears for Cliff's future as a pop singer were well founded. Professing a deep religious commitment was anything but trendy at a time when London was swinging, the Pill was encouraging a permissive society, Mary Quant had introduced the mini-skirt, John Lennon was claiming The Beatles were more popular than Christ, and a series called *All Gas and Gaiters* had hit the screen as one of the first TV comedies to allow laughs at the expense of the Church.

Cliff had not taken his decision to speak out lightly, however, and he quickly clarified to the press how it came about: 'Someone suggested it's sissy to proclaim your Christian beliefs, but I don't think it is. I feel great all the time and know it is because of my beliefs. I've felt this way for two years now and it has relieved me of the petty jealousy one gets in showbusiness and helped me to help others.

'I did a Billy Graham study course of about five weeks and found it stimulating. Then I had a letter asking me if I would speak at a meeting.'

Cliff admitted he was a bundle of nerves when it came to the crunch at Earls Court. 'I was petrified,' he said. 'There was a desk in front of me and I put my arms on it as I spoke. Then, when I sang, I put my arms to my sides and had terrible pins and needles. I tried to raise my arms to emphasise the words in the song, but I couldn't, and at the end I walked off with my arms still pinned to my sides. When I sat down I was so scared, so emotional, I couldn't even bend my arms.

'It took me a long, long time to pluck up enough courage to tell the world: "I'm a Christian." But when I did, I knew I had scored. Now I can make something of my life.'

For Cliff Richard's millions of fans there was essentially only one question they all wanted answering: did this mean the end of his career as a pop singer? At first it appeared he was indeed preparing to turn his back on showbusiness and totally devote all his time and energies to Christianity. In view of a number of contracts he had already signed and was therefore committed to, his swansong was likely to take some time. But Cliff seemed deadly serious about quitting.

'It did cause a few problems,' Cliff explained, 'because I kept thinking to myself: well, all my friends who were Christians were not in showbusiness and they were heavily involved in Christian things like teaching and school and they were totally involved in their beliefs and I thought I am going to have to give up singing.

'I started making plans to stop, although I hadn't planned to give it up immediately. But the first time I made it public at that point, I didn't know what it would mean. I got up on the Billy Graham platform in 1966 and told the press and I was blinded by flashbulbs from the amount of photographs they took. Then people said to me: "You could lose a lot of fans."

'I planned to give up showbusiness completely. I said to my manager: "I want to get out," which was a bit of a shaker for him, but he accepted it. He just said: "All right." I went to see if I could get a place in teacher training college and I took an O level in religious instruction.'

Cliff took the O level exam in secret in Lewes, Sussex. He was ushered into a room on his own and several schoolmasters took it in turns to preside over the famous examinee to watch that he didn't cheat. 'Imagine me cheating while doing a religious exam!' Cliff laughed.

However well intentioned Cliff was at the time, not everybody believed he could abandon showbusiness altogether. Tellingly, Hank Marvin declared: 'I think he'll continue to make records and TV shows and do some appearances on stage, because I think he basically needs showbusiness, it's part of him. He needs an aura of adulation around him at times, and for that reason I don't really believe he'll give up singing.'

Within weeks, *Melody Maker* informed its readers: 'Cliff will be studying in his spare time. He won't be giving up pop and he still has contracts he's committed to for many years.'

Confusion over Cliff's future was inevitable, especially when Cliff's fan club, which numbered 42,000, announced it would be closing down. Even after it was made very clear in a press conference that Cliff was giving up showbusiness, his loyal fans refused to believe he would simply cease to sing, and they urged him to continue his showbiz career alongside his Christian activities.

A fan called Mary Clifford even set about organising a 'Stay in Showbiz, Cliff' campaign. By the end of 1966 she had managed to collect 19,000 signatures for a petition, which was handed in to Cliff at the Palladium, where he was topping the bill and compering live the first *Sunday Night at the London Palladium* show of the new season.

The petition appeared to have been in vain when it was announced in November that Cliff was unlikely to make any personal appearances in 1967, save for the odd summer concert.

And in an interview with the *New Musical Express*, Cliff stressed: 'I'm not being self-righteous. I just want to get out of this business because I feel I have to ... Don't think I regard everybody in showbusiness as sinful. I love the atmosphere and the life. If I didn't want to teach religious instruction in a secondary school, I'd stay in it till Doomsday. When I give up this life, it's not going to be a complete break; I don't think people realise I'll still be making records. I just want to be an ordinary teacher in an ordinary secondary school. I don't care if some people think I'm a phoney, they're entitled to their opinions.'

Around the time Cliff was stating he wanted to be an ordinary teacher in an ordinary secondary school, he was packing in the crowds in the pantomime *Cinderella* and enjoying a big hit from the show with 'In the Country'. Cliff commented: 'In July I made my pronouncement to the world and then in the December we broke all box-office records and I thought to myself: well, maybe the fans don't mind.'

By January 1967, Cliff had reached a compromise with himself and felt able to go on the BBC Light Programme's (the radio station that was replaced by Radios 1 and 2 in 1967) religious show *Five to Ten* to say: 'I've found I can mix both my Christian life and my showbiz life because I treat my showbiz life as, we are biblically told, a job that we're going to give to God.

'It was a bit embarrassing because I had called the press together and said I was leaving. I then had to call them back together six months later and say I am not leaving. You can imagine they had a bit of a field day, saying things like: "We knew he couldn't do it." I am sure it was the right step to take. I realised I could stay involved with my beliefs.'

The catalyst for his momentous decision to carry on in showbusiness was the offer of a film role in *Two a Penny*, a £150,000 movie to be made and funded by the Billy Graham Organisation. 'They wanted a Christian with film experience and that rather whittled it down to me,' Cliff recalled. 'So I did the film, and while I was doing it I thought: wait a minute, here am I thinking I can't be involved in showbiz, and yet I am involved. This very film is total artistic involvement as an artist because I am a Christian.'

In *Two a Penny*, Cliff plays a conniving, money-grabbing, drug-dealing, wayward art-school layabout called Jamie Hopkins. Jamie also happens to be so randy that when his similarly unscrupulous, but sexually shy girlfriend Carol, played by Ann Holloway, refuses to put out, he nearly rapes her in the bushes before rounding on her to complain: 'Sex is natural when two people are supposed to be in love.'

For newly committed Christian Cliff, the role of Jamie was certainly casting against type, but he was anxious not to play the nice boy who goes on to be converted at a Billy Graham crusade in the film's finale. Instead, it was left to amoral Carol to find spiritual redemption at one of Graham's religious meetings and eventually persuade her boyfriend Jamie to mend his ways.

Naturally, it was not easy for Cliff to play the bad guy but, because the film gained only a very limited release, few of his fans saw him as hateful Jamie. Cliff was, of course, anxious to appear in Billy Graham's film for nothing, but union regulations dictated he must be paid a fee of £40 a week – a fee he promptly returned to the Billy Graham Organisation.

Two a Penny, with Dora Bryan playing Cliff's mum and Avril Angers as a sexually predatory former showgirl, may not rank among Cliff's finest movie vehicles, but at least he proved to himself that he could carry on as an entertainer and still pursue his Christian beliefs. The film afforded Cliff the chance to sing, and among his numbers were 'Twist And Shout', The

Isley Brothers' favourite that had recently been enjoying new popularity thanks to versions by The Beatles and by Brian Poole and The Tremeloes.

'*Two a Penny* was closely followed by an offer of six religious television programmes,' said Cliff, 'and that was the first intimation I had that I could make use of the media. It became apparent to me that God was saying: "This is the way you must go."'

It took fully seven years before all Cliff's doubts vanished completely about whether he had made the right choice to continue with his career. Complete vindication came only after Cliff went to Bangladesh in a bid to help the Evangelical Alliance Relief Fund (TEAR Fund), a leading relief and development charity that works in partnership with Christian agencies and churches worldwide to tackle the causes and effects of poverty.

'In 1973 I stopped feeling guilty,' he explained. 'It was then that I went to Bangladesh and spoke to some nurses there who were being supported by the TEAR Fund. I wanted to be there to help them, but a nurse turned to me and said: "Can you give an injection? If you can't, you're no use to us here." My job, I discovered, was to raise money for them.

'I'm grateful for what I've got. Gratitude is a much greater motivator than guilt. I give to charity through tithing, donating a tenth of my money. I don't believe that I should feel guilty. I should feel grateful and give back.'

Just two days after Cliff's dramatic announcement at Earls Court, Cliff's mother quietly married for the second time – to Derek Bodkin, the former chauffeur Cliff had provided for her four years earlier. Derek had not worked for the Webbs since the death of Cliff's father, but he had remained a friend of the family and especially close to Dorothy. Derek was only 24, one year younger than Cliff, when he and Dorothy wed, and news of his marriage to a 45-year-old mother of four inevitably raised eyebrows.

The wedding took place at Epping register office, and the first Cliff got to know of it was when he received a call at Pinewood Studios from his mother from a public telephone box in Epping inviting him to the reception at Rookswood.

At the time, Cliff was filming *Finders Keepers* and the movie was on schedule enough for Cliff to get away from the set to join in the wedding celebrations. After the chaos at her daughter Donna's wedding, Dorothy had been determined her own wedding should be kept low key and had told as few people as possible about her big day.

Cliff made it back to Rookswood in time to take photographs of the happy newly-weds on the lawn and wave them off on honeymoon, for which Cliff made his white E-type Jaguar available. Although the wedding took Cliff by surprise, he knew that his mother's relationship with Bodkin was heading that way. 'At first I was rather shocked, but I'd known Derek for a few years and, after all, my mother's happy. So who cares?' he said. 'It's her life. I hope she and Derek – I can't call him Dad – will be very happy.'

Cliff immediately arranged for his mother and Derek to honeymoon at a villa he had bought in Portugal and he promised the newly-weds he would buy them a new home as a wedding present.

'My sisters and I naturally want our mother to build a happy life,' he said. 'So I shall buy them a house of their own in Essex, not far from where we live now.' True to his word, Cliff bought them a modern detached house, not in Essex, but in Broxbourne, Hertfordshire. He also bought two more houses in Broxbourne, one for his sister Jackie and another for an aunt so they could all live close by each other.

Once Dorothy had moved out of Rookswood, the old house was never the same again for Cliff. Donna had married and departed and now, with his mother living elsewhere and sister Jackie also on the point of marrying, the vast mansion was home to just Cliff and Joan, who was still a schoolgirl. It seemed pointless for just the two of them to rattle around in a home where many of the rooms were never used, and Cliff very quickly made up his mind to sell it. Within three weeks of his mother's remarriage, Rookswood was sold for £43,000, a handsome return in two years on his original investment of more than £30,000.

The speed of the sale left Cliff homeless for a short while, but he was able to continue staying for four months with Bill

Latham and Bill's mother, Mamie, at their home in Finchley. This arrangement was such a success that together they then bought a small detached Georgian house in Northcliffe Drive, Totteridge, north London, before moving to a fabulous new £70,000 home in the prized St George's Hill estate in Weybridge, Surrey.

Mindful that moving south was said not to suit north Londoners, Cliff was at first reluctant to go and look over a house in St George's Hill while still living in Totteridge. Finally, he agreed to travel to Weybridge for lunch and was persuaded to take a look at a fabulous house on an estate built around a golf course with private roads and lush woodland.

To buy it, Cliff would need to find just £4,000 more than he would get from the sale of his Totteridge home. The obvious attractions of a swimming pool and an acre of ground made his mind up for him. Much later, in 1989, he bought a house he liked even better on the same estate, which also had a tennis court and a swimming pool. As a typical Cliff touch, he installed a jukebox in the changing room by the pool and stocked it with a wealth of golden oldies, including records by Elvis, The Shadows and even some of his own.

Cliff found the Weybridge location ideal. The house was set in enough grounds for him to enjoy its beautiful garden and walk his dogs, while it only took 45 minutes to get into London. In time he also set up offices in nearby Claygate.

Bill's close and long-lasting friendship with Cliff inevitably prompted malicious gossip that there was more to their relationship than met the eye. But in a rare newspaper interview when Cliff was two years short of his fiftieth birthday, Bill told the *Daily Express*: 'The homosexual innuendoes are bound to happen. Cliff is single. He is middle-aged. We have lived together in what I will tell you is a perfectly natural friendship situation. But I can understand that some people put two and two together and make five.'

He added: 'The press have always been convinced that there's some sort of closet side of life which they have always been frustrated in finding out. I know it does not exist. I also genuinely have never known why they think it should.'

At the end of 1967, Cliff was able to look back on a year of startling changes but one in which he had established to his own satisfaction and in the minds of his fans that he could be both a Christian and an entertainer.

The year had seen him chalk up three more Top Ten hits – 'It's All Over', 'The Day I Met Marie', one of Hank Marvin's best compositions, and 'All My Love', Cliff's fortieth single. And two weeks before Christmas, Cliff was confirmed by the Bishop of Willesden, Graham Leonard, at St Paul's Church, Finchley, in north London.

Significantly, although the song was written by Hank, The Shadows were not featured on the recording of 'The Day I Met Marie'. Cliff has always considered this to be one of his best records, and a favourite because he felt he was progressing towards a real production sound with the use of a gentle, soft-gut guitar intro and a strident brass and circus sound in the middle.

It was very different from anything he had recorded before and he was acutely aware of the difference. He has said that this departure from the norm made life a lot easier for him when The Shadows eventually broke up. 'I didn't have that panic, which I might have had, if I'd only ever used only them. When they did break up, I didn't feel the jolt as I might have done.'

14. MIDDLE MUSIC

You started as a recording star. It's all very well to be a film star and a radio star, an evangelist and this, that and the other, but you seem to have lost the interest to be a recording star. But that's how you made your name.

Bruce Welch

Along with just about everyone else in the music business, Cliff Richard took hardly any notice in October 1962 when 'Love Me Do', a debut single by an unknown group from Liverpool, slipped into the UK Top Twenty. *The Young Ones* was still in the final editing stages and Cliff was much in demand and deeply absorbed in keeping his finger on the many pulses of his astonishing, multi-faceted career.

'Love Me Do' was a promising enough first record but it was not ground-breaking enough to suggest to Cliff, or anyone else outside of Merseyside, that The Beatles were likely to pose any great threat to his position as Britain's top pop attraction. 'I never dreamed that The Beatles would be such a success,' he's admitted, 'especially with a name like that. It made me think of insects and I was sure they would have to change their name to get on.

'One of my fondest memories of The Beatles is that whenever I went on tour in those days, in places like South Africa and Australia, the radio stations would ask for my favourite record.

I could never think of one at the time and then I heard "Love Me Do". I really liked that, so I chose it as my favourite. I took "Love Me Do" with me to South Africa and every time they asked me if they could play a record for me I'd say, "Yes please," and hand them "Love Me Do". I'm sure it didn't help their career at all, but I always think I had a part in their success in South Africa.'

Even when Beatlemania was at its peak and the guitar-driven Mersey sound was all the rage, Cliff still managed to hold his own against the proliferation of groups who dominated the charts. There is a general perception that the Fab Four swamped the old guard and that singers like Cliff were temporarily pushed out of the pop picture completely. Cliff said, 'People think we were snowed under by The Beatles. But I never thought we were. People forget what everybody else was doing because of all the media attention heaped upon The Beatles.

'There's no doubt that The Beatles took pop music into another realm. It had to happen. Someone had to do it, and they did it. It couldn't have been us because we started too early. But we were pioneers, and they came after the pioneers, built upon that foundation and took it soaring away.

'It's amazing how things seem to have five-year cycles. We started in 1958, and almost to the day five years later you get a new group coming up who get a reaction similar to what we got. And they sort of took over, but we were still touring and selling out and the records were still in the Top Ten.'

While EMI's creative genius of a producer George Martin was helping The Beatles scale ever more innovative musical heights in the studio, EMI's Norrie Paramor was also, in his own way, without Martin's inventive approach, trying to steer Cliff out of his comfort zone towards more expansive material.

Under Norrie's aegis, Cliff began quietly progressing in the recording studio, experimenting, for example, with the use of acoustics and Hank playing one of the first electric twelve-string guitars on Cliff's Top Ten hit 'I'm the Lonely One' in 1964.

Bruce Welch and Hank Marvin continued to come up with prolific hit material for Cliff, but manager Peter Gormley and

Norrie Paramor nevertheless kept encouraging Cliff to widen his musical horizons. In the spring of 1964 when The Beatles were enjoying their fourth number-one hit, 'Can't Buy Me Love' from their first film *A Hard Day's Night*, Cliff was at number four in the charts with 'Constantly', an Italian ballad Norrie had found for him.

Cliff acknowledged, 'By this time I was thinking of having a career that was more than just as a rock 'n' roll singer. In my mind there was no reason why I shouldn't stay around. I had gone past the deathly five-year period. I knew I wasn't going to be suddenly disappearing. So to do "Constantly" and other ballads like "The Twelfth of Never" was a natural progression in my career.

'"The Twelfth of Never" was a Johnny Mathis song and again it was Norrie who suggested I record it. I just thought it was an absolutely fantastic song. It was natural for me as an artist to want to get into things which were really quite different. I feel if I hadn't done those, I could never have recorded "Miss You Nights" . . . It's a whole different style of singing.'

In a further effort to spread his wings musically when Beatlemania was at its peak, Cliff flew to Nashville, the home of country music in America, to lay down some new tracks. Cliff remembers that he did not get off to the best of starts in the studio. 'Being terribly British, I asked the guy there: "How far away from the mic should I be?" and he said: "You're the goddam singer. Just sing, and I'll do the rest." It was a dreadful putdown and I was terribly nervous and scared. But it was great.'

Cliff was thrilled to be recording in the same studios that Elvis had used and felt privileged that his backing for the sessions was provided by members of Elvis's legendary vocal back-up group, The Jordanaires.

Among the Nashville tracks Cliff cut was 'The Minute You're Gone', which became a number-one hit in the UK in 1965, and 'Wind Me Up (Let Me Go)', which reached number two the same year. Now that The Beatles had led the way in opening up the American market for British groups and singers,

Cliff naturally had high hopes for 'The Minute You're Gone' in the US. But once again they were quickly dashed.

'I'd thought now that I'd made number one smack in the middle of The Beatles period, that's all it took,' he said. 'At that period anyone who was number one over here made the Top Ten or the Top Twenty over there. But my company didn't even release it in America,' Cliff revealed with undisguised disappointment. 'They said: "Oh no, it's a B-side. It's not suitable for our market." That whole American scene dogged me for years.'

Significantly, 'The Minute You're Gone' was Cliff's first UK chart-topper without The Shadows. For some time, Norrie Paramor had begun to make use of orchestras on Cliff's records. Songs such as 'Constantly' had required strings and a rhythm section rather than strident guitars, and although there was no real split as such, Cliff gradually began making more and more records without The Shadows – even if he was still recording songs they had penned.

Despite the absence of The Shadows when it came to recording sessions, Cliff continued to tour with them as his backing group. In concert, when it came to Cliff's ballads, The Shadows proved perfectly adept at providing the appropriate backing to present to a live audience.

'It was a gradual separation,' said Bruce Welch. 'It wasn't a case of "you're not going to play on my records any more". Everyone thinks there was a tremendous big split in the middle of the '60s. But there was no sort of argument.'

Hank Marvin agreed: 'It got to a stage where we were doing less and less together, and eventually, in 1968, The Shadows virtually broke up. This was not Cliff and The Shadows, this was just that The Shadows ceased to exist as a working band, so it wasn't possible, even if we had wanted it, for Cliff and The Shadows to work together. There was never a break-up as such.'

Cliff's final single featuring The Shadows was 'Don't Forget to Catch Me' from the album *Established 1958*, made to celebrate ten years at the top.

Despite a blip in the summer of 1965 when 'The Time in Between' became Cliff's first single not to reach the UK Top

Twenty, the hits steadily kept coming, including a cover of a Rolling Stones song 'Blue Turns to Grey'. So it was a considerable surprise for many in the music business when the BBC announced that Cliff Richard had been chosen to sing for Britain in the 1968 Eurovision Song Contest.

Much ridiculed as a contest in which Norway always seemed to garner 'Nil points', it appeared to many that Eurovision was beneath a singer of Cliff's calibre to enter: the songs were mediocre at best, and the voting was politically tactical. The sceptics felt that Cliff was on a hiding to nothing. If he won, then it was only to be expected, given his international popularity, and if he lost then it would be a serious slap in the face for such an established star with a successful track record.

Cliff saw it otherwise. After lengthy discussions of the pros and cons with Peter Gormley, they both chose to regard Eurovision not as a potential banana skin, but as a golden opportunity not to be missed.

There was method in their apparent madness. The 1968 contest, thanks to Sandie Shaw's Eurovision win with 'Puppet on a String' the year before, would be staged in England at the Royal Albert Hall in London, thereby guaranteeing enormous home interest in the event and in Cliff's performance in particular. Whichever song was chosen for Cliff to sing would inevitably give him a UK best-selling record and quite probably an international hit as well.

The format for finding Britain's song for Europe involved the BBC inviting songwriters to submit their compositions. A panel then whittled down the entries to half a dozen for Cliff to sing in turn to a TV audience. The public then voted to determine the winning song to represent the UK. It was certainly one way for Cliff to attract the pick of any new songs on offer. 'We were confident we could find one song that would be our next record anyway, and have the bonus of two hundred million people watching it on Eurovision,' said Cliff, explaining why he was so keen to take part. The chance to perform to such a vast audience in seventeen different countries was enticing.

Among the final six contenders for the song to represent the UK were compositions by such notables in the pop music world as Mike Leander, Tony Hazzard, and the songwriting duo of Bill Martin and Phil Coulter, who had written Sandie Shaw's 1967 Eurovision winner. Cliff sang all six in turn on the BBC's *The Cilla Black Show*, and on 12 March, 250,000 votes came in from viewers, of which 171,000 nominated Martin and Coulter's cheerful, back-slapping sing-along number, 'Congratulations'.

The universal celebratory appeal of the lyrics and its catchy tune made 'Congratulations' the hot favourite to win when the contest was staged on 6 April. And right up to the closing moments, it appeared that Cliff would indeed triumph, until Germany contrived to award six points to Spain's entry, 'La La La', by a female singer called Massiel, thereby bringing Spain's total up to 29 and pipping Cliff by just one point.

The result came as such a shock to everyone that even the normally unflustered presenter Katie Boyle, in charge of the vote collection from the various foreign delegations, was moved to have a recount.

Cliff was desperately disappointed, and the result still rankles today. 'We was robbed, absolutely robbed,' he said in 2006, 38 years after the event. 'Had Ireland and Yugoslavia given me one point each, I'd have won by one point. I lost to a girl who sang "La La La", which is not remembered that well today, except by me. It's burned into my memory.'

The huge consolation for Cliff was that 'Congratulations' became his first number-one UK hit for three years and earned him his first gold disc for five years. It soon achieved sales of over a million, and 56 versions in various languages were hurriedly released around the world. Bill Martin commented: 'The ironic thing is that Germany, whose votes lost us the contest, placed an order for 150,000!'

Cliff had the satisfaction of 'Congratulations' comfortably outselling Massiel's winner across Europe. The record eventually proved to be his biggest worldwide seller up to that point and it even crept into the American Hot Hundred. But, with rival cover versions by two seasoned American solo singers, Perry Como and Bobby Vinton, competing for sales, Cliff's 'Congratulations' was once again not the hoped-for success in America.

'It just won't happen for me there, and I won't change my career to make it,' Cliff stated while 'Congratulations' was topping the charts in Britain, Belgium, Denmark, Holland, Sweden and Norway and in the Top Ten in New Zealand, Germany, Spain and France.

Despite American apathy, Cliff's 'Congratulations', still a favourite at football grounds and at any sort of a celebration, remains one of the biggest international hits in the history of the Eurovision Song Contest.

It was an important chart-topper for Cliff in every way, coming as it did at a time when the likes of The Beatles, The Rolling Stones, and Jimi Hendrix were holding musical sway, and Tom Jones and Engelbert Humperdinck were challenging Cliff for the title of Britain's leading solo male singer. 'Congratulations', moreover, proved Cliff's continuing ability to have a massive mainstream hit at a time when he was also going off on gospel-folk singing tours with The Settlers.

Cliff's participation was indisputably a timely boost for the Eurovision Song Contest. Since its inception, Eurovision had been stigmatised by the poor quality of songs and oddball, often strangely attired performers singing unfathomable words for international juries, whose voting was frequently utterly illogical or blatantly biased.

A singer of Cliff's stature gave the contest some much needed credibility, and Cliff went on to represent Britain again five years later, in 1973, this time at the Nouveau Theatre in Luxembourg, singing 'Power to all our Friends'. An audience of more than three hundred million people in 32 countries watched him come third.

In the run-up to the contest, 'Power to all our Friends', Cliff's fifty-ninth single, took the singer into the UK Top Ten for the first time for three years and sold well all over Europe – vindication again of his willingness to embrace a competition so frequently ridiculed. But, once again, America failed to embrace Cliff's European success. Cliff himself pointed out that four different record labels and seven appearances on *The Ed Sullivan Show* had failed to help him make an impact of any real note.

As for the Eurovision Song Contest, Cliff remained philosophical. 'I've done it twice and lost both times and still sold over one million copies of both songs. And that's the only way to look at it,' Cliff consoled himself after he failed to win for a second time.

'Power to all our Friends' was Cliff's first hit with a new record producer, David Mackay. After nearly fifteen years of almost unbroken success as Cliff's producer, Norrie Paramor decided he had taken Cliff as far as he could. Norrie was keen to move to Birmingham to become conductor of the BBC Midland Radio Orchestra and suggested a new producer with a different approach would be good for Cliff anyway.

In truth, Cliff was starting to feel the same way. Norrie had been finding it increasingly difficult to come up with fresh and new top-quality material for Cliff. Cliff, for his part, felt he wasn't getting the kind of songs he wanted to record. He would receive a little note from Norrie attached to the demo of 'Goodbye Sam, Hello Samantha', for example, which read: 'This is just right for Cliff.' But although the record became a Top Ten hit in 1970, it wasn't the way Cliff wanted to go musically.

Explaining the break with Cliff, Norrie simply said he was getting older and that Cliff needed a younger producer. 'He obviously wants to get a younger image and keep it,' said Norrie. 'It was time to say: "Thanks very much, Cliff, for having me as your producer for many years. I've enjoyed it and I hope you have." He definitely needs a young approach.'

After Dave Mackay produced '(You Keep Me) Hangin' On' in 1974, which reached number thirteen in the charts, Cliff went through the whole of 1975 without a single hit. Having averaged three and sometimes four hits a year since he burst on to the scene, it was an unwelcome lull, but wholly understandable, since Cliff recorded nothing that year and 'Honky Tonk Angel', the only single released, was withdrawn at Cliff's own instigation amid much controversy.

'Honky Tonk Angel', a country-and-western song Bruce Welch had found for Cliff in America, was regarded by the record industry as a fine comeback single for Cliff after a disappointing year in terms of hits in 1973 and just one chart entry in 1974. The new song seemed destined to be a big hit. But it was never to be, thanks to Cliff being totally unaware that 'honky-tonk angel' was an American slang term for a hooker.

Bruce Welch, who co-produced the single with Hank Marvin, explained: 'One of Cliff's Christian friends said to him: "Cliff, how can you sing a song about a subject like this?" And he said: "A subject like what?" He rang the American Embassy and asked: 'Can you tell me what honky-tonk angel means?" And they said: "It's a woman of low repute, sir."

'Obviously we all knew what it meant, and all that mattered to me was that it was a great song. But Cliff was true to his beliefs and he went on TV and said he was withdrawing the record.'

Thereafter Cliff refused to promote the single, thus allowing it to fade quietly away after the initial headlines in the press. Cliff's refusal to support his latest single came as a shock to everyone in the industry, not least to EMI's head of promotion at the time, Eric Hall, who had lined up 'Honky Tonk Angel' as Noel Edmonds's record of the week on the Radio 1 DJ's show, further promotion on *Top of the Pops* and on Mike Mansfield's hugely popular ITV pop show, *Supersonic*. In addition, he had booked Cliff in to sing the song on Russell Harty's chat show. 'I had all these wonderful shows,' said Eric, and then I was told: "We can't do it." Are you mad? It was obvious it was about a hooker.'

Cliff did appear on Russell Harty's show, but mainly to explain why he would not be singing his latest single. He said of 'Honky Tonk Angel': 'It's not exactly a prostitute, but there are bars where they play honky-tonk piano and there are certain ladies that frequent the bar, good-time girls as someone put it. And I thought: well if it is going to upset a minority, but usually a large minority, then I'll show them that I don't have to do it.'

The fiasco was a bitter disappointment for Bruce Welch: 'As a producer you find the material, book the musicians, do the sessions, get all the performances – if it's a hit it's the artist, if it's a flop it's the producer's fault.

'I thought "Honky Tonk Angel" was a good song, and a few years ago, when EMI put out a box set of Cliff's singles, I played "Honky Tonk Angel" and listened to it for the first time for nearly thirty years. Then I rang Cliff and said: "Have you listened to Honky Tonk Angel? What a great record it is, what a great vocal performance from you, the backing vocals, all of it." He said: "Yes you're right, it's a great record."'

If 'Honky Tonk Angel' was Cliff's only single of 1975, Cliff himself believed, in retrospect, it was a necessary fallow recording period in which he and musical associates around him could search for songs that were a cut above the pleasant but largely unremarkable numbers he had been putting out on record.

When the time came to make another album after this respite, Cliff's manager Peter Gormley threw down a challenge to the music industry. He declared that whoever came up with the best songs should be given the opportunity of producing the new album. It was an opportunity that one-time Shadow Bruce Welch seized with both hands.

As a record producer, Bruce's experience was strictly limited to tracks by Olivia Newton-John, a beautiful young Aussie singer who was making a name for herself in Britain. But having worked with Cliff for so long, Bruce believed he had an advantage in that he knew exactly where Cliff's recording career had been going wrong and, just as importantly, as a good friend he also had the courage and conviction to tell him to his face. Never one to beat around the bush during their long friendship, Bruce was always able to say what he thought.

'I felt Cliff wasn't concentrating on his music,' said Bruce. 'He was concentrating on his religious life as his main outlet for everything and dabbling with music. I don't think he was taking as much care of his records as perhaps he should have done. Some of the songs were a little bland, I thought.'

Cliff has since admitted as much: 'What happened was that I became incredibly focused on my faith. I let go a little of the reins of my career. I was much happier to just turn up at the studio and put my voice on to a track that was already pre-recorded and in a way that probably showed a little in sales.'

Bruce said: 'When the opportunity came up from Peter Gormley, I went looking for numbers that would stretch his vocal talent.' All those years of sitting around harmonising with Cliff or trying out different songs on tour buses or in hotel rooms had given Bruce a clear idea of just what Cliff could achieve vocally. He said, 'I knew what Cliff's voice could do, if he had the material – for instance, singing in falsetto or stretching his vocal chords, which at the time he tended not to do.

'So I started looking for songs. I asked all my mates here in England, all the publishers and all the top songwriters. I finished up in Los Angeles, and there was a mate of mine, Lionel Conway, who ran Island Music, and in his office he played two or three numbers to me on cassettes, as they were in those days.

'I wasn't sure about them and didn't want to upset Lionel, so I asked if I could take them back and listen to them again when I returned to England. Once I was back home I listened to the three numbers and didn't like any of them. Then I just happened to flip one of the cassettes over and a song called "Miss You Nights" was on the other side. Lionel hadn't played it to me. I had found the most fantastic song – by default. It was such a great contemporary ballad, with a magnificent lyric.

'When I first heard it, shivers went down my spine – and you very, very rarely get a song that does that to you. So I rang Peter Gormley and went down to his home in Weybridge and played it to him. He loved it too.'

Taking up the story, Cliff recalled: 'When Bruce first played it to me, he came to my home and I have this balcony with big sliding doors, and it was a beautiful day and we both leaned on the rail looking out at the greenery. And halfway through the song I said: "Look at my arms," and he said: "Look at *my* arms," and all the hairs on our arms were standing up on end. It was goosebump time magnified. "Miss You Nights" has been constantly a joy for me to sing over the years.'

Bruce also picked up on the potential of another song, 'Devil Woman' by Terry Britten, lead guitar player in Cliff's band, written while they were on tour. 'Cliff had heard it about a year before,' said Bruce, 'but no one had done anything with it. We had a recording session and the first three songs we did were "Miss You Nights", "Devil Woman" and "I Can't Ask for Anymore Than You".'

All three were destined to become huge hit singles for Cliff, and Peter Gormley was so impressed with the session and the quality of material Bruce had assembled that he told him to press ahead with an album – which evolved into the LP *I'm Nearly Famous*. 'Musically it was a rebirth for Cliff and it amazed the music business,' said Bruce. '"I Can't Ask for Anymore Than You" surprised everyone because it was in a high falsetto that Cliff had hardly ever used before.'

Bruce and Cliff discussed the musical direction to be taken, and they both agreed that this time Cliff would record nothing that sounded remotely like 'Congratulations', 'Summer Holiday', 'Living Doll' or 'Bachelor Boy'.

Right from the start of their collaboration, Cliff involved himself in the actual production of his records to a far greater extent than before. He had started showing an unusually marked interest in the whole process of recording while making his previous album, *The 31st of February Street*, produced by Dave Mackay. Cliff's interest was partly inspired by the fact that he had written five numbers himself for the album. 'Not many people bought it,' he admitted, 'but if they'd bought it they would have heard the beginnings of *I'm Nearly Famous*. It was a very laid-back album, perhaps too low key, but it was very different and perhaps part of my transitional period. I needed that year of change.'

Bruce detected a new enthusiasm from Cliff in the studio. 'From the word go Cliff was at the recording sessions helping to pick the numbers,' Bruce remembered of the sessions for *I'm Nearly Famous*. 'He even came to the track sessions, which he never did before. Before, he used to walk in and put his voice on when everything was finished.'

Cliff started warming up his throat as soon as he got up in the morning, before heading for the studio. But once in the studio, he found Bruce a stickler for tuning. 'I used to give him two or three goes at a song to warm his voice up,' Bruce said, 'and then I'd press the buzzer and say: "Cliff, can you please sing it in the same key as the backing track!"

'We were not scared of a good argument in the studios. It was a bit of a joke between us. Cliff would say: "I just want to try it this way, Bruce," and I'd say: "Try it your way and we'll do it mine. I'm in charge of production." It was a standing joke between us.'

One major disagreement between Bruce and Cliff was over the interpretation of the lyrics of "Devil Woman". The song contains a line about "neighbourhood strays", which Bruce interpreted as a reference to prostitutes, but which Cliff interpreted very differently.

'"Devil Woman" is a prime example of Cliff and I not agreeing on what it's about,' said Bruce. 'We're not talking about cats, not in this instance, but he's convinced we are. He's convinced we are warning about the occult and the dangers of the occult.'

Tony Rivers, then Cliff's vocal arranger, gave further insight into Cliff's naïvety in a TV interview: 'The song is talking about ladies wandering the streets. But, bless him, he didn't realise that. That's how naïve he is.

'We were at rehearsals once and we were all sitting around and there was a foot pedal that one of the guitar players had that made a flangey sort of sound. This pedal is called – wait for it – a big muff, Electric Lady's big muff. And Cliff said: "I've got a great idea for an album cover – my face super-imposed on this big muff." I said: "Cliff, you cannot possibly do that, it's the worst idea you've ever had. It'll sell, mind you!" And he went: "Oh no, that's not what it means, is it?"'

I'm Nearly Famous, with its three massive hit singles, rejuvenated Cliff's career. It put him back high in the album charts and gained him renewed respect within the music industry after years of mediocrity. He had regained his credibility courtesy of Bruce Welch.

The stunning single 'Miss You Nights' might have been an even bigger hit if it had been released after 'Devil Woman'. The latter was scheduled to be released first, but was held back so as not to be confused with ELO's 'Evil Woman'.

'Bruce's productions were fabulous,' Cliff reflected. 'I really enjoyed working with him, because the song is the beginning and end of everything.'

Terry Britten's 'Devil Woman' also earned Cliff, at long last, a placing in the American Top Ten singles chart, the record eventually peaking at number five. News of this longed-for US success was a moment to savour and Cliff remembers clearly where he was and how the news was relayed to him. 'We were doing a concert tour of the East and on the last night in Hong Kong, Bruce Welch was in the band and while I was talking into the mic to introduce a song, he just came over to me and whispered: "Eighteen with a bullet."

'It was that phraseology that he used and I knew exactly what he meant. There's only one country in the world that uses bullets and I knew we had made it in the States.' (In the US, the music industry uses the word bullet to describe a record that is shooting up the charts.)

Bruce remembered: 'I got a message from the wings to say "Devil Woman" was a big hit, so I just wandered across the stage to Cliff and told him. He could hardly believe it.'

Cliff added: 'Of course, I didn't think it was going to get to number five in America. I didn't think we were going to get a gold disc out of it either. It sold about a million and a half copies.

'Now, if I was asked to leave something behind or if, for instance, somebody came from outer space and wanted to know what I did for a living, I'd be tempted to play them "Devil Woman".'

Elton John, a fan since his mother took him to see Cliff in panto when he was a small boy, takes a great deal of credit for breaking Cliff in the States. 'Devil Woman' was issued on Elton's Rocket Records label in America and he was a prime mover behind its release and promotion.

Elton instantly took to Cliff from the first moment they met in Australia. The Rocket Man, who affectionately calls his great pal Rod Stewart 'Phyllis', quickly took to calling Cliff either 'Sylvia Disc' or the 'Bionic Christian'. 'I thought he would be quite conservative because of his religious views,' said

Elton of their first meeting. 'But when I actually met him, we stayed up drinking until six in the morning together and we were absolutely legless!' Cliff has said he has been drunk only three times in his life and this was clearly one of those occasions.

Some time later, Cliff flew by Concorde to New York for a lavish launch party for RCA and Rocket Records at the then highly fashionable nightclub Studio 54, a legendary discotheque famed for its decadent hedonism and glitzy clientele – a scantily dressed Bianca Jagger once made a spectacular entrance at the club seated on a white horse.

Cliff said of the party: 'They had some of the most weird and wonderful people, but mostly weird. I thought: well, there are many Christians in the world who would think I shouldn't be here, but I don't know. I don't necessarily agree with some of these people's lifestyles, but I did see some weird things and some people who are at the different end from me spiritually.

'What disturbed me was that they sniff things and smoke things. The funny thing was that I lasted longer than any of them. Someone handed me a bottle to have a sniff at and I thought: there's me sweating and freaking out after three hours, I don't need a bottle. I just needed a bass and drums. They kept having to rest, but I was still dancing away after five hours. I had a great time. I loved it.'

After the success of *I'm Nearly Famous*, Bruce Welch produced two further albums for Cliff – *Every Face Tells a Story* and *Green Light*, both of which yielded a clutch of hit singles.

On the back of three hit albums in a row, Bruce then set about seeking out more new songs for Cliff's next album, only to discover from a chance remark by an engineer at Abbey Road Studios that Cliff had discarded him. Bruce learned that Cliff was off to Paris to make a new album – without him. Cliff's collaborator this time, he discovered, would be Terry Britten.

Bruce was far too worldly to expect that he would be Cliff Richard's record producer for life. But he was hurt and livid that neither Cliff nor Peter Gormley who, after all, was manager to them both, had not told him to his face that they wished to move on and try a new approach with a new producer.

'It's all water under the bridge now,' Bruce told the authors of this book. 'I think Cliff has said he doesn't like confrontation. But I'm the opposite, and I had words with Cliff. I was fuming, furious, and I told him so.'

Despite the bad feeling at the time, Bruce did not hold a grudge, and before long he had got hold of yet another song which he knew would be ideal for Cliff to record and had no hesitation in offering it to him. He came across 'We Don't Talk Anymore' written by Alan Tarney, one of the musicians who had worked on *I'm Nearly Famous*. Bruce heard the song for the first time while he and Tarney were co-producing a British female singer, Charlie Dore.

Bruce recognised 'We Don't Talk Anymore' as a potential monster hit and felt it was tailormade for Cliff. He immediately rang Peter Gormley to express his excitement, but stressed that if Cliff wanted to record it then the proviso was that he, Bruce Welch, would be the producer.

Cliff proved to be as enthusiastic as Bruce about the song. It was recorded in June 1979 and the following month it was number one in the UK charts – Cliff's first chart-topper since 'Congratulations' eleven years before. It also became Cliff's best-selling single ever, notching up sales of over five million around the world, and gave Cliff another Top Ten hit in America.

Ironically, after much internal argument within the record company, the Bruce Welch-produced track 'We Don't Talk Anymore' was included on the Terry Britten-produced album *Rock 'n' Roll Juvenile* – spearheading the LP for which Bruce had been overlooked.

'The period with Bruce and with Terry Britten gave me a period when I was taken seriously as an album artist,' said a grateful Cliff. 'Those guys played such a major role in my life. I'm very grateful to them because they pushed me and pushed me.

'I must consider myself one of the most fortunate pop singers that ever existed to have someone like Alan Tarney write you songs like "We Don't Talk Anymore", when you know almost anybody else on the planet who sings would be able to do just as good a version of this or perhaps even a better one. This is my favourite of all the songs I've recorded, in terms of being a pop singer singing something that is so purely pop and wonderful.'

One area in which Cliff has regularly excelled down the years is the Christmas singles market, and in 2006 he would have had another seasonal number one with *21st Century Christmas*, but for Leona Lewis's spectacular debut after winning ITV's talent show *The X-Factor*.

While acknowledging his seasonal success, Cliff qualified it in a Radio 2 interview at the end of 2006 by saying: 'Everybody thinks of me as an artist who has Christmas hits, but in actual fact when you boil it down over almost fifty years of recording, I've only had two Christmas number ones and four other releases that were Christmas songs and a couple of other hits that were hits at Christmas, but were not Christmas songs.

'I do still look for Christmas songs, but it's harder for me now because I've had such great success with "Saviour's Day" and "Mistletoe and Wine". The song that I believe should have been number one but wasn't was "Little Town". That was the classic of all the Christmas songs I've ever done.'

The Cliff Richard Christmas hit that attracted more attention and controversy than any other was "Millennium Prayer", released in November 1999. Taken from a Christian musical called *Hope and Dreams*, it matches the words of the Lord's Prayer to the tune of 'Auld Lang Syne'. EMI, who had been Cliff's record label for 41 years at the time, rejected it. 'They said they didn't see it as a single,' Cliff said, 'so I took it to Papillon, who were thrilled.'

But to Cliff's intense disappointment, many major radio stations chose not even to include it in their playlists. Even Radio 2 decided it did not have broad enough appeal for its listeners, even though Cliff described 'Millennium Prayer' as 'a theme for us as a nation'.

The perception in the press was that the record was effectively banned. This caused a storm of controversy, fuelled by some churches urging their parishioners to buy it because they believed the Christian aspect of the millennium had been generally overlooked.

Despite the lack of airplay, 'Millennium Prayer' topped the charts and, coupled with the proceeds of a Cardiff concert, raised around a million pounds for the charity Children's Promise. It was also a big seller in various different countries around the world, reaching number two in New Zealand and number one in Australia.

'It was not the happiest hit I've ever had,' Cliff reflected with understatement. 'I couldn't believe the opposition to what was really just a prayer that was taught by Jesus, and a charity record to boot. Never mind, it sold one point four million in five weeks.'

'Millennium Prayer' represented another remarkable milestone in Cliff's recording career. When the record hit number one, it meant he had now enjoyed chart-topping hits in five consecutive decades.

15. THE EVENT

To me he's almost St Cliff, he's such a special person.

Jet Harris after Cliff asked his former bass guitarist to appear
with him in *The Event* at Wembley Stadium, 1989

It's a testimony to Cliff's remarkable staying power that the
end of each of the last three decades of the twentieth century
saw him provide an emphatic answer to anyone who dared to
wonder whether his popularity was on the wane. It was almost
as if Cliff deliberately targeted 1979, 1989 and 1999 as special
years of resurgence so that he could begin a new decade full of
confidence in his career.

Cliff began the 1970s as one of the BBC's top television stars.
His prime-time BBC 1 show *It's Cliff Richard* drew huge
audiences over the first thirteen weeks of the new decade. And
in 1979, twenty years and twenty-five days after his first
number-one hit, 'Living Doll', Cliff shot to the top of the charts
for the tenth time with 'We Don't Talk Anymore'.

It was his biggest-selling worldwide hit up to that point and,
piquantly, during its stay at the top, Norrie Paramor, the
producer who had done so much for Cliff's recording career,
passed away.

The massive chart-topping success of 'We Don't Talk Anymore' sparked a resurgence that saw Cliff begin the new decade

by taking 'Carrie' to number four in the charts in February 1980. He then proceeded to chalk up no less than six more Top Ten hits over the next four years. Included among them was Cliff's distinctive version of one of his all-time favourite songs – 'Daddy's Home' by Shep and The Limelites.

In 1980 Cliff turned forty, and on 23 July that year he and his mother arrived at Buckingham Palace in his Rolls-Royce to the sound of a crowd singing 'Congratulations' to collect an OBE. For the presentation in the white and gold palace ballroom, Cliff wore a black lounge suit set off by a red tie, bright red trainers and a rose in his buttonhole. 'I haven't got any morning dress,' he explained of his investiture outfit, 'so I thought I'd wear something colourful. I've been to the palace before and I knew there was a lot of red about the place.'

Ever since starring in pantomimes at the London Palladium back in the 1960s, Cliff had always harboured the thought that one day he would like to star in a West End musical. He saw a musical as a natural progression for his career, but only if the right vehicle presented itself. And in 1987 the opportunity to fulfil this long-held ambition came his way, courtesy of Dave Clark, former leader of 1960s pop group The Dave Clark Five.

Clark offered Cliff a starring role in *Time*, a spectacular sci-fi musical he was producing and staging in the West End with his own money. It would be an expensive production with a good pedigree – and Clark had also written a concept album to accompany the show, with tracks by Stevie Wonder, Julian Lennon, Freddie Mercury, Ashford and Simpson, Dionne Warwick, Burt Bacharach and Sir Laurence Olivier, as well as Cliff.

Time is essentially a morality tale in which planet Earth is tried at a celestial court for becoming a danger to the civilised universe. The defence for the misuse of Earth is in the hands of a pop singer, played by Cliff. The musical offers several messages that appealed to Cliff, and he readily committed to a year in the show. Among these messages are 'the answers are to be found in your heart, be wise', 'the quality of your life is brought about by the quality of your thinking' and 'there is a power stronger than logic and greater than hope; the power of love'.

221

Thanks largely to the prospect of Cliff appearing in his first stage musical, *Time* broke all advance-booking records for London's West End theatre and tickets for Cliff's year-long run completely sold out. The show eventually played to more than a million people.

Even though the critics were less than kind when *Time* opened in April 1986, Cliff enjoyed his role immensely.

'It was one of the nicest experiences I've had,' he said. 'It was fantastic. Everyone said to me when I decided to do a year in the show: "You're going to be bored." And I wasn't at all. I didn't miss a show. It was just a fabulous experience. It was so visually startling it was actually doing something that no other show was doing. It was the first of the high-tech shows. We had unbelievable lighting rigs, people came down from the ceiling on ropes. It was a stunning-looking show and because of that it got slaughtered.'

Dave Clark gave Cliff a public vote of thanks on stage on Cliff's last night on 11 April 1987, and it was only when he took himself off for a well-deserved holiday that Cliff realised how much the strain of performances eight times a week had taken out of him.

'After leaving *Time*, I missed it terribly,' he said. 'I went straight away on holiday to the Caribbean islands and I found I was in bed for about ten or eleven hours a day. I didn't know I was that tired. When I did the show I felt really good every night – the adrenalin flowed and every night felt like a first night. But when you stop you are suddenly aware and your body says: "Wait a minute." '

Once back in England, Cliff showed his continuing enthusiasm for *Time* by going to see the show four times after former teen idol David Cassidy had taken over his pivotal role. 'I'm a *Time* man,' Cliff said. 'I love it.' The whole experience set him thinking about perhaps staging his own musical one day.

By 1989, Cliff was approaching fifty and he ended the decade in extraordinary style. He silenced any doubters that his star was waning by staging *The Event* at Wembley Stadium, a two-day thirtieth-anniversary celebration of his life in music in which he sang to two separate audiences of 70,000 on successive days.

A year in the planning and six weeks in the rehearsing and preparation, *The Event* was as much a triumph for Cliff's determination as it was for anything else. 'It cost two point four million pounds to put on,' he revealed, 'and we only did it twice. Mel Bush, the concert promoter, thought I was wonderful. I kept saying: "OK, spend it," to everything he suggested. My business manager asked me why I was doing it, and I said: "Don't worry, we'll sell the TV rights and get something from it." '

He did precisely that. The TV rights to *The Event* were snapped up by ITV and screened at Christmas 1989 as a major highlight of ITV's festive programme schedule. It attracted a huge audience. *The Event* was also released as a double album, which reached number three in the album charts, and in addition it became a best-selling DVD. The concert was filmed by eighteen different cameras and was broadcast on both TV and radio.

Prior to its TV screening, Cliff revealed just how much *The Event* had meant to him. 'I've never played to so many people in my life before,' he said. 'People started arriving early in the morning and were quite happy to wait until five o'clock for the show to begin. There was no need for crowd control in the stadium. The police said that the only problem they had was that people gave the horses too many sticky buns.

'I've spent three decades performing for the fans and I wanted to make this very a special celebration, a great experience for us all. I spent six weeks preparing for the show. I phoned people up to ask them to appear in the *Oh Boy!* section and got in touch with some of The Vernon Girls to re-form their group.'

Among those welcomed on stage to take part in the celebrations was Jet Harris, who commented afterwards: 'That was the most wonderful moment of my life after everything I'd been through, standing beside Cliff in front of 70,000 people for two nights, and then coming back on stage for the finale. All The Shadows were there and it was great seeing them all.'

Charitably, Jet insisted that the passing of time had enabled him to feel no animosity about taking the Wembley stage with

Cliff. Cliff's dalliance with Carol Costa when she was Jet's wife was history as far as the guitarist was concerned.

'It's certainly not something that I think about now,' said Jet, 'and, looking back, you're talking about us when we were just a bunch of children.

'I'm very fond of Cliff and the support he has given me, inviting me to his concerts and sending me a card for my fiftieth birthday. Those sort of things have meant a lot to me and given me great strength. To me he's almost St Cliff, he's such a special person.'

Commendably, Jet's eulogy was willingly given, despite the stark disparity in the cards life had dealt Jet and Cliff since their early association. After the Wembley concerts were over, Jet and Jacqueline, the new woman in his life, got on the coach at Victoria for the journey back to Gloucester on the return portion of their £12 return tickets, and went home to their council house.

Cliff admitted he was unusually nervous in the run-up to *The Event*. 'The night before the first concert, I didn't sleep at all,' he confessed. 'I kept writing notes to myself about the show . . . I stepped on the stage and I couldn't believe it. I was the catalyst for all this. I was the cause of the traffic being jammed on the North Circular.

'I just looked out over the sea of people and cried. Looking at the recording now, I'm embarrassed. But I just couldn't help it. The tears ran down my face. I just became emotional. *The Event* was an unimaginable high. I spent six weeks trying to recover from it. I'll never forget it.'

Cliff clearly did not envisage *The Event* as anything approaching a swansong. 'In the next ten years I want to do everything again,' he declared, 'but even better. My ambition still burns hot and I'd like to be remembered as the best.

'I'm not worried about getting old. At eighteen I was expected to have hits. Now I don't have to prove anything any more. I'm not fighting and struggling for success. I was an early teen idol and I'm grateful that I've still got those fans. But it gave me a tremendous buzz to look at the audience at Wembley and people of all ages who'd come to see me.'

Cliff Richard is a man who definitely knows his own mind. And once it is made up, he sticks by his decision. Cliff always has the courage of his convictions, and is not afraid to take on challenges that might bring criticism or even ridicule. The next challenge he found was in Emily Brontë's remarkable novel of 1847, *Wuthering Heights*. Heathcliff was a character so striking and so compelling that Cliff wanted to bring him back to life.

There was something about the powerful, brooding Heathcliff and his doomed and passionate love for Cathy that fascinated Cliff Richard, and he decided he had to play the role. Cliff knew perfectly well that even voicing such an ambition would attract adverse comments and instant opposition. After all, it hardly seemed like obvious casting. The squeaky-clean pop star with the wholesome image was surely a million miles from the bearded brute of a man who set Cathy's heart trembling on the Yorkshire moors. Not to mention the fact that Cliff was by now about twenty years older than Heathcliff.

Cliff first came up with his plan to star in this high-profile role in 1990 and, in his customary honest and open way of running his life, he soon went public with his idea. The pundits and commentators quickly rushed to fill acres of newsprint with advice generally poking fun at him.

But Cliff was not to be put off: there was something in Emily Brontë's only novel that captured his imagination. At the time, friends who bothered to read the book pointed out that Heathcliff as a child is described as a 'dark-skinned foundling'. The echoes of Cliff's own difficult childhood, when he arrived in England from India and found other children quick to bully him and call him 'nigger', were loud and clear.

Of course, Heathcliff goes on to do some dreadful things in the novel. Crucially, he fails to hear Cathy say that Heathcliff is 'as much to me as the rocks are to the earth beneath' and, after wrongly believing he has been rejected, he leaves to seek his fortune and marries the unfortunate Isabella, who soon flees in terror because he treats her with unspeakable cruelty. Heathcliff's behaviour is what helped make him such an attractive prospect to Cliff, along with some of the wild and abandoned aspects of the stirring story.

'All my life I've been very controlled and regulated,' he said at the time. 'I don't lose my temper. I don't scream and shout and I don't have tantrums. Of course, there are times in my life when I feel incredibly angry and I want to hit someone or something, but I don't let it bubble over. I sit on my hands and stay cool on the outside – even though I am boiling mad on the inside! There are moments when I wish I could lash out physically, but I put them behind me. We all have demons inside us. I don't know why people worry about whether I can be bad. It's much harder to be good. People say I'm a goody-two-shoes who can't sing anything other than "Living Doll". That's not true.'

Cliff realised that playing a character as explosive as Heathcliff would give him a rare freedom of expression and licence for some seriously bad behaviour that he knew he would really enjoy. But he also knew some of his fans would be shocked to see him in a show in which he savagely beats up his wife while calling her 'a pitiful, slavish, mean-minded bitch'.

Ignoring untold column inches of negative publicity, Cliff pressed ahead with his plans. His musical version of *Heathcliff* was originally intended to open in November 1994. The first five tracks, written for the show by Sir Tim Rice and John Farrar, were recorded for the album and considerable momentum was built up. But perfectionist Cliff decided the project was not yet quite right and more time was needed for writing, rewriting and more complex technical planning.

That work continued through 1995 and became really intensive throughout the autumn. Cliff took time out in October to very gratefully accept his knighthood at the investiture at Buckingham Palace, but he was very busy visiting Los Angeles to work on the album to go with the show. There were countless production meetings, a UK radio promotional tour and several television appearances across Europe to support the release of the album *Songs From Heathcliff* and the singles 'Misunderstood Man' and 'Had to Be'. And Cliff's leading role in November's Royal Variety Show offered the perfect platform for a preview of the upcoming musical.

Tickets for *Heathcliff* went on sale on 4 March 1996 and instantly provided the perfect answer to the sneering critics and doubting pundits. An astonishing £2,305,000 worth of tickets were sold on the first day of issue. Cliff was shocked and pleased in roughly equal measure. He said simply: 'I am staggered and amazed.' Fans had been queuing for days and sleeping in tents at night in Birmingham and London to make sure of getting to see their hero.

In London, the queue took eight solid hours of ticket-selling to clear, and one of the first customers to reach the box office handed over £4,500 in cash for 150 seats costing £30 each. 'There have been a lot of disparaging remarks about Sir Cliff, but this proves he is an industry all on his own,' said Peter Harlock, the managing director of Hard Sell, the agency handling the *Heathcliff* sales. 'In monetary terms this must be a record for first-day sales. I've never seen anything like it.' The show did not even open until October in Birmingham before moving on to Manchester, Edinburgh and London, yet on that first day of sales the four theatres sold more than 97,000 tickets.

Cliff was delighted by the response of his ever-faithful fans. But he had been so determined to stage this expensive and elaborate musical that he was well prepared to risk his own money. He had been warned that it could have cost him around £3 million if the show did not prove popular, but he said that he was happy to back himself: 'I have come to a position in my life when I could feasibly lose two and a half or three million pounds. I would feel it, but it would not destroy my lifestyle.'

Cliff took the bold decision to become his own producer and cast himself in the leading role he so desperately wanted to play because no one else would offer that sort of adrenalin-pumping opportunity. 'No one else was going to give me a part like *Heathcliff* because they see me as a pop star,' said Cliff. 'So I had to create it for myself.'

He knew that even if the show exceeded his wildest dreams, it would never make him a profit. 'However successful the show becomes it will never make me a penny,' said Cliff shortly before the musical opened. 'The running costs are too high.

'Before I started, I sat down with my accountant and he reassured me that I wouldn't lose my house or my car and I wouldn't be begging on the street. If it closed after four months, which is what I hoped it would achieve, then I would lose about £1.5million of my own money. If it ran for six months, then I would just about break even. Why did I do it? Because if I can't do something that I care about after all these years of hard work, then what's the point? Everyone thinks they know best what I can and cannot do, so the only way to give myself that chance is putting my money where my mouth is.'

The closer the launch date came, the happier Cliff felt about his decision. He was confident enough to go on Radio 2 and tell Gloria Hunniford that he accepted it had been a surprise to many people to learn that he was going to take the stage as the earthy hero Heathcliff and he knew: 'A lot of people would expect me to fail at it. Well, I am going to thumb my nose at them all and say, "To heck with you – I am not going to fail." I've had great practice getting into character for *Heathcliff* because I've been derided for five years for doing it.'

The age difference was raised many times, but Cliff was undeterred: 'For years people have been telling me how young I look. I am the perfect person to play a thirty-eight-year-old.' An album of songs from the show was recorded with Olivia Newton-John and, after an exhaustive string of auditions, the beautiful Helen Hobson was picked to play Cathy. 'Her voice was exceptional,' said Cliff, and certainly it was a partnership that worked well on stage.

One of the most enjoyable aspects of the production for Cliff was being part of a team. Being a solo singing star can be a lonely business at times and Cliff really revelled in the camaraderie of the company. 'I really enjoyed working with actors, because it's so completely different for me as a concert artist,' he said. 'When you're singing to a crowd you sing to them, your reaction is to them. In a show you have to ignore the audience to a great extent because you're acting with your fellow actors. It's a whole different way of looking at things.'

The success of the project was very important to Cliff. Years later in a Radio 2 interview with Cilla Black he said: 'I had to do *Heathcliff* and it didn't really worry me what anybody else thought. Long before we opened they had started to criticise. Tim Rice wrote a lovely letter to *The Times* saying he had been criticised for writing the lyrics to *Heathcliff* and he hadn't put pen to paper yet! That's how bad they got.

'Gone are the days when people wished you good luck for a project. They didn't wish me luck in it. They hoped for failure, and this is a negative area of our society ... We need the critics to keep us on our toes, we really do, but I'm afraid they've lost their heart, whereas we've still got ours. We are still vulnerable, sensitive individuals and if they want to hear this, I'll tell them. They really hurt us! ...

'In the end, because they were so nasty before I had started, it goaded me to doing it. I suddenly thought: why are they trying to tell me how to do things? They can't sing. They can't act. They can't dance. They can't do anything. They can barely write!

'So I thought to myself, I'll do it. Of course, I did get the whiplash and it doesn't really matter now. But I'm so glad I did it, because I think we have a product we can use again.'

Despite the savaging from the critics, nearly half a million people had seen *Heathcliff* by the time the curtain came down on the show for the last time. Cliff may have been inwardly smarting from the criticism, but he could point to combined sales of more than 300,000 copies of the two albums from the production: *Songs from Heathcliff* and *Heathcliff Live*. A video of the production also topped the music video charts.

While plunging all his energies into *Heathcliff* over a period of four years, Cliff's average quota of three to four singles a year was considerably reduced, but he managed to maintain a steady presence in the album charts, thanks to EMI releasing several compilation albums.

And there was no doubting Cliff's standing in the nation's affection. He was invited to sing in front of Buckingham Palace as part of the VE celebrations in 1995, and he was a popular choice on the bill of yet another Royal Variety Performance.

On 25 October 1995, he was knighted by the Queen – an immensely proud moment for the singer, who took his three sisters along with him to Buckingham Palace for the ceremony. Cliff was also just one of very few pop stars who were invited to attend Princess Diana's funeral in 1997.

In 1998, forty years after he first brought audiences to their feet at major concert venues, Cliff resumed touring on the back of *Real as I Wanna Be*, his first non-*Heathcliff* album of original material for five years. It was moderately successful and, importantly, Cliff had the satisfaction of proving he was still a singer who could move with the times.

Cleverly, he pulled the wool over the eyes of some of commercial radio's ostensibly hippest DJs who normally would not play a Cliff Richard record for all the tea in China. Advance white-label copies of a remix of 'Can't Keep This Feeling In', Cliff's first single from the album, were sent to various radio stations purporting to be by a brand new artist by the name of Blacknight 001.

The hypocrisy of these stations was exposed when several DJs were totally fooled and gave the record very favourable reviews. One station even deemed it to be 'wicked rap'.

'I found myself in two black charts and soul stations started to play it,' Cliff said proudly. 'But as soon as they found out it was me, radio stations stopped playing it. I couldn't understand it, but at least I'd made my point.'

Point proved, the singer's true identity was finally revealed when a DJ with Choice FM conducted a phone-in interview with the exciting newcomer. Asked about himself, he told startled listeners: 'I'm Cliff Richard.'

Cliff was somehow forgotten when the nation's official millennium celebrations were planned for New Year's Eve in 1999. It was not as though he had slipped out of the public consciousness – not long before he had sold out twenty shows at the Royal Albert Hall, which proved so popular that he went back for a further twelve sell-out shows. In all, 160,000 fans flocked to the Albert Hall to see Cliff perform with seventy musicians from the London Philharmonic Orchestra.

Such lionising by the public somehow counted for nothing when the millennium festivities were planned. Hordes of dignitaries were invited to join the Queen and Prime Minister

Tony Blair for the major celebrations at the Dome in Greenwich – but the country's foremost performer over four decades was not among them. Typically, however, Cliff overcame this undeserved slight by planning fourteen nights in concert at Birmingham's NEC, climaxing with a special charity extravaganza on New Year's Eve for which, astonishingly, some fans queued for ten days to get tickets.

'As the old Father Time of pop, I'd rather presumptuously assumed that I would be asked to do something,' Cliff told music aficionado and journalist Simon Kinnersley. 'So of course it's sad not to be part of the millennium plans. I'd been waiting for ages for someone to say something, so, when nothing came, I decided it was up to me to make things happen.

'I remember when I was young and you'd wait around to see what the best New Year's Eve party might be before making up your mind, and in the end you do nothing. Well, I was determined that wouldn't happen So, when no one asked me, I decided I'd get on with it and make something happen myself.'

Cliff was partly motivated in staging his own millennium concerts by the fact that he had already decided to take a year off and wanted to go into his twelve-month hiatus on a high. After forty years of relentless work, he had begun to realise it was high time he stopped recording and touring and simply allowed the world to revolve around him for once. For too long his career had dictated how he lived his life. In the year 2000 Cliff would be celebrating his sixtieth birthday, and it seemed a fitting time for him to live life on his own terms and just do as he pleased.

'For the first time in my life I've been holding up a mirror to life and the way I live,' he confided. 'Hearing that one of my contemporaries, Dusty Springfield, who was touring at the same time as me in the 60s and is now suffering from cancer, is not only sad, but it also reminds me of what a friend said to me a long time ago: "Why wait to retire at sixty-five? Why not do it when you're forty and still young and fit?"'

'I want to take things a little easier and take control of my life. I always thought that I was in control of my career and I could do whatever I wanted. But, equally, it's been controlling me. I've been a hostage to it, without recognising it. There's been no time for me; my diary has always been full for a year ahead.

'It's funny, because I've always thought that I had the choices, but in fact even though I've enjoyed it immensely, my career has been a treadmill of recording, promoting the new record, touring, then back to the studio and starting off all over again. It's been like that for forty years.'

Cliff went on to stress: 'I've no intention of retiring. I'd like to have a go at doing different things. I'd love to do a play for perhaps six months.

'I feel there are new priorities in my life. I want to break free from my career, but not discard it. I love what I do, but I'm lucky enough that I don't have to do something if I don't want to. I can afford to say no. I also no longer fear the idea of doing nothing. If I want to spend the day lying on a sofa reading a book, then that's what I'll do. I don't feel that I have to go into the studio and record another song.

'It's a very exciting time. I feel that the future is ahead of me, the question is: how do I want to fill it?'

One thing he was looking forward to doing more of was indulging his passion for tennis. A keen player and spectator, he also established the Cliff Richard Tennis Foundation in 1991, which has encouraged thousands of primary schools to introduce the sport into the curriculum. Anticipating his 'year off' in 2000, he said, 'Wimbledon fortnight is always blocked off in my diary, but now I want to be free so that if I want to go to the US Open, I can just get on a plane and go to New York.

'For the first time, and I never thought I would feel or say this, I can see that if the perfect partner stepped into my life, then I would change absolutely everything and reorder my life.

'When I was younger my mother always wanted to see me settled, happy and married. And I always used to reply that I'd managed two of those things, which was pretty good, and we used to laugh about it. But, like all mothers, I think she liked the idea of her son having a secure home life.

'Later on she changed her mind and said that I shouldn't get married. She could see how committed I was to my work and what my lifestyle involved, and she could recognise that it simply wasn't compatible with being married. The fact is that if I had got married years ago, it couldn't possibly have lasted.

'Looking back, there are two times in my life when I could have got married. The point is that on both occasions I stepped out of the relationship. Now it might have been because I felt my career was more important, or maybe it was more simple – that I didn't love them enough. In the end I had to ask myself the question: did I want to live with them for the rest of my life? Obviously, deep down I knew that the answer was that I didn't. I didn't care for them deeply enough.'

The first of those two relationships was in the 1960s, with dancer Jackie Irving, and the other was nearly twenty years later, with blonde tennis star Sue Barker. The couple met at a Shadows concert in 1981 when he was 41 and she was 25 and they were seen together so frequently afterwards that they made no secret of what they called their 'friendship'.

At first it was light-hearted. Just after the marriage of Prince Charles and Lady Diana Spencer in July 1981, Cliff joked: 'Someone has to take over from Charles and Di.' Cliff dedicated his summer 1982 record 'Now You See Me, Now You Don't' to Sue and, in his customary honest way, he said: 'If we decide we'll get married, don't worry, we'll make sure everyone knows. But it's early days yet.'

The pressure on the new golden couple grew. Reporters and photographers were constantly asking them when they were going to get married when they had only known each other for a few weeks. Cliff was already very adept at handling the voracious media, but even he found the torrent of personal enquiries very embarrassing. He said: 'After each new story we started ringing each other up to apologise, until we made a pact to ignore what was printed about us.'

The constant attention certainly did not help the relationship, but it was not the reason it ended. In essence, it foundered because Cliff felt he was losing the freedom he had enjoyed for so long as a singleton.

Soon after the romance was over, Cliff tried to explain his feelings in *Woman* magazine: 'The fact of the matter is that we tried, but our love was not that kind of love. If we had got married, I think it would have been a big mistake. We still have a really good friendship. We can talk to each other on the phone anytime.'

Asked on TV if he had been in love with Sue, Cliff replied: 'Yes, definitely. It fascinates me that I can feel love for somebody, and yet when it comes to getting married, I didn't want to get married.'

Talking of his feelings coming up to his sixtieth birthday, he reflected: 'I've realised that marriages tend to go wrong through a lack of commitment and that most of them suffer because the people involved aren't prepared to acknowledge this is the most important thing in their lives. If you don't feel that way, then you shouldn't go into it.

'I believe that if I'm going to make a marriage work then I must invest the same level of energy and determination that I've done with my career and if I don't feel that then don't do it.

'I'm certainly not interested in living with a girlfriend. I don't believe that takes you anywhere. If you're going to make that declaration of love, then do it properly and get married. Don't do it in a half-hearted manner.

'I've never felt broody or wanted to be a father,' he insisted. 'Nor do I feel that's something I'm ever going to regret. The first thing is being in a relationship where you want to make that bond – and that's not happened to me yet – rather than just having children. It's not been an issue providing my mother with grandchildren, because she's got lots already, so it's not something I worry about.'

The fact that Cliff has never married has, perhaps inevitably, led to questions about his sexuality. But this has never been an easy subject for him to discuss. As recently as February 2007 he terminated an interview in Dubai when a journalist demanded to know if he was gay.

It is a question that Cliff does not believe he has any need to answer. After all, others have answered the question for him, including Delia Wicks, his girlfriend in 1960, who, in an interview years later, said he was not gay, and Una Stubbs, whose 1963 romance with Cliff turned into a lifelong friendship.

Una is a great defender of Cliff's stance and a fervent admirer of him as a person. She was interviewed about her relationship with Cliff on an edition of *The South Bank Show* in 1993 and said firmly: 'There have always been suggestions that he's homosexual. That has always happened ever since I've known him. If he was homosexual would that matter? The fact is, he isn't.'

In October 2000, Cliff celebrated his sixtieth birthday with family and friends aboard the 4,250-tonne *Seabourn Goddess* on an eight-day Mediterranean cruise from Nice to Malaga. On his actual birthday, 14 October, Shirley Bassey sang 'Happy Birthday' and Cliff successfully blew out the sixty candles on his cake with ease.

The celebrations were the highlight of a year of change that included Bill Latham, his mentor for some thirty years, moving out of the singer's home. Cliff's friends saw a late blossoming in Cliff the man. Without the responsibilities of recording, the pressure to notch up hit records and sell out concert venues, Cliff's year off saw him more at ease socially than his closest friends could remember for some while.

This late blossoming of Cliff, according to some of those closest to him, could partly be attributed to a growing friendship with Father John McElynn. A New York born Roman Catholic priest, McElynn was born in 1953 and had been a missionary in Panama before committing to the Congregation of the Mission, a religious order dedicated to evangelising to the poor.

A tennis lover like Cliff, McElynn was introduced to the singer at a tennis tournament and the two men got on well straight away and quickly became friends. Eventually McElynn moved into Cliff's Weybridge home and took on the mantle of mentor previously held by Bill Latham as well as general factotum and organiser of Cliff's diary and social life.

In time, he went on to become Cliff's travelling companion, property manager, confidant and adviser, and other friends noticed that Cliff became progressively more comfortable and at ease with himself as McElynn began to exert greater influence over his life. Gloria Hunniford observed that he helped Cliff 'spread his wings'.

The year 2000 also saw him pick out a prize plot of land in Barbados, where a beautiful new hilltop holiday home in a gated community and overlooking the Caribbean would be built to his specifications at Sugar Hill. Cliff bought a plot for a house, but ended up building a palace. In years to come it would prove to be the perfect retreat, and not just for Cliff: he lent the house to Tony Blair and his family in the summers of 2003 and 2004.

On a personal level, Cliff's only serious worry during the 1990s and beyond has been the health of his mother, who has developed dementia. But determined that some good would come out of his mother's plight and his own anguish, Cliff spoke out to the BBC Radio 4 programme *You and Yours* in September 2006 to mark World Alzheimer's Day.

With great compassion Cliff said simply that he knew that something like Alzheimer's really hits at the heart of a family and at the centre of all relationships. He pointed out that, technically, his mother, who was then 86, does not have Alzheimer's, but dementia. He said, 'It's the same kind of destruction of the brain cells. She is living, but the dementia takes away the life. My mother doesn't have a life. I've talked with my sisters and said, "You know, I feel as though I have already mourned my mum, because the person that we have with us is not the vibrant woman that we all knew."'

Throughout his long and successful career, Cliff had always told himself that his beloved mother would never go into a nursing home. He swore that as he could comfortably afford it, she would always be able to live in her own home, with whatever help she needed. It was in 1996, when she was living in a house adjoining that of Cliff's sister Joan and her family, that they began to realise Dorothy was ill.

As Dorothy's memory deteriorated, Joan and her family worried about Dorothy's safety, so they removed the kitchen knives. Then Dorothy started to do things like leaving the gas on and later she would just go wandering off down the road. It got to the point where Joan was at her wits' end and she admitted to Cliff that, with her own family to take care of, she simply could not cope.

The family found an excellent home for Dorothy to receive the round-the-clock care she needed, but even then there were heart-wrenching moments when Dorothy would plead with them: 'Oh, don't leave me here.' But after a few months they found that if they could distract her, so that she looked the other way, they could leave without the pain of upsetting her and she would instantly forget them.

Cliff described his experiences to BBC listeners with enormous sensitivity and the programme-makers received a huge response from people who found his broadcast both helpful and uplifting. Cliff said: 'In one respect it is a gentle disease. My mother knows nothing about political uproars, or about terrorists. She does not know what time it is or how bad the weather is outside. Now we find we have really nice visits, but I am not sure she can recognise us.'

It is very important to Cliff that Dorothy is remembered as the person she once was, so he has insisted there is a large picture of her displayed on the wall of the home. 'We found a fantastic photo of my mum,' said Cliff. 'She was in her early forties, just preparing to go to one of my film premieres, and she looked great. So that when these good folks come in the home they can see that this is really the woman we are looking after.'

Cliff accepts that his mother's dementia is the hardest thing he has ever had to deal with. 'And it is the same for my sisters, too,' he said. 'It is desperately difficult to come to terms with the fact that this has happened to our mother and there was nothing we could do to stop it. It is almost unbearable sometimes.'

Cliff's strong faith helps to sustain him and on radio he said: 'I don't know why these things happen to us, but they do, and we have just got to knuckle down and say that if we are upset, then God is even more upset. If we trust Him then we have eternity ahead of us.'

EPILOGUE

I'm going to have to stop at some point, if only because I've fallen over.

Cliff Richard

Above the sturdy wrought-iron electronic security gates guarding the entrance of Quinto do Moinho, there, proudly displayed for all to see, is the owner's coat of arms. And this farm-cum-winery in the small town of Guia, Portugal belongs to Sir Cliff Richard.

Cliff bought Windmill Farm, which gets its name from a picturesque windmill overlooking the garden, in 1993. And the coat of arms – approved by heraldic authorities – greets visitors at the gates with several clues as to the identity of its owner.

Based on designs suggested by fans, it features a bird on the top, denoting the singer, and it stands on a rock – signifying rock 'n' roll. It's also surrounded by gold discs.

Four flames represent The Shadows, and netting refers to Cliff's love of tennis. The coat of arms also contains the cross of Christ, the helmet of salvation and a quote from the Bible, 'Sing a new song'. Beneath the crest hangs Cliff's OBE.

A long drive leads up to Cliff's magnificent whitewashed 250-year-old farmhouse with its bright yellow shutters and blue patterned tiles. Above the main building is an old tower that once housed a dilapidated water tank, but that has been taken out and the tower restored to hold a splendid bell Cliff found in a disused church in Scotland.

Extensions have been added, terraces created with terracotta tiles or pink calcada stones, and bougainvillea and plumbago cling brightly to the walls. A swimming pool with a blue windmill motif on the bottom shimmers invitingly. Nearby is a raised terrace with a fountain and a restored Algarvian cart with its wheels gaily painted yellow.

Inside, the elegant dining room has a terracotta floor and a traditional cane-and-pole ceiling. The main living area, known as the ballroom, has a salmon marble floor and the lounge has the same terracotta red-and-black floor, a green alcove with beautiful blue vases and red-and-white-striped armchairs.

Cliff had always wanted his own farm and this wonderful eleven-bedroom villa, a mixture of authentic rural beauty and elegance, not far from the sea, is one of Cliff's favourite places on earth.

When he first moved in, the farm had neglected vines, which were considered too old to bear much fruit, and Cliff had them taken out to make way for ten acres of fig trees.

A chance meeting with an Australian wine expert resulted in the planting of sixteen acres of vines instead, of four different grape varieties.

In his late teens Cliff drank the occasional glass of cider, but didn't discover wine until he was 21 and filming *Summer Holiday* in Greece. Over forty years later, fired with enthusiasm and never one to take a challenge or a new interest lightly, Cliff set about the process of making wine, even though he didn't at first even realise that all grapes, whether they're red or white, make white wine. Red wine's colour is determined by the red grape skins being left in the tanks.

A state-of-the-art winery called Adega do Cantor – the winery of the singer – on a neighbouring estate was soon producing Cliff's own wine, complete with his distinctive windmill logo, with spectacular results.

'I've had fantastic reviews for my wine, better than I've had for some of my albums,' Cliff can say with a laugh.

His Vida Nova (meaning new life) Tinto 2004, one of 9,000 competing for honours, was awarded a coveted bronze medal at the International Wine Challenge in London, where the wines are all blind-tasted by experts.

Cliff's willingness to work the land, and his obvious, enduring love of Portugal – he spends every summer at his villa from the last day of Wimbledon to the end of August – has endeared him to the locals. The neighbouring town of Albufeira has even named a street after him near the beach – Rua Sir Cliff Richard, Cantor. One summer before opening his winery, Cliff sang to 25,000 people on the beach and followed up by throwing a party offering roast pork and lashings of his own wine. Cliff even draped himself in a Portuguese flag to greet his guests.

Cliff maintains he is no great businessman, but manages to surround himself with the right people. And now, apart from his award-winning wine, he has interest in hotels and fragrances bearing the names of some of his hits. But, despite these welcome business successes, Cliff says he will always be first and foremost a singer. And the remarkable statistics of his recording career will certainly ensure his place in the rock 'n' roll hall of fame. 'I know a lot of people think I'm a no-no as a musical entity,' he has said, 'but when they're writing textbooks, I will have to be in there. People will hate it, but I will have to be in there.'

And there's no sign of Cliff calling it a day. 'If people are still prepared to come out and see me, and if I can still hold a melody, and only I would know this, then I'd be very happy to continue to entertain,' he recently told his good friend Gloria Hunniford in a TV interview for the Biography Channel.

'If the record sales drop down to zero I could stop making records, but if people want to come out and be entertained at a concert, I'd be happy to do that.'

Early in 2004, a British television programme for Channel 4 called *The Ultimate Pop Star* revealed that Cliff Richard had sold more records in the UK than The Beatles and more than Elvis Presley, thereby establishing Cliff as Britain's highest-selling artist on the singles charts. Figures showed that Cliff's sales of 20,969,006 singles was the highest by any artiste, followed by The Beatles with 20,799,632 and Presley with 19,293,000.

Cliff's tally, more than the singles of Abba and Queen combined, was based on the 125 singles he had released up to that point, including 'Santa's List', which had peaked at number five in December 2003.

'Some people think that I've just been lucky, but the harder I work the luckier I get,' he has said. 'If it was just luck that kept the hits coming, my good fortune would have run out long ago. Instead I've had an average of three hits a year during my career.

'The real secret of my success is that I've not had to follow myself. You know how it happens. You have two number ones on the trot, and if your third record isn't a number one people say that your career has ended. Instead I've had lots of number threes and number twos. When I have a number one people then say: "I knew it was coming all along."'

Cliff is rightly proud of his career, and his records. 'I wish more people would appreciate that rock 'n' roll is an art form. I defy Pavarotti to sing "Good Golly Miss Molly" while performing a dance routine. In rock 'n' roll, you have to find a way of dancing, getting enough breath and singing in tune. But we're written off. I think rock 'n' roll is the best thing that ever happened to music and to showbiz.

'The reason why I have survived is that I have something far stronger and far greater to live up to. My faith has kept my feet on the ground and it's made me feel more confident.'

By any standards, Cliff Richard's career has been phenomenal, and when he turned 65 on 14 October 2005, he chose that milestone to announce he was going back on the road on his *Here and Now* tour, his first UK national arena tour for several years.

Buoyed by selling out his concerts at the Royal Albert Hall in 2004, Cliff was confident enough to announce he would go ahead with a tour of main arenas in England and Ireland towards the end of 2006. Naturally, they were a sell-out.

In bullish mood, he said: 'Bus pass, pipe and slippers? Don't you believe it. The buzz I get from performing to a live audience is just as real and exciting as it ever was – and hopefully I've a few years left in me yet.'

ACKNOWLEDGEMENTS

The authors wish to express their deep gratitude to the many individuals who have made this book possible. Heartfelt thanks go to all those who have figured in Cliff Richard's life who agreed to be interviewed for this book.

Special thanks are due to Bruce Welch for his fascinating and extensive insights, and to Simon Kinnersley for sharing with the authors his multiple interviews with Cliff Richard and with Jet Harris.

The authors also wish to acknowledge many TV and radio programmes as invaluable sources, notably *The South Bank Show*, Channel 4's *The Real Cliff Richard*, Tim Rice's series of interviews with Cliff about his string of hits for BBC Radio, and several shows broadcast on BBC Radio 2 about Cliff's success and the rock 'n' roll era in general. Ray Flight and his *Oh Boy!* website also provided vital information.

Special thanks are due to Pete Murdie for his great help with research.

For their co-operation, help and encouragement, past and present, thanks are due to: Joe Brown, Charles Catchpole, Barbara Davis, Ingrid Dodd, Vince Eager, Rod and Joy Gilchrist, Jim and Jorma Hampshire of Canterbury Rock, Ann Infield, Clive Jackson, Claire Kingston, Moira Marr, Fraser

Massey, David and Sarah Mertens, Norman Mitham, Mickie Most, Roy Orbison, Jennifer Palmer, Peter Radford, Keith Richmond, Ian Samwell, Claire Sefton, Paula Trewick and Lynn Trunley-Smith.

The authors would like to acknowledge as additional important sources: *New Musical Express*, *Melody Maker*, the *Sun*, the *Daily Mirror*, the *Daily Express*, the *Daily Mail*, *Woman's Own*, the *Sunday Mirror*, *News of the World*, *The Times*, the *Sunday Times*, the *Guardian*, *Hello!*, and *OK!*.

In a book containing many pop chart statistics, every effort has been made to ensure accuracy, and the authors would like to acknowledge the Guinness book *British Hit Singles* and Mike Read's book *The Cliff Richard File* as reliable sources of data.

Grateful thanks to Robert Kirby, Kate Quarry, Davina Russell and all at Virgin Books.

Personal thanks from Tim are due to Shona Johnston for teaching him the chords to 'Travellin' Light', thereby sparking a lasting love affair with the guitar, and to Tim's admirably knowledgeable guitar teacher, Rob Urbino, for his patience and enthusiasm.

INDEX